Counting-Out Rhymes: A Dictionary

Publications of the American Folklore Society
Bibliographical and Special Series
Volume 31, 1980

Counting-Out Rhymes
A Dictionary

Edited by
**Roger D. Abrahams
and Lois Rankin**

University of Texas Press
Austin and London

Library of Congress Cataloging in Publication Data

Main entry under title:
Counting-out rhymes.
   (Publications of the American Folklore Society,
bibliographical and special series; v. 31)
   Bibliography: p.
   1. Counting-out rhymes.   2. English language—
Rhyme—Dictionaries.   I. Abrahams, Roger D.
II. Rankin, Lois, 1940–   III. Series: American
Folklore Society.   Bibliographical and special series; v. 31.
GR485.C68   398.8   79-22260
ISBN 0-292-71057-7

To Dorothy Howard and
to the Memory of Carl Withers

Contents

Preface

This volume is a companion-piece to *Jump-Rope Rhymes: A Dictionary* and grows from the same personal project—an attempt to give order to a mass of items of childlore in English. It is hoped that such compendia will make the materials of folklore available not only to folklorists, but also to those concerned with the language and motor development of children, child culture, and socialization in general. I was extremely fortunate to find a coeditor, and especially one as industrious, careful, and enthusiastic as Lois Rankin. In fact, she had been coeditor of the earlier volume in all but name, as she was then serving the American Folklore Society as manuscript editor. It was she who developed the final formulation of the bibliographical entries for the jump-rope book, a technique we follow here.

Our collaboration was a simple (if arduous) one. She inherited a manuscript of mine which was more or less complete to 1965 but in far from publishable shape; she gave it the order and clarity of reference and cross-reference you will find herein. I found a number of other sources which I had missed the first time around, and I sent these—usually in photocopy form—to her. Again I asked Herbert Halpert and Ken Goldstein to search their libraries and files for out-of-the-way references, and again the two of them responded with alacrity and a wealth of exotica—materials we were still receiving two years after our initial plea! Many many thanks to them. As with the former volume, materials supplied by Dorothy Howard and the late Carl Withers were helpful in filling in the distributional record. These two central personalities in the collection and study of children's lore have kept alive popular and scholarly interest in these children's materials.

R.D.A.

Introduction: Getting to *It*, or A Special Way of Beginning

by Roger D. Abrahams

Counting-out is one important way of getting into play, used by children of about ages six to eleven. It provides a frame and a break between the stream of ordinary activity and the specially licensed behavior we call playing. It is a formulaic and ritualized way of focusing energies for those who wish to play games more complex than "Tag," but less coordinated in focus than team sports. It is the special way of beginning games and contests which comes after the simple touching of "Tag" and before the more elaborate ways of *choosing-up sides*. In fact, the most common term in American English is probably *choosing-up* rather than *counting-out*. Beginnings are always difficult when the experience is prospectively a special and licensed one; counting-out provides an activity in which the beginning is conventionally brought into play, therefore apparently not under the control of any one of the players. Counting-out rhymes are the formularized and conventional performative acts by which *it* is chosen *out* and games are begun.

It is essential that these rhymes be recognized as performatives (this derives from the speech act theory of J. L. Austin), as speech acts which actually do what they say they are doing at the point of utterance. This places them in the same category as "I dub thee knight" and "I pronounce you man and wife," but only as long as the play world is maintained. They have the power to transform individuals from one role to another, but unlike the other performatives they exist only within the ritualistic context of game and have no carryover into other domains of life. Being *it* is far from a permanent condition.

The formulae of counting-out are relieved of the need

to communicate anything but the message "Everything that follows is play." Thus, the hocus-pocus language of the rhymes is central to their licensing function. Among other operations, it marks the shift of worlds by switching the pronoun system of reference from the personal to the impersonal; there are no meaningful *I*'s or *you*'s in any "Eeny meenies"; there are only *it*'s. The distinction is not trivial.

With these rhymes we are involved with a number of fictions, of course. Playing rests on the presupposition that there may be significant patterns of movement and motive which are not under the obligation to produce anything; and if something happens to happen, the consequences of the product are not to be personally assigned (at least in the ideal). We know, however, from our long experience at playing that this relief from consequences is a very limited license; it applies only when the rules are closely followed and the personal integrity of others maintained. We do not commonly lose sight of our other selves while engaged in play, for to do so is to risk the consequences of having the play spill back over the frame into the "real" world. Under such conditions we may be called to account for our destructive or over-serious behavior—usually by being called a *bad sport*. But we also know that play will not be meaningful if we are not fearful, at all times, of the motives of the real world invading play. As Gregory Bateson notices, the message "This is play" must be accompanied by another voice asking "Is this really play?" for the special balance of enjoyment and anxiety to be brought to bear in playing.[1] To put it in its simplest terms, when someone becomes *it* we must simultaneously know that *its* touch will not harm us in any way and yet dread this touch in the deepest way. (*It* is called *the devil* in some game-traditions). Furthermore, just as we are both delighted by and fearful of the proximity of *it*, we also must want both to be *it* and yet to become *not-it* as quickly as possible. The *it*-principle is one of unalloyed power; branding someone in this way makes the player a pariah, but a very attractive one who can positively affect the lives of everyone around.

Perhaps the only role more powerful than *it* is that of the one who gets to do the choosing-up, the counting-out, as Kenneth S. Goldstein has demonstrated in the only study that we have been able to find on the strategies of counting-out.[2] There are numerous devices which one employs to manifest this power by modifying the formulae. To be sure, the existence of the rhyme seems to establish that an impersonal and traditional means is being brought into play to establish who is going to be imbued with the power of *it*; but there are all sorts of ways in which the counter may expand or contract the formula to make sure that the right person will be chosen. To the "Eeny meeny" routine may be added, for instance, "My mother told me to choose this one," and if this is not sufficient, "And out goes you," and if more is needed, "You dirty old dishrag, you." Enough is enough in everything but counting-out and dealing with the Internal Revenue Service and the mortician.

Furthermore, the condition of being *it* is characteristic of games which need some help in beginning but which seem to have no equivalent formula for ending. These are not really games in which winning or losing is important. The only appropriate ending to the condition begun with "One potato, two potato" seems to be "Olly olly in free," a serendipitous decision not to play any more—or at least not to play *that game* any more.

What seems to be involved when counting-out rhymes are employed is the making complex of the simple activity of getting into play. The rhymes establish a distance between the *real* and the *play* worlds more profound than that implied by simply saying "Tag, you're *it*." Moreover, the games which are framed in this way are ones, like "Kick the Can" and "Hide and Seek," in which negotiations of status and classification have become intermingled; thus the initial choosing of *it* established the vocabulary and the rhetoric by which the role of the distribution of power can be negotiated.

This process is not that far removed from the "Tag, you're *it*" approach in terms of how power to choose is seized. Danielle Roemer has noted a number of these scenes of role manipulation when children come out to play.[3] Appropriately, she has called the first stage of the negotiation for who will lead the *choosing-up*, "the bid." The process she describes also employs, in the bidding, a choice of which rhyme will be employed, and the power to explain how the counting will be done:

JACK: Wait a minute. I got it. I got it. I got it.[bid]
Put out these [puts out his fists].
Engine, engine . . .

In this case, the role of counter was simply appropriated. In the next, acquiescence was solicited and received, through a recognition that choosing up initially involves a choice of rhymes.

SAUNA: I have a good 'un.
CANI: O.K.
SAUNA: Put your hands in, 'K?
KATIA: 'K.
SAUNA: Monkey, monkey . . .

If one takes on the role of counter, it must be carried out with fluency or the bidding will begin again, with someone else often winning. Similarly, the competitive bidding may result in more than one person beginning the counting-out, in which case the loudest (or strongest) usually triumphs.

That counting-out is a game to begin a game is, then, apparent. Indeed, there are certain elaborate rhymes included in this volume which are commonly employed apart from any other game, especially "Intery, mintery, cutery, corn" (no. **287**).

There have been some important collections of counting-out rhymes in English: Bolton and Withers are the two that come to mind immediately.[4] Little attempt has been made in these collections to come to grips with either the contrived strangeness of these rhymes or how they are employed in the increasingly complex process of socialization among children. Just why this should be is difficult to ascertain, for they are certainly as rich, as abundant, and as available as, say, riddles. Among others, Martha Wolfenstein and Brian Sutton-Smith have found in such joking enigmas some key insights into childhood developmental processes, the former with regard to testing out motives of power and sexuality, the latter with regard to discernment of staged levels of verbal and concept control.[5]

These rhymes, then, are a sonorous accompaniment to negotiations in an ego-centered classification and reclassification contest. The play world encourages precisely this playing around with received social and cultural orders, much as riddling does in the confronting of the child's concepts of the order of things. What Sutton-Smith points out with regard to riddles at ages six to eighteen describes important features of other kinds of play, including games: "at about the age when riddles peak, children show their initial competence in problems of verbal classification, reclassification and multiple classification." [6] The major point of counting-out is to establish the order of play and players in many dimensions by repetition of numbers and number-like classifiers. Counting-out does just what it announces itself as doing; it makes ciphers of players, allowing them to enter into the temporarily declassified and meritocratic world of play, a world in which you are what you become through your ability to control your body while mastering the rules of the game—and the rules for changing the rules.

But the game play begun by this elaborate framing device is more than just a classificational scheme in preparation for a possible reclassification through reordering. We are involved with learning to understand "multiple classification" here as well, that complex state of mind in which someone (or something) can stand for something and its very opposite, and at the same time! In its riddling equivalents, the message is boldly presented:

What has ears and cannot hear?
  Corn.

What is it the more you take from it the larger it grows?
  A ditch.

What goes up the chimney down but not down the chimney up?
  An umbrella.

These are only verbal contradictions, however, and in games the contradictory states are considerably more existential. In the games begun with counting-out, the ones being chosen are in a perilously ambiguous state, for they are endowed with the dreadful yet desirable power of being *it*. *It* is, in such cases, a semantic conflation of *in* and *out*, making counting-out a process both of distinguishing who's *in* and who's *out*, and of breaking down that distinction right away through the powerful quality of touch. I don't wish to make undue claims for the practice (there are a number of other ways we learn about social complexity through experiencing such contradiction), but nowhere is the existential dilemma of power and vitality more clearly to be confronted. To put it in utilitarian terms for the moment, as Sutton-Smith points out: "Children achieve an organization of personal and social behavior in play which far exceeds their ability outside of play. Thus in the hide and seek model of seven years, children achieve a role reversibility which they cannot achieve in their other social behavior until about eleven years."[7] Certainly one factor in developing this ability to change roles is arrived at through the conventionalization of both the roles and the impersonalized way of choosing them. But we might also explore the possibility that the world in which such role transformation can be brought off occurs because of the protective covering provided by counting-out, a verbal routine that makes a litany of the earliest verbal orders one learns: numbers, letters, days, and colors.

In a sense, counting-out then represents a statement of verbal control beyond phonology, such as Sutton-Smith demonstrates in the riddles of this age group. Following Piaget, he notes (as mentioned above) that at this age "children show their initial competence in verbal classification, reclassification and multiple classification."[8] However, in counting-out, and jumping rope, the ambiguous classificational play is accompanied by physical movement within the agonistic frame of reference. I refer to this as "beyond phonology" only because on first blush these rhymes often seem nonsensical, a simple playing around with sounds for their own sake, while sense is being made on the level of the social world within play. Though these rhymes often seem to involve gibberish, as Sanches and Kirshenblatt-Gimblett argue, when viewed in the context of both their history and the other rhymes used interchangeably, even the "Eeny meeny" and "Intrery mintery" routines can be seen to be models of ordering nonsensified, "put into neutral" as it were.[9] Though these rhymes do not operate under any apparent need to make sense, in fact, like most nonsense, they provide a recognition and an underscoring of the earliest verbal devices of ordering. The process is one of choosing mainly by using numbers. The context insists on this. "Eeny meeny" is, after all, a functional substitute for "One potato, two potato." All of the rhymes invoke a kind of defamiliarization of lexical series, a foregrounding of the routine set by saying the series strangely. All of this contributes to the multiple statements going on in choosing-up, all of which are reducible to one—"Everything within this frame is play . . . isn't it?" The linguistic inversions simply announce the onset of other kinds of play. Physical play is preceded by verbal play, both of a highly conventionalized sort, and both replete with motives of conflict and negotiation of roles. Without this before-play play, the thrill of the chase and the test could never be so exquisite.

A good part of the thrill of being *it* (or being the one who counts out) is in the awe this inspires in the other players. Play cannot be carried out effectively, in fact, without this intensity of focus. But the power is also one which causes others to test and retreat from you. To keep the power too long, moreover, is to bring on boredom; it must be effectively passed on precisely as a measure of one's competency in the game. To pass it on too quickly, on the other hand, is also to risk making the game boring. When some imbalance between getting to be *it* and passing it along is encountered, the group will tend to respond by graduating to a more complicated game, as occurred in the early graduation from "Tag" to "Iron Tag," "Stoop Tag," and so on. The development of contest-forms is, indeed, a process of careful gradation and growing complexity, from "Tag," to "Hide and Seek" type games, to ones involving choosing up sides, like "Capture the Flag," to team sports. With each change the rules become more complex, the roles more varied, stylized, and convention-bound, and the focusing energy of *it*-ness altered from hand to eye ("I spy Johnny") to control over a power object.

The employment of *choosing-up* techniques is part of the diversification in the vocabulary of power. Controlling these rhymes is a way of introducing word play into action play, of making a statement about how the simple laying on of hands is not enough to dramatize ability and control; verbal routines parallel conventional moves and plays both in the counting-out and in the game afterward.

Use of these rhymes occurs at the same age as learning to joke. The physical trick, or *catch*, involves a similar deployment of verbal negotiation for a temporary physical dominance available to anyone who would seize the opportunity.

A: Did you get my letter?
B: No.
A: I must have forgotten to stamp it. [A stamps on B's foot.]

A: Adam and Eve and Pinch-Me went down to the river to swim. Adam and Eve fell in. Who was left?
B: Pinch-Me.
A: Gotcha.

Being chosen *it* is perhaps the biggest catch of all.

Notes to the Introduction

1. Gregory Bateson, "A Theory of Play and Fantasy," in *Steps to an Ecology of Mind* (San Francisco: Chandler, 1972).

2. Kenneth S. Goldstein, "Strategy in Counting-Out," in *The Study of Games*, ed. Elliott M. Avedon and Brian Sutton-Smith (New York: John Wiley & Sons, 1971), pp. 167–178.

3. Danielle Roemer, unpublished paper.

4. Henry Carrington Bolton, *The Counting-Out Rhymes of Children* (London: Elliot Stock, 1888); Carl Withers, *Counting Out* (New York: Oxford University Press, 1946).

5. Martha Wolfenstein, *Children's Humor* (Bloomington: Indiana University Press, 1978 [reprint]); Brian Sutton-Smith, "A Developmental Structural Account of Riddles," in *Speech Play*, ed. Barbara Kirshenblatt-Gimblett (Philadelphia: University of Pennsylvania Press, 1976), p. 113.

6. Sutton-Smith, *Speech Play*, p. 115.

7. Brian Sutton-Smith, "Current Research on Play, Games and Sports" (Developmental Studies preprint series, Program in Developmental Psychology, Columbia Teachers College, 1975), pp. 4–5.

8. Sutton-Smith, "A Developmental Structural Account of Riddles," p. 113.

9. Mary Sanches and Barbara Kirshenblatt-Gimblett, "Children's Traditional Speech Play and Child Language," in *Speech Play*, ed. Kirshenblatt-Gimblett, p. 93.

Counting-Out Rhymes: A Dictionary

A Guide to the Dictionary

Rhymes

Texts

A representative text has been chosen for each rhyme and is given completely except where the rhyme is essentially repetitive. Spelling and punctuation are occasionally altered for consistency or to aid understanding.

Common variations appear within parentheses in the text. Italicized material within quotation marks indicates a response by a player other than the counter; italics alone are used for the word or syllable on which a player is counted out or chosen *it* if that word or syllable is not the last of the rhyme.

Alphabetization

In the alphabetical arrangement of rhymes, punctuation is ignored and contractions are treated as though they were spelled out. Numbers and "Doctor" are spelled out; "Mr." and "Mrs." are not. Rhymes beginning with articles and "O," "Oh," or "And" are alphabetized according to the second word. The practice of calling "Dip!" to begin the counting-out process is not reflected in the texts, although "dip" and "ip" do appear when the words are necessary to the rhyme pattern.

Comments on the rhymes

Some rhymes are found in connection with other play activities. The identification of such activities and general comments on the texts appear in italics beneath the rhyme text. The inclusion of a rhyme in *The Oxford Dictionary of Nursery Rhymes*, edited by Iona and Peter Opie, or in Roger Abrahams's *Jump-Rope Rhymes: A Dictionary* is also noted here.

Cross-references

The first line of a variant rhyme, if unlike the first line
of the representative text, is included in the alphabetical arrangement of texts, with cross-reference to the
representative text. These variant entries are not num-
bered. The seemingly endless possible ways of spelling
gibberish words has resulted in an extraordinary but
unavoidable number of cross-references. Every effort
has been made to reduce cross-referencing without sac-
rificing usefulness and completeness.

Notes to the rhymes

Sources for each rhyme are listed beneath the rhyme. In
the source entry, year of publication is given in parentheses. Provenience, where ascertainable, appears in
brackets, together with the year the rhyme was re-
corded if this date is known and differs significantly
from the year of publication. Notation on substantive
variation from the representative text, if any, follows. In
the case of frequently reported gibberish rhymes, con-
siderations of space required limiting notation on variation to first lines and nongibberish endings.

Sources are in chronological order according to the
earliest date each source attributes to a rhyme. This
date may be year of collection, year of publication, or,
when a variant is reprinted from another source, the
date that determines the chronological placement of
the source being quoted.

Sources giving only texts reprinted from another
source are joined to the original source by an equal
sign. In entries for sources giving some variants that are
reprinted and others that are not, information on the
original sources appears in the notes on variation from
the representative texts.

It should be mentioned that some sources do not
assign a particular function to the rhymes they give,
usually presenting them in general terms of children's
jingles or games. Rhymes from these sources are included only if they belong in a rhyme category whose
counting-out function has been clearly established by
other sources.

Publication information can be found in Works Cited
at the end of the *Dictionary*. Abbreviations used in the

notes to the rhymes are as follows:

AA: American Anthropologist

GMW: Green Mountain Whittlin's

HF: Hoosier Folklore

JAF: Journal of American Folklore

JRR: Roger Abrahams, ed., *Jump-Rope Rhymes: A Dictionary*

Misc. of Rymour Club: Miscellanea of the Rymour Club

NCF: North Carolina Folklore

NF: Northeast Folklore

NYFQ: New York Folklore Quarterly

Old Lore Misc.: Old Lore Miscellany of Orkney, Shetland, Caithness, and Sutherland

PADS: Publications of the American Dialect Society

SFQ: Southern Folklore Quarterly

TFSB: Tennessee Folklore Society Bulletin

Transactions: Transactions of the Historic Society of Lancashire and Cheshire

WF: Western Folklore

L.R.

A

1   A, B, C, and D, pray playmates agree;
E, F, and G, well so shall it be;
J, K, and L, in peace we will dwell;
M, N, and O, to play let us go;
P, Q, and S, love we may possess;
W, X, and Y, will not quarrel or die;
Z and ampersand, go to school at command.

Bolton (1888), 118 [England].

A, B, C, bouncing B. *See* **192**.

2   A, B, C,
Catch the cat by the knee;
L, M, N, O,
Let the poor thing go.

Bolton (1888), 119 [Ireland] = Daiken (1949), 10.

3   A, B, C, deffigy, aitchygy K,
L, M, N, oppi Q, restivy W, X, Y, Z.

Notes and Queries, 1st ser., 10 (September 9, 1854), 210
   [England] = Bolton (1888), 118.

4   A, B, C, D, E,
F, G, H, I for It.

Clifton Johnson (1896), 166. Ends ". . . F, G, H, *I*."
Opie (1969), 30 [Pendeen, England].

5   A, B, C, D, E, F, G,
H, I, J, K, L, M, N, O, P;
Q, R, S, T,
U are out.

Also found as a jump-rope rhyme; see JRR, p. 5.

Newell (1883), 201 [Ohio] = Bolton (1888), 119.
Emrich and Korson (1947), 119.
Opie (1969), 30 [England]. Ends "U-are-He."

6 **A**, B, C, D, E, F, G,
H, I, J, K, L, M, N,
O, P, Q, R, S, T, You.

Opie (1969), 30 [England].

7 **A**, B, C, D, E, F, G,
Saying that puts out thee!

Bolton (1888), 118 [Massachusetts].

8 **A**, B, C, D,
Tell your age to me.

Withers (1946), n.p. With playing explanation.

A, B, C,
Mother caught a flea. *See* **429**.

A, B, C,
My Grannie caught a flea. *See* **430**.

9 **A**bena, babena, baby's knee,
Hallsom, pallsom, sacred tea;
Potatoes roast, single toast,
Out goes she.

Bolton (1888), 108 [Limerick, Ireland].

Acka, bacca (backa, baka). *See* **10**.

10 **A**cker backer, soda cracker,
Acker backer boo.
Acker backer, soda cracker,
Out goes you.

Cf. "My mother, your mother, lives across the way." Also found as a jump-rope rhyme; see JRR, p. 5 ("Acca, bacca").

Bolton (1888), 109 [Rhode Island, Connecticut, Delaware, New Jersey, New York, Oregon, California]. Seven variants; one begins "Hackabacker, chew tobacco," one "Acka, backa," one "Occa, bocca bona cracka," one "Ecker, becker, soda cracker."

Clifton Johnson (1896), 166. Ends "My father chews tobacker, / Out goes you."

Waugh, *JAF*, 31 (1918), 46 [Ontario, 1909]. Begins "Ocka bocka stona crocka."

Anderson, *Evening Ledger* (May 17, 1916) [Kentucky]. Ends "If your father chews tobacker, / Out goes you."

Whitney and Bullock (1925), 140 [Maryland]. Begins "Acka baka."

Heck, *JAF*, 40 (1927), 37. Ends with "Eggs, butter, cheese, bread" rhyme (**152**).

Hudson (1928), 116 [Mississippi]. Begins "Ikka bokka."

Maryott, *SFQ*, 1 no. 4 (1937), 45 [Nebraska]. Two variants, one beginning "Aka baka bona cracka."

Saxon et al. (1945), 445 [Louisiana]. Begins "Ooka dooka."

Withers (1946), n.p. Two variants: one begins "Ecka, decka, donie, crecka," and ends "Ease, cheese, butter, bread, / Out goes you!"; the other begins "Oka, bocca, stona crocka."

Emrich and Korson (1947), 122. Begins "Ikka, bokka."

Withers (1948), 86. Begins "Acka, bacca."

Brewster (1952), 168 [North Carolina]. Ends "If your Daddy chews tobacker, / He's a dirty Jew."

Randolph, *SFQ*, 17 (1953), 245. Begins "Icka backa soda cracker."

Leventhal and Cray, *WF*, 22 (1963), 243 [California].

Opie (1969), 42 [United States]. Two variants: one begins "Icka backa," one ends "If your father chews tobacco / He's a dirty Jew."

Knapp (1976), 26, 27. Two variants; one from Hawaii is "Boys are rotten, made of cotton, / Girls are dandy, made of candy, / Pick a pack of soda crackers / Out goes you."

Addi, addi, chickari, chickari. *See* **467**.

11   **A, E, I, O, U,**
      Which shall be tick?
      It must be you.

Burne (1883), 572 [Shropshire] = Northall (1892), 342.
Evans (1956), 9.

12   **A, E, I, O, You.**

Opie (1969), 30 [England].

13   Ahee and a high and a hump stump fumadiddle,
Set back a faniwiddle,
In come a nitcat sing song kitty gitche kimeo.

From the nineteenth-century minstrel song "Kemo Kimo."
Cf. **70**, **314**.

Maryott, *SFQ*, 1, no. 4 (1937), 40 [Nebraska].

Ah, ra, chickera. *See* **467**.

Aihie, mailie, tribily, trick. *See* **128**.

Aila, maila, tip-tee tee (Aily, maily, tipsy taily).
   See **140**.

Aina, maina, mona mike. *See* **139**.

Aina, peina, para, peddera, pimp. *See* **500**.

Ain, tain, fethery fip (tethera, pethera, pimpi). *See*
   500.

Airy, eyery, ickory Ann. *See* **408**.

Aka baka bona cracka (soda cracker). *See* **10**.

Ala mala ming mong. *See* **131**.

Ala, mala, tipsy, tee. *See* **140**.

A-le, ma-le, tipte-tee. *See* **140**.

14 Algy, balgy, ripshee rah;
Ripshee, rapshee, rolla.

Howard, *NYFQ*, 16 (1960), 137 [Australia; reported by older
persons, not current among school children in 1954–1955].

15 Allalong, allalong, linkey, loo.
Merry goes one, merry goes two.
Allalong, allalong, linkey, loo.
Merry goes one, merry goes two.
I'll lay a wager with any of you
That all my marks make thirty and two.

Bolton (1888), 8, 120 [New York, Georgia, West Virginia,
Virginia] = *Old Cornwall*, 1, no. 6 (October 1927), 44.
Three variants. With playing instructions.
Withers (1946), n.p.

16 All around the butter dish,
One, two, three;
If you want a pretty girl,
Just pick me.
Blow the bugles,
Beat the drums
Tell me when your birthday comes.

Related to the game "Round the punch bowl." Cf. **122** *for
the last three lines.*

Withers (1946), n.p. With playing instructions.
Emrich and Korson (1947), 122. With playing instructions.
Withers (1948), 84.
Howard, *NYFQ*, 16 (1960), 143 [Australia, 1954–1955].
"Round and round the butter dish, / One, two, three. /
Please, little man, will you go He? / No; then we shall see. /
Bread, butter, sugar, tea, / You are not he."
Opie (1969), 36 [England]. Begins "Round and round the
butter dish"; last three lines omitted.

All last night, and the night before. *See* **320**.

Allory, mallory, tipsy, tee. *See* **140**.

17   All the monkeys in the zoo
         Had their tails painted blue.
         One, two, three—out goes you.

Withers (1946), n.p. [from Brooklyn College students, 1936–
    1945].
Evans (1956), 21.

18   Amka, marieka, dronneka, dross,
         Skyttel, piper, foss.
         Bim, bam, rotlingang,
         Ess, pess, aff!

Bolton, JAF, 10 (1897), 319 [Strömöe, Faröe Islands].

Ana, mana, dippery Dick. See **128**.

Ana, mana, miny (mina), mo. See **133**.

Ana, mana, mona, Mike (mi). See **139**.

Ana, mana, tippety fig. See **129**.

19   Andy, mandy, sugar-candy,
         Out goes he.

*Cf. the nursery rhyme "Handy spandy, Jack-a-Dandy"
(Opie, Dictionary, pp. 232–233). Also a jump-rope rhyme; see
JRR, p. 8 ("Amos and Andy").*

Bolton (1888), 108 [Michigan].
Withers (1946), n.p.
Goldstein (1971), 174 [Philadelphia, 1966–1967].

20   Ane's nane
         Twa's some,
         Three's a curly Andrew.

         Three's a pistol, four's a gun
         Five's the laird o' Bouqie's son,
         And six is Curlie dougie.

Simpkins (1914), 304.

Anerie (Anery), twaarie (tary, twaaery, twaery, twaory, twary), . . . See **21**, **410**.

21 Anery, twary, tickery tan,
Obbs, jobbs, an Englishman;
A bird i' the air, a fish i' the sea,
A bonny young leddy cam' doon to see me.

> *Related to a number of other gibberish rhymes.* Cf. **403**, **408** (Gregor [1891] entry).

> *Notes and Queries*, 1st ser., 10 (September 9, 1854), 210. Begins "One-ery, two-ery, tick-er-y, ten; / Bobs of vinegar, gentlemen."
> "Counting-Out Rymes," *Misc. of Rymour Club*, 2, part 2 (1913), 94 [Fifeshire].

Ane twa dickery seeven. See **410**.

Ane, twa, three, four,
Mary's at the cottage door. See **421**.

22 Ane, twa, three, fower,
Staan ye oot ower.

> Gregor (1891), 30 [Scotland].

23 Annie Bell, she kens hersel';
She lives below the steeple,
And every time she rings the bell,
She wakens all the people.

> Reid, *Misc. of Rymour Club*, 2, part 2 (1913), 70 [Scotland].

Any, many, mony, my (mowt). See **139**.

24 An Apple, an orange,
A kirk or a college,
A string o' laamar beads,
A bunch o' blue ribbons,

A happeny bap, peat, sod,
Dyvot, or clod.

Gregor (1891), 31 [Foveran, Scotland].

25   Apple core, bite no more,
      In the snout, point him out.

Musick and Randolph, *JAF*, 63 (1950), 429 [southern
Missouri].

26   Apple Davie, currant Tam,
      Sugar rollie, black man.

Gregor (1891), 30 [Scotland].

27   Apple, peach, pear, plum,
      When does your birthday come?

Withers (1946), n.p. With playing instructions.
Harry Harris, *Evening Bulletin* (May 30, 1949), 10. Begins
"Pear, apple, peach and plum." With playing instructions.
Ritchie (1965), 44 [Edinburgh].
Opie (1969), 60 [England]. Begins "Eachie, peachie, pear,
plum."
Knapp (1976), 33.

Apples and oranges. See **24, 28, 440**.

28   Apples, oranges,
      Cherries, pears, and a plum,
      I think you're dumb.

Goldstein (1971), 174 [Philadelphia, 1966–1967].

Are you going to coff, sir? See **269**.

29   Around the house, arickity-rary,
      I hope ye'll meet the green canary:
      You say ay—I say no,
      Hold fast—let go!

Gullen (1950), 13.

A-rub, a-dub-dub. See **486**.

As eenta, feenta, ficket a feg. See **129**.

As Eenty Feenty Halligolum. See **126**.

A-seenty-teenty, heather beathery. See **500**.

30 As fair as fair as it can be,
The king of Egypt said to me,
The one that comes to number three
Must be he. One—two—three.

> *Ending to extend other rhymes.*

Opie (1969), 35 [Portsmouth, England].

31 As I came by the bear's tree,
All the bears looked at me,
White puddin', black trout,
I choice thee first one out.

G.W.R., *Old Lore Misc.*, 5 (1912), 6 [Kirkwall, Scotland].

As I climbed up the apple tree. See **42**.

As I climbed up the crazy (hickory) steeple. See
39.

As I gaed (gied, geed) up an apple (aipple) tree.
See **42, 49**.

As I gaed up the brandy hill. See **43**.

As I geed up a fairy tree. See **42**.

As inty, tinty, lathera, mothera. See **500**.

As I was going down Inky Pinky lane (street). *See* **36**.

As I was going down piggy wiggy track. *See* **40**.

32   As I was going over London bridge,
I met a dead rat:
I one it, you two it, *etc*.

> *The player who says "eight it" is out. Usually collected as a catch.*

> Reid, *Misc. of Rymour Club*, 1 (1911), 105 [Edinburgh]. "As I went up the London road, / I met a stupid donkey, O; / Me one, you two, me three, you four, / . . . you *ate* it."
> Gullen (1950), 13 [Argyleshire]. Begins "As I went oure the Muckle Brig."
> Opie (1959), 66 [Swansea, England]. Begins "As I was walking up a scabb't lane, / I met a scabb't horse."
> Sutton-Smith (1959), 71 [New Zealand].

33   As I was going up the stairs,
I heard a chinaman say his prayers:
Izza bizza bing bong,
Izza bizza boo,
Izza bizza bing bong,
Out goes you!

> *Comes from the children's song "That Crazy Bald-headed Chinee," a recent version of "His Old Gray Beard A-waggin'."*

> Rutherford (1971), 52 [Newcastle upon Tyne, 1965].

34   As I was in the kitchen
Doing a bit of stitching
Old Baldie Humle
Cam an' stole ma thumle.
I up wi' a wee cherry-stone
An' struck him on the knuckle-bone.
You are out, out goes one and out goes she.

> *Often collected as a jump-rope rhyme; see JRR, p. 12.*

Maclagan (1901), 249 [Argyleshire].

As I was on St. James steeple. *See* **39**.

35   As I was walking (down) by the lake
I met a little rattlesnake.
I gave him so much jelly-cake,
It made his little belly ache.
One, two, three, out goes she.

> *Also often found as a taunt and as a jump-rope rhyme; see*
> JRR, p. 12.

Babcock, *AA*, o.s., 1 (1888), 274 [District of Columbia]. Be-
gins "As I went up the golden lake."
Bolton (1888), 113 [Connecticut, New Jersey, New York].
Three variants; one begins "As I went up the silver lake."
Gregor (1891), 31 [Grantown, Scotland].
Clifton Johnson (1896), 165. Begins "As I went up Salt Lake."
Monroe, *AA*, n.s., 6 (1904), 48 [Massachusetts]. Begins "As I
went up to silver lake."
Heck, *JAF*, 40 (1927). Begins "As I went up the golden gate."
Boyce and Bartlett (1946), 30.
Withers (1946), n.p. Begins "As I went by the garden gate."
Emrich and Korson (1947), 122.
Howard, *NYFQ*, 16 (1960), 139 [Australia, 1955]. Two var-
iants, beginning "A little green snake" and "As I went up to
silver lake."
Turner (1969), 14–15 [Adelaide (1957) and Melbourne
(1967), Australia]. Two variants: "Little green snake (A big
fat snake) / Ate too much cake / And now he's got / A
belly-ache."
Ritchie (1965), 49 [Edinburgh via Adelaide]. Begins "A little
green snake."

As I was walking down Inky Pinkie Lane. *See* **36**.

As I was walking up a scabb't lane. *See* **32**.

As I went by the garden gate. *See* **35**.

36   As I went down the Icky Picky lane
I met some Icky Picky people.

What colour were they dressed in—
Red, white, or blue?
"Red."
R-E-D spells red.
And that's as fair as fair can be
That you are not to be it.

Cf. **40.**

Opie (1969), 58 [Gloucestershire, 1898; current in Manchester, Welshpool, Trowbridge, Enfeld, Shrewsbury, Ruthin].
Rutherford (1971), 50 [Hull, England, 1920's].
Turner (1969), 10 [Canberra (1961) and Geelong (1967), Australia]. Two variants ("As I was going [went] down inky pinky lane [street]") asking "the colour of the Union Jack. / Red, white, or blue?" The player on whom "blue" falls selects a color; the counter resumes with the appropriate lines: "Red is for danger, for danger, / Red is for danger and out goes you"; "White is for wedding, . . ."; or "Blue is for beauty, . . ."
Ritchie (1965), 44 [Edinburgh]. "As I was walking down Inky Pinkie Lane / I met some Inky Pinkie soldiers. / I asked them what colour their flag was," etc.

37 As I went oure the Hill o' Hoos,
I met a bonnie flock o' doos.
They were a' nick nackit,
They were a' brown backit;
Sic a bonnie flock o' doos,
Comin' oure the Hill o' Hoos.

See Opie, Dictionary, pp. 405–406.

Reid, *Misc. of Rymour Club*, 1 (1911), 102 [Edinburgh].

As I went oure the Muckle Brig. See **32.**

38 As I went out to sell my eggs,
I met a man wi' painted legs,
Painted legs and tipped toes,
That's the way the ladies goes.

See Opie, Dictionary, p. 220.

Gregor (1891), 32 [Grantown, Scotland].

39   As I went up a steeple,
I met a lot of people.
Some were white and some were black,
And some the color of a ginger-snap.

Bolton (1888), 113 [Connecticut, New Jersey]. Two variants;
one, "hickory steeple."
Monroe, *AA*, n.s., 6 (1904), 47 [Massachusetts].
Waugh, *JAF*, 31 (1918), 43 [Ontario]. Begins "As I was on St.
James steeple," ending ". . . some were the color of my hat. /
—B-l-u-e."
Whitney and Bullock (1925), 138 [Maryland].
Brewster (1952), 165 [North Carolina, ca. 1928]. ". . . crazy
steeple."
Guy B. Johnson (1930), 166 [St. Helena Island, North
Carolina]. Begins "Once I went up the heeple, steeple."
Boyce and Bartlett (1946), 30.

40   As I went up Hicty-picty hill
I met two frichty-picty children.
They asked me this and they asked me that,
And they asked me the colour of my best Sunday
hat.

Cf. **36**.

Opie (1969), 58 [England: Somerset, 1922; Swansea, Golspie,
St. Peter Port]. Begins "As I went up the Piccadilly hill / I
met some Piccadilly children."
Gullen (1950), 13.
Sutton-Smith (1959), 70 [New Zealand]. Begins "As I was
going down piggy wiggy track, / I met piggy wiggy children."

41   As I went up in a pear tree,
With all the pears around me,
There came a man from Tamworth town
And swore, by Jube, he'd knock me down.
I up with a pear and hot (hit) him there.
I up with another and hit his brother.
O-U-T spells out goes he.

Northall (1892), 343.

As I went up Salt Lake. See **35**.

42   As I went up the apple tree
All the apples fell on me.
Bake a pudding, bake a pie,
Did you ever tell a lie?
You know you didn't, you know you did.
You broke your mother's teapot lid.
She blew you in, she blew you out.
She blew you into sauerkraut.

See also **49**. Also a jump-rope rhyme; see JRR, p. 15 ("Bake a pudding").

Opie (1969), 61 [England, Scotland, Wales, United States since nineteenth century]. Ends "You broke your mother's teapot lid. / What colour was it? / 'Blue.' / No, it wasn't, it was gold, / That's another lie you've told."

Gregor (1881), 171 [Scotland]. "As I gied up the apple tree / A' the aipples stack t' me. / Fite puddin', black trout, / I choose you oot / For a dirty dish clout."

Newell (1883), 203 [Ohio].

Bolton (1888), 113 [Kansas, Rhode Island, Massachusetts, Virginia, Wisconsin, New York, New Jersey]. Five variants; one ends "I took one, my brother took another, / And we both jumped over the bridge together. / One, two, three, out goes she!"; one, "I climbed up the apple tree, / John had a stone and he fired it at me. / I shook the apples down. / And they fell on the ground."

Gregor (1891), 28 [Scotland]. Four variants beginning "As I geed (went) up the aipple (fairy) tree"; first two lines followed by common "Black puddin', fite troot" type endings.

Leon, JAF, 8 (1895), 255 [New Brunswick]. Ends "Make a pudding, make a pie, / Just you stand by."

Clifton Johnson (1896), 160–161. Two variants, beginning "As I climbed up . . ."

Monroe, AA, n.s., 6 (1904), 49 [Massachusetts].

Gardner, JAF, 27 (1914), 325 [New York].

Soifer, Story Parade, 6, no. 7 (July 1941), 16 [Brooklyn, 1916]. Ends "She whipped you up, / She whipped you down, / She whipped you all around the town."

Whitney and Bullock (1925), 139 [Maryland]. Two variants, one beginning "Did you ever tell a lie?"

Heck, JAF, 40 (1927), 36.

Gardner (1937), 229 [New York].

Maryott, SFQ, 1, no. 4 (1937), 56 [Nebraska].

Boyce and Bartlett (1946), 30. Ends "I took one, my brother

took another / And we both jumped over the bridge together."

Withers (1946), n.p. Ends "I took one, my brother took
another, / And we both jumped over the bridge together."

Emrich and Korson (1947), 122.

Justus (1957), 45 [Tennessee]. "I walked under an apple
tree, / Down some apples fell on me. / One—two—three—
four— / O-U-T goes out the door."

Fowke (1969), 112 [Canada]. Begins "When I went up an
apple tree"; ends "No, I never told a lie / But I ate my
mother's sweet apple pie, / With a dirty dish-cloth around
her knee. / When this counts out, count one, two, three, /
And out goes she!"

43   As I went up the Brandy hill,
I met my father wi' gude will.
He had jewels, he had rings,
He had mony braw things;
He'd a cat and nine tails.
He'd a hammer wantin' nails.
Up Jock, down Tom.
Blaw the bellows, auld man.

Cf. **59** for the last two lines. Also found as a nursery rhyme;
see Opie, Dictionary, pp. 101–102.

Blackwood's Edinburgh Magazine, 10 (August 1821), 36.

Gregor (1881), 170, 174; (1891), 32 [Scotland]. Two variants beginning "As I gaed up"; one ends "Old man had a
coat, / He rowed aboot t' the ferry boat; / The ferry-boat's our
dear, / Ten poun' in the year. / I've a cherry, I've a chest, /
I've a bonny blue vest, / I've a dog amo' the corn, / Blowin'
Willie Buck's horn; / Willie Buck hiz a coo, / Black an fite
aboot the moo, / It jumpit our the Brig o' Muck, / An ran awa
fae Willie Buck" (cf. **568**).

Bolton (1888), 102 [Indiana]. Used also as the ending for two
"Intery, mintery, cutery, corn" rhymes (**287**).

Davis (1906), 211 [New England] = Botkin (1947), 905–906.
Begins "Up on yonder hill."

Emrich and Korson (1947), 119. Begins "Upon yonder hill."

Gullen (1950), 14. Ends "The auld ram took a dance, / First to
London, then to France" (cf. **103**).

As I went up the fairy tree. See **42**.

44   As I went up the garden, I found a little farden,
I gave it to my mother, to buy a little brother.
My brother was a sailor; he sailed across the sea,
And all the fish that he could catch, was one, two,
    three.

Reid, *Misc. of Rymour Club*, 2, part 2 (1913), 69 [Scotland].

As I went up the golden gate (lake). *See* **35**.

As I went up the London road. *See* **32**.

As I went up the Piccadilly hill. *See* **40**.

As I went up (to) the silver (golden) lake. *See* **35**.

45   At the battle of the Nile
I was there all the while,
I was there all the while;
So you hop over the stile.

See Opie, Dictionary, p. 70.

Bolton (1888), 119 [Connecticut].

Auckland City Council, A.C.C. *See* **66**.

46   Auld Robin in the lock
Suppin' sowans oot a trock.

Maclagan, *Folk-Lore*, 16 (1905), 453.

47   The Auld wife
The cauld wife
The bed fou o' banes.

Maclagan, *Folk-Lore*, 16 (1905), 453.

Awkum, bawkum. *See* **198**.

Azeenty teenty figgery fell. *See* **129**.

B

48   Back side, front side,
Looking for a little ride;
In and out and up and down
Goes in red and comes out brown.

Goldstein (1971), 175 [Philadelphia, 1966–1967].

49   Bake a pudding, bake a pie,
Send it up to Lord Mackay,
Lord Mackay's not at home,
Send it up to the man o' the moon,
The man o' the moon's making shoes,
Tippence a pair,
Eery, ary, biscuit, Mary,
Pim, pam, pot.

See also **42**, **142**.

Gregor (1891), 24, 28, 30 [Scotland]. Five variants; three
begin "As I went up the apple tree"; one, "Bake a pudding,
bake a pie, / Stan ye oot by."
Turner (1969), 10 [Sydney, Australia, ca. 1900]. "Bake a pud-
din', / Bake a pie, / Take 'em up to Bondi; / Bondi wasn't in, /
Take 'em up to black gin; / Black gin took 'em in— / Out
goes she." ("Bondi" is a suburb of Sydney; "gin," an
aboriginal woman.)
Maclennan (1909), 51 [Scotland].
Simpkins (1914), 304. Begins "As I gaed up an apple tree."
Gullen (1950), 13. Begins "As I gaed up an apple tree."
Ritchie (1965), 45 [Edinburgh].

50   B-A-L-T-I-M-O-R-E spells
Baltimore

Whitney and Bullock (1925), 139 [Maryland].

51   Barber, barber, shave a pig,
How many hairs to make a wig?
Four and twenty that's enough,
Give old barber a pinch of snuff.

Usually a nursery rhyme. See Opie, Dictionary, pp. 66–67.

Bolton (1888), 113 [England, Rhode Island].
Emrich and Korson (1947), 117.

Barney, Barney, buckwheat straw. *See* **197**.

52   **B**ee, bee, bumble bee,
Sting (Stung) a man upon his knee.
Sting a pig upon his snout.
I say you are out.

    Also found as a jump-rope rhyme; see JRR, p. 150 ("One, two, three / Bumble, bumble, bee").

Bolton (1888), 117 [Maine, Massachusetts].
Gardner, JAF, 31 (1918), 530 [Michigan].
Whitney and Bullock (1925), 139 [Maryland].
Bennett, Children, 12 (1927), 21. Ends "Stung Johnny on the knee, / Stung the monkey on the snout."
Maryott, SFQ, 1, no. 4 (1937), 61 [Nebraska].
Brewster, SFQ, 3 (1939), 179.
Withers (1946), n.p. Begins "One, two, three, a bumble bee."
Potter, "Counting-Out Rimes," Standard Dictionary (1949), 255.
Brewster (1952), 167 [North Carolina].
Randolph, SFQ, 17 (1953), 248 [Arkansas].
Grayson (1962), 73.

A **B**ig fat snake. *See* **35**.

53   **B**illy, Billy Burst—
Who speaks first?

    The first to speak is "out" and the doggerel repeated until only one remains.

Bolton (1888), 11 [Ontario].
Withers (1946), n.p.

54   **B**lack balls, four a penny,
You are out!

Reid, Misc. of Rymour Club, 2, part 2 (1913), 69 [Scotland].

55   Black bau, grey clüd, green grass, tap rüd;
Stand doo fur do's oot.

Saxby (1932), 63 [Shetland].

56   Black fish (hen, puddin'), white (black, fite) trout
(troot).
I choose you out.

Common ending to many rhymes from Scotland.

Gregor (1891), 28 [Scotland]. Five variants. Alternate last
line, "Eery, aary, ye're oot."
"Counting-Out Rhymes," *Misc. of Rymour Club*, 2, part 2
(1913), 94 [Scotland]. Ends "You are to be put out / Of this
G-A-M-E spells game, game, game, / Out goes he."

57   Black puddings, white puddings,
One, two, three.
Sausage and liver
For you and me.
Who sells the best in the land?
We say Kennedy's.

MacColl and Behan, Folkways 8501 (1958) [Dublin].

58   Black shoe,
Brown shoe,
Black shoe,
Out.

Opie (1969), 31 [Barrow-in-Furness, England].

59   Blacksmith very fine,
Can you shoe this horse of mine?
Yes, master, that I can,
As well as any other man.
Bring the mare before the stall.
One nail drives all.
Whip Jack, spur Tom.
Blow the bellows, good old man.

Usually a nursery rhyme; see Opie, Dictionary, p. 366. Cf.
43 *for the last two lines.*

Gregor (1881), 175, and (1891), 25 [Scotland]. "John Smith, a
    folla fine, / Can t' shoe a horse a' mine. / Shoe a horse, / Ca a
    nail, / Ca a tacket in its tail, / Black fish, fite trout. / Eerie,
    aarie, ye're oot."
Bolton (1888), 116 [Georgia].
Emrich and Korson (1947), 117–118.

Black Top taxi. See **469**.

Black troot, white troot. See **56**.

60   **B**lue hoss, red hoss,
    Out goes the boss.

Bolton (1888), 111 [western Tennessee].

Blue shoe, blue shoe. See **503**.

61   **B**oilika, bublika, devila-pot,
    Boilika, bublika, hellika hot!
    Boil black blood of big black man;
    Boilika, bublika, Ku Klux Klan!

Bolton (1888), 54 [Michigan].

62   **B**omb, bomb, the girls are marching
    Calling (*girl's name*) to my door
    She is the one that's going to have fun
    So we don't need me any more.

The *"calling-in, going-out" format suggests a jump-rope
rhyme.*

Brill, GMW, 24 (1972), 3.

A **B**ottle of ink. See **395**.

Boys are rotten. See **10**.

63   Boy Scout,
Walk out.

> Cf. **458**.

Opie (1959), 4 [England, Scotland, Wales since 1911].
Howard, NYFQ, 16 (1960), 140 [Australia, 1954–1955].
Ritchie (1965), 45 [Edinburgh]. Ends "Girl Guide / Step
   aside."
Those Dusty Bluebells (1965), 22 [Ayrshire].
Turner (1969), 10 [Geelong, Australia, 1967].
Fowke (1969), 109 [Canada]. "Boy Scout, watch out! / Girl
   Guide, step aside!"
Opie (1969), 31 [England and Scotland]. Four variants; "Boy
   Scout, walk out" with "Girl Guide, step aside" and "With
   your breeches inside out" endings; Glasgow version: "Oot
   Scoot, you're oot."

64   Braw news has come to town,
Braw news is carried;
Braw news has come to town,
So-and-so is married.

First she got a kail-pot,
Syne she got a ladle,
Syne she got a dainty wean,
Syne she got a cradle.

> See Opie, Dictionary, pp. 241–242.

Our Meigle Book (1932), 166 [Scotland].

65   Bread, butter, sugar, tea.
You are not he.

> *Often used as rhyme ending.*

Howard, NYFQ, 16 (1960), 142 [Australia, 1954–1955].

Briar, wire, limber lock. See **287**.

66   Brisbane City Council, B.C.C.
Brisbane City Council game not he.

Howard, NYFQ, 16 (1960), 140 [Australia, 1954–1955].
Turner (1969), 14–15 [Melbourne, 1957]. "Melbourne City
   Council, one, two, three."
Sutton-Smith (1959), 69 [New Zealand]. "Wellington, "
   "Auckland," or "Christchurch" city councils and appro-
   priate initials; last line ". . . you're not he."
Opie (1969), 32 [Alton, England]. "London County Council,
   L.C.C. / Board of Education, you are he."

67   Bubble gum, bubble gum in a dish.
How many bubble gums do you wish?
"Three."
One, two, three, and out you must go
With your mother's big fat toe.

Also found as a jump-rope rhyme; see JRR, p. 21.

Heck, JAF, 40 (1927), 37. Begins "Ish, fish, codfish."
Guy B. Johnson (1930), 165 [St. Helena Island, North
   Carolina]. Begins "Cod fish, cod fish"; ends "Four spells
   four an' you're clean out / Wid yo' mudder dirty dish clot'
   in yo' mout'."
Withers (1946), n.p. Begins "Ish, fish, codfish."
Fowke (1969), 109 [Canada].
Carey (1970), 77 [Maryland]. "Fish, fish / In the dish."
Knapp (1976), 26.

The **B**utcher, the baker, the candlestick maker. See
   486.

Butter, eggs, cheese, bread. See **152**.

Butter, leve (levi), bone (boni), story. See **139**.

68   By the hokey, by the pokey,
By the pinky, by the panky,
How do you do.
Very well I thank ye.

Robertson, NF, 3, no. 2 (Summer 1960), 32 [Shelburne
   County, Nova Scotia, 1875].

69   By the holy evangile of the law
      I marry this Injun to this squaw;
      On the point of my jack-knife
      I pronounce them man and wife.
      One, two, three,
      Out goes he.

>   *Also a jump-rope rhyme; see JRR, p. 22.*

      Bolton (1888), 114 [District of Columbia].

C

70   Cairo karo, captain cairo,
      Boma netchie kind bow,
      Simmernicker, bomma nicker,
      Rolly bolly rinktum,
      Rolly bolly rinktum do do.

>   *From the nineteenth-century minstrel song "Kemo Kimo."*
>   *See also* **13**, **314**.

      Randolph, SFQ, 17 (1953), 247 [Farmington, Arkansas].

71   Calcium, potassium,
      Magnesium beer,
      Nitrogen, oxygen,
      Hydrogen dear,
      Compound unit, atom fat,
      You're the fool
      Who's not at bat.

      Maryott, SFQ, 1, no. 4 (1937), 41 [Nebraska].
      Emrich and Korson (1947), 119.

72   Call lummy koo,
      Out goes you.

      Sutton-Smith (1959), 69 [New Zealand].

73   Captain Cook chased a chook
All around Australia.
He jumped a fence
And tore his pants
And then he was a sailor.

Ritchie (1965), 49 [Edinburgh via Adelaide].

74   Capting, what's the fare to Boston?
Eleven shillings.
Eleving! Great heavings!
I thought 'twas only seving.

Bolton (1888), 114 [New England].

75   A Cart of dross tumbled the horse,
A cart of dross is out.

Gregor (1891), 29 [Grantown, Scotland]. "Horse, cart, thimble."
Reid, *Misc. of Rymour Club*, 2, part 2 (1913), 69 [Scotland].
Opie (1969), 31 [Aberdeen, Scotland]. "Horsie cartie rumble oot."

76   A Car went up the hill
And conked out.

Opie (1969), 31 [Bristol, England].

77   Cat, cub, catch coon,
Cling, clong, clackem.

Bolton (1888), 111 [New York].

Chaps to count the queen's name. *See* **84**.

Charley, barley, buck and rye. *See* **141**.

78   Charlie Chaplin
Sat on a pin,
How many inches

Did it go in?
"*Four.*"
One, two, three, four.

> *Usually a jump-rope rhyme; see JRR, p. 25.*

> Opie (1969), 57.

79   Charlie, Charlie, stole some barley
Out of the baker's shop.
The baker came out and gave him a clout
That made poor Charlie hop.

> *See Opie, Dictionary, p. 115.*

> Howard, *NYFQ,* 16 (1960), 141 [Australia, 1954–1955].

80   Charlie over the water,
Charlie over the sea,
Charlie broke the teapot (kissed a black girl)
And blamed it on me.

> *Cf. the jump-rope rhyme "Johnny on the Ocean" (JRR, p. 101).*

> Howard, *NYFQ,* 16 (1960), 141 [Australia, 1954–1955]. Two variants, one ending "Charlie in the ferry boat, / Out goes he."

81   Che, chi, cho, chitter,
One of these old men
Must be old gitter (getter).

> Dew (1898), 80 [Norfolk, England].

Chick-a-ma-Craney Crow. See **567**.

82   Chickamy, chickamy, crany crow,
I went to the wall to wash my toe.
When I came back one of my chicks was gone.
What time is it, old witch?

> *Usually a game rhyme.*

Bolton (1888), 120 [New York]. Two variants; one, "Hippiney, pippiney, craney crow / The cat's asleep, the crow's
aware, / It's time to give my chicken some meat. / Down in
the cellar and get a good supper; / Up again, up again! What
time is it, old buzzard?"
Withers (1946), n.p. Begins "Cricky, cracky."
Emrich and Korson (1947), 120. Begins "Chicky, cricky."
Musick and Randolph, JAF, 63 (1950), 429 [Missouri]. Two
variants; one "Chickee chickee ma craney crow."
Evans (1956), 14. Begins "Cricky cracky."

Chick, chick, chatterman. See **311**.

Chickee chickee ma craney crow. See **82**.

Chickery, chickery, my black hen. See **213**.

83   Chickety choo, choo, choo cha,
Knockaby nooby knockaby da,
Oddawy dusty canty coo,
Ollipy follipy china moo.
In China once there lived a man,
His name was Tiddy-ran-tan.
His legs were long, his feet were small,
This Chinaman couldn't walk at all.

Turner (1969), 10–11 [Kalgoorlie, western Australia, ca.
1905].

Chicky, cricky, craney crow. See **82**.

Ching, Chong, Chinee man. See **311**.

Chink, Chink (Chinky, Chinky), Chinaman. See
311.

84   Choose to count the King's men,
Hellelujah, A-men.
A-men, too sweet,
Jennie wi' the bogie feet,
You are out.

Gregor (1891), 29 [Scotland]. "Chaps to count the queen's name, / Hallelujah, amen."
Maclagan, *Folk-Lore*, 16 (1905), 450. "First tae count the king's name / Corra, ina, amen."
Bluebells My Cockle Shells (1961), n.p. [Ayrshire].

Christchurch City Council, C.C.C. See **66**.

85 Clap hands, clap hands
Till Mammie comes hame.
Mammie will bring something,
But Daddy will bring nane.

> *Usually an infant amusement; see Opie, Dictionary, pp.*
> *196–197.*

Maclagan, *Folk-Lore*, 16 (1905), 453.

Cod fish, cod fish. See **67**.

86 Copy cat, dirty rat,
Stole my mother's baseball bat.
Turned it in, turned it out,
Turned it into a speckled trout.

> *Usually a taunt.*

Leventhal and Cray, *WF*, 22 (1963), 239 [California].

87 Cork the bottle, cork the bottle;
One, two, three.

Reid, *Misc. of Rymour Club*, 2, part 2 (1913), 70 [Scotland].

88 Cowboy, cowboy,
Which way shall we go?
North, South, East, West,
O-U-T.

Howard, *NYFQ*, 16 (1960), 141 [Australia, 1954–1955].

Cricky, cracky, cranery, crow. See **82**.

89   Cups and saucers, plates and dishes;
My old man wears calico breeches.

> *Also a jump-rope rhyme; see JRR, pp. 34–35.*

Brewster (1952), 167–168 [North Carolina, ca. 1923].

90   Cups, plates, china, bowls,
Cups, plates, china, bowls.

Gregor (1891), 30 [Scotland]. Alternate last line: "An two and two's out."

D

91   Dainty Davie, curly pow,
Wet the grass, an' mak' it grow.

Maclagan, *Folk-Lore*, 16 (1905), 453.

92   Daisy Deborah Deliah Dean,
Fresh as a rose and proud as a Queen!
Daisy Deborah, drawn from the pool
By Harry and Dick, came dripping to school.
Daisy Deborah, wet as a fish,
Her mother says bed,
While her father say pish!

> *Used for "pairing off."*

Bolton (1888), 7 [New Hampshire].
Emrich and Korson (1947), 121.

Dash, dash, dash,
My blue sash. *See* **289**.

93   Deanna Durbin wore her turban
In-side-out!

Also adapted as a jump-rope rhyme; see JRR, p. 36.

Opie (1959), 113 [Swansea, England].

94   Dearly beloved brethren,
Is it not a sin,
That, when you peel potatoes,
You throw away the skin?
The skins feed the pigs,
And the pigs feed you;
Dearly beloved brethren,
Is that not true?

Found in connection with the finger-game "Here is the church, and here is the steeple"; see Opie, Dictionary, p. 125.

Reid, *Misc. of the Rymour Club,* 1 (1911), 107 [Edinburgh].

95   Oh, **D**ear me,
Ma grannie catcht a flea. *See* **430**.

96   Oh, **D**ear me! What a flower I be!
Three young men came a-courting me.
One was blind, the other couldn't see;
And one fell down and broke his knee.
Out goes she.

Related to the taunt "Mama, mama pin a rose on me." Cf. the jump-rope rhyme "Mother, Mother, Mother, pin a rose on me" (JRR, p. 128).

Gardner, *JAF*, 31 (1918), 534 [Michigan].

Delia, Domma, Nona dig. *See* **129**.

97   **D**ic-dic-tation,
Cor-por-ation,
How many buses
Are in the station?
"Five."
One, two, three, four, five.

Those Dusty Bluebells (1965), 23 [Ayrshire]. Ends "What
were the buses' colour? / 'Red.' / R-E-D. And red you must
have on."

Opie (1969), 58. Two variants; the other begins "Dic-a dic-a
dation, / My operation. / How many stitches / Did I have?"

Dickery, dickery, dare. *See* **215**.

Dickory, dickory, dock. *See* **216**.

Dicky, Dicky, alla-ga-mo. *See* **248**.

98   **D**id you ever, ever, ever,
In your life, life, life,
See a nigger, nigger, nigger,
Kiss his wife, wife, wife?

> *Also found as a jump-rope rhyme; see JRR, p. 37 ("Did you
> ēv-a, īv-a, ōv-a").*

Gardner, *JAF*, 31 (1918), 531 [Michigan].

99   **D**id you ever see a bear
Walk a tightrope in the air?
If you did it was all a dream.
So out you must go for saying so.

Sutton-Smith (1959), 72 [New Zealand].

Did you ever tell a lie? *See* **42**.

100   **D**ie, do, Bendigo
Sprendigo and Romeo.

Turner (1969), 11 [England, ca. 1870; Melbourne, 1910].

101   **D**ip, dip, alla ber da,
Dutch cheese, sentima,
Sentima, alla ber da,
Dutch cheese, scram.

See also **276**. *Also found as a jump-rope rhyme; see* JRR, *p. 45 ("Dutch cheese and sauerkraut.")*

Bolton (1888), 112 [Massachusetts]. "Dutch cheese and
sauer-kraut, / O-U-T puts you out."
Emrich and Korson (1947), 119. Same as Bolton (1888) entry.
Opie (1969), 51–52 [southern Britain]. Four variants; other
beginnings are "Ip, dip, alaba da" and Ip, dip, dalabadi."

Dip, dip, dip,
My blue ship. *See* **289**.

Dip, red, white, blue. *See* **470**.

Dirckty, dirckty, dock. *See* **216**.

102 **D**octor, doctor, can you tell
What'll make a sick man well?
Take a bowl full of lice;
When the lice begin to crawl,
Take a spoon and eat them all.

Cf. *the jump-rope rhyme "Mother, mother, can you tell"*
(JRR, *p. 125).*

Bolton (1888), 118 [Connecticut].

Doctor! Doctor! how's your wife? *See* **361**.

103 **D**octor Foster's a very good man,
Whipped (Teaches) his scholars now and then;
When he whipped them, made them dance (And
    when he's done he takes a dance)
Out of Scotland (London), into France.
One, 2, 3, out.

Cf. **536**. *Usually a nursery rhyme; see Opie, Dictionary, pp.
168–169. Cf. also the jump-rope rhyme "Doctor Long is a very
good man"* (JRR, *p. 38).*

Opie (1969), 39 [England, ms. of 1795]. Ends "Out of England
into France; / He had a brave beaver with a fine snout, /
Stand you there out."

Chambers (1841), 121 [Scotland]. "Master Foster, very good
man, / Sweeps his college now and then."

Gregor (1881), 169, 170, 175. Four variants; two begin "Mr.
Smith," one ends "He wears a green beaver wi' a snout,"
two (one beginning "Mr. Frog") end "Oranges, oranges"
rhymes (**440**).

Napier, *Folk-Lore Record*, 4 (1881), 175. "Mister Foster";
ends "Up to London, o'er to France, / With a black beaver,
and a red snout; / Stand you there for you are out."

Babcock, *AA*, o.s., 1 (1888), 274 [District of Columbia]. "Doctor Franklin whipped his scholars / Out of Scotland into
Spain / And then back again."

Bolton (1888), 118, 119 [Pennsylvania, District of Columbia,
western Scotland]. Three variants: "Dr. Foster," "Mr. Foster" (with "beaver" and "snout"), and "Dr. Franklin"
("whipped his scholars / Out of Scotland into Spain / And
then back again").

Gregor (1891), 26 [Scotland]. Five variants. Three feature
"Mr. Dunn," "Mr. Smith," and "Mr. Macpherson" wearing
bonnet and snoot in fifth lines. Two versions ("Johnnie
Frog" and "Mr. Frog") end "Jenny, good spinner" rhymes
(**307**).

G.W.R., *Old Lore Misc.*, 5 (1912), 7 [Kirkwall, Scotland].
Begins "Mr. Drum"; ends "White fish, black trout, / Eerie
orrie, you're oot."

Emrich and Korson (1947), 118.

Doctor Franklin whipped his scholars. *See* **103**.

104   Doggie, doggie (woggie).
Step right out.

Bolton (1888), 108 [Connecticut]. Begins "Oggy, doggy."
Evans (1956), 28. With playing instructions.
Castagna, *NYFQ*, 25 (1969), 227 [New Rochelle, New York].

Donald Duck, he had no sense. *See* **561**.

105   Don't give me the dish-cloth wet,
Allie, Annie, Tony, Bet.

Now run out and play about,
Since you've wrung the dish-cloth out.

Bolton (1888), 111 [New York].
Emrich and Korson (1947), 118.

106 Down in the jungle
Living in a tent,
Better than a pre-fab—
No rent!

> *Also used for ball-bouncing.*

Opie (1959), 105 [Caistor, Lincolnshire, 1952].

107 Down went McGirty to the bottom of the sea,
Do re me! Out goes she!

Maryott, *SFQ*, 1, no. 4 (1937), 58.

108 Draw the snake.
Kill the snake.
Catch the blood.
Who dares to tap?

Cassidy, *PADS*, no. 29 (April 1958), 25 [Pennsylvania].

109 Oh, Dreary me,
Mother caught a flea. See **430**.

Dutch cheese and sauer-kraut. See **101**.

E

Eachie, peachie, pear, plum. See **27**.

110 Each, peach, pear, plum,
Out goes Tom Thumb;

Tom Thumb won't do,
Out goes Betty Blue;
Betty Blue won't go,
So out goes you.

See also **119**. *Also found as a jump-rope rhyme; see* JRR, *p. 46 ("Eachie peachie pearie plum").*

Opie (1969), 36 [England, first two lines current since ca. 1915].

Turner (1969), 11 [Melbourne and Adelaide, Australia, 1935]. First two lines only.

Opie (1959), 116 [Luncarty, near Perth, 1954]. "Eexie, peeksie, pearie, plum, / Out steps Tom Thumb; / Tom Thumb in a basin, / Out pops James Mason; / James Mason in a cellar, / Out pops Cinderella; / Cinderella in a fix, / Out pops Tom Mix; / Tom Mix is a star, / S-T-A-R."

111 Eachy, peachy, peary, plum,
Throwin' tatties up the lum,
Santa Claus got ane in the bum,
Eachy, peachy, peary, plum.

See also **580**.

Opie (1959), 386 [Forfar], and (1969), 38 [Scotland].

Ealy mealy dibbly Dick. See **128**.

Eanae, meanae, meinae, mo. See **136**.

Eani, meani, macker, racker. See **120**.

Eany, meany, maca, raca. See **120**.

Eany, meany, miny, mow,
Catch a thief by the toe. See **134**.

Eary, ory, hickory on. See **408**.

112 Ease, ose,
Man's nose (broze);

Caul parritch,
Pease brose.

See also **204**, Gregor (1891) entry.

Gregor (1881), 173, 175 [northeast Scotland]. Two variants:
one, "Eis, aas, oos, ink, / Peas, pottage sma' drink, / Twa an
twa's a tipenny loaf, / Twa an twa's it"; the other ends "A
potty fou / O' water broze."
Napier, *Folk-Lore Record*, 4 (1881), 175.
Bolton (1888), 108, 110 [west Scotland, Oregon]. Two variants; one begins "Eze, oze."
Edward Nicholson (1897), 306 [Scotland].
Gregor (1891), 21 [Scotland]. Sixteen variants. Other beginnings are "Ese, ose," "Eesy, osy," "Eese, ose," "Eese, oose
(ouse), aase, ink," or "Eese, aase (aese), oose, ink (zink)."
The endings are of four types: "Ese, ose, oot"; "A potty [or
'cuppie'] full of water brose"; "Peyse porridge, sma drink"
(the "man's nose" line is omitted, and three variants give
two additional lines); and "My dog's dead, / The cat's away
to the craidle wi' a sair head, / Canna crack a biscuit, canna
smoke a pipe, / Little Johnnie Middleton's breeks is ower
tight" (cf. **147**).
Maclennan (1909), 54 [Scotland]. "Easie-osie, mannie's
nosie."
Waugh, *JAF*, 31 (1918), 45 [Ontario, 1909].
G.W.R., *Old Lore Misc.*, 5 (1912), 7 [Kirkwall, Scotland].
"Eese oze; man's nose, / Pot full of water brose. / Lick
McKeever's muckle bubby nose, / Eerie oorie, you're out."
"Counting-Out Rhymes," *Misc. of Rymour Club*, 2, part 2
(1913), 96 [Edinburgh]. "Easy, osey, mannie's nosey, / Easy,
osey, out."
Our Meigle Book (1932), 166 [Scotland].
Ritchie (1965), 39 [Edinburgh]. Begins "Easie, osie."
Rodger (1969?), 19 [Scotland]. "Eezie, ozie, mannie's brosie, /
Eezie, ozie, oot."

Easie, osie. See **112**.

113   East strike, West strike,
The one that you love best strike.

See also **329**.

Heck, *JAF*, 40 (1927), 37.

Easy, osey. See **112**.

Eatum, peetam, . . . See **149**, **204**.

Eatle autle, blue bottle. See **147**.

Eat me, teat me, terry berry, ram tam toosh. See **127**.

Eatum, peatum, . . . See **139**, **149**, **204**.

Eaver Weaver, chimney sweeper. See **203**.

Ecka, decka, donie, crecka. See **10**.

Eckary, Airy, Ory, Anne. See **211**.

Ecker, becker, soda cracker. See **10**.

114   Eckery, peekery, jeckery, jye,
Stan ye oot by.

Gregor (1891), 30 [Scotland].

Eckety, speckity, spice so lickety. See **212**.

Eckie, picklie, eleka fa. See **276**.

Eddle oddle, black bottle. See **147**.

115   Eddle, weddle, limber lock,
Five miles in a clock;
I sat, I sunkel,
Daylight spunkle,
Fellasy dear,
To come to beer;
Invite you in to kill a fat
Little white dog and a mountainy cat;
For that same reason pull in your foot.

Cf. **287**, **567**.

Bolton (1888), 103 [Ireland].

Bolton, *JAF*, 10 (1897), 321 [Somerset, England]. "I-rum, bi-rum, brimberlock, / Six wires to the clock; / Hitspin, turnawin, / Tiffy, taffy, out and in."

116   E do me do,
So fa la la.
Ecka pishatal
And a jingasota.
Watermelons, watermelons,
A nickel for two.
Out goes you.

Evans (1956), 20.

Eeckie, ockey, black bokie. *See* **147**.

Eeenerty, feenerty, fickerty, fae. *See* **129**.

Ee-e-ry, o-e-ry (or-e-ry), ick-e-ry, Ann (bum). *See* **408**.

Eekery eckery mony mike. *See* **139**.

117   Ee-ley ley, olley ee,
Olma, tohma, fillie, fee,
Honda, konda, Mary, onda,
That last one out stands yonder.

Bolton (1888), 108 [California].

118   Eelie olie
Dugs tolie
Eelie olie
Out!

Ritchie (1965), 46 [Edinburgh].

Eely, meely, . . . *See* **140**.

Eena deena (deina) dina do (dass, doe, doh, dus, dust). See **119**, **133**, **141**.

119 Eenah, deenah, dinah, doh (duss, dhest),
Catla weela wila woe (wuss, wust),
Spit spot must be done (Pin, pan, musky dam),
Twiddlum, twaddlum, twenty-one.
O-U-T spells out and out you must go.

See also **410** for the ending.

Halliwell (1849), 135 [London]. Begins "Igdum, digdum, di-dum, dest."

Ellis, *Transactions of the Philological Society* (1878), 365–367. Eight variants, beginning "Eena, deenă [deină], dūs," "Eena deena dina dust (duss)," "Heena, deena, dina, dust," and "Igdum, digdum, didum, dest" and including Halliwell (1849) and *Mill Hill Magazine*, 5 (October 1877) versions. Alternate or extended endings are "One out, two out, three out / Out goes he," "One dead, two dead, three dead," and "A rotün dotün dirty dishclout / Now all you boys and girls / Are fairly push-ed out."

Bolton (1888), 98–99 [Massachusetts, England, Ireland]. Seven variants. One each from Halliwell (1849); *Notes and Queries*, 1st ser., 10 (November 4, 1854); and *Mill Hill Magazine*, 5 (October 1877). From Ireland: "Eena, deena, dina, dass, / Bottle 'a weena, wina, wass; / Pin, pan, muske-dan, / Eedleum, deedleum, twenty-one! / Eery, ory, out goes she!"

Notes and Queries, 1st ser., 10 (November 4, 1854), 369 [Guernsey]. Third line: "Tittle, tattle, what a rattle."

Daiken (1949), 2, 5, 10, 570. Four variants; two from Bolton (1888), one beginning "Haina, daina, diena, duss."

Northall (1892), 343, 347. Three variants; one each from *Notes and Queries*, 1st ser., 10 (November 4, 1854), and Ellis, *Transactions* (1878).

Opie (1969), 44 [England, 1859, 1891, 1922]. Three variants; one begins "Een-a, deen-a, dine-a, dust" and ends "O-U-T spells out, / A nasty dirty dish-clout; / Out boys out!"; one, "Zaina, daina, dina, disk," from Gregor (1891).

Turner (1969), 11 [central Victoria (ca. 1875) and Melbourne (ca. 1910), Australia]. Two variants: one begins "Eeny meeny miney-mo" with "Each peach pear plum / Out goes Tom Thumb" ending (**110**); the other has as third and fourth lines "A way flour flock, / Allago pallago we wo wis."

Mill Hill Magazine, 5 (October 1877) [England]. Ends "O-U-T spells out, / With a dish, dash, dirt or clout, / Out goes he."

Gregor (1891), 14, 31 [Scotland]. Two variants: one begins
"Zaina, daina, dina, disk," with the third line "Each, peach,
must be done"; one ends "O-U-T spells out, / With a rotten,
totten, dirty dish-clout."

Leon, *JAF*, 8 (1895), 255 [Massachusetts, Ireland]. Two variants; one begins "Hana dana tina das."

Sutton-Smith (1959), 63 [New Zealand, 1895, 1900]. Three
variants; two end "Each peach pear plum, / Out goes Tom
Thumb. / O-U-T spells out"; one begins "Eeny meeny minney mo."

Bolton, *JAF*, 10 (1897), 314, 319. Two variants: one from
Cape Toron; one, first two lines only.

Dew (1898), 80 [Norfolk, England]. Two variants beginning
"Einey, deeney, deiney diss (duss)."

Enid Porter (1969), 209 [Cambridgeshire, late nineteenth
century]. "Eene deena vinah voh / Catra veen vinah, voh /
O-U-T spells out goes she."

Maclagan, *Folk-Lore*, 16 (1905), 450. Begins "Ina, dina, dinalo, dash."

Davis (1906), 210.

Waugh, *JAF*, 31 (1918), 45–46 [Ontario, 1909]. Begins "Ena,
dena, dina, dust."

"Uncle Sandy," *Word-Lore*, 1 (1926), 224.

Wood and Goddard (1940), 570.

Evans (1956), 13.

Howard, *NYFQ*, 16 (1960), 135, 136 [Australia]. Two variants, beginning "Eena, deena, dinah, do" and "Eeny,
meeny, miny, mo"; both end "Each peach, pear, plum, / Out
goes old Tom Thumb."

Eena, meena, hickory, Dick. *See* **128**.

120   **E**ena meena macker racker
Rare, ro, domino,
Juliacker, alapacker,
Rom, Tom, tush.

Opie (1969), 40–41, 53 [Scotland, England, Wales, Australia,
New Zealand, since 1920's]. Eighteen variants, beginning
"Eeny, meeny," "Eeni, meeni," "Iney, meney," "Ina,
mina," "Eany, meany," "Ena, mena," "Eenie meenie,"
"Eani meani," "Eny, meeny," and "Eena, mena." Discussed
in relation to other gibberish rhymes. The rhyme is sometimes introduced with "I went to a Chinese laundry / To
buy a loaf of bread; / They wrapped it in a tablecloth / And

this is what they said." Three embryo forms of the rhymes are given: "Ena dena, dasha, doma" (1909); "Eener, deener, abber, dasher" (1910); and "Haberdasher, isher asher" (1916) (*see* **123**).

Turner (1969), 11 [Melbourne, 1920, 1962]. Two variants: "Eena, meena, micka, macka" and "Eeny meeny macka racka."

Daiken (1949), 2.

Ritchie (1965), 45 [Edinburgh]. Two variants.

Those Dusty Bluebells (1965), 22 [Ayrshire]. "Eenie meenie macaracha, / A M dominacha, / Cheek-a-pop-a, lolly-pop-a, / Am bam bush."

Fowke (1969), 111 [Canada]. "Eeny meeny macker racker, / Rear ride down the racker. / Chicka poppa lollipop, / A rum tum trash."

Eena, meena, micka, macka. *See* **120**.

Eena, meena, mina, mo (moe). *See* **121, 122, 136, 141**.

121   Eena, meena, mina, mo.
Fox and hens and Dinah Doe,
Allicum, ballicum, bulkney, bo,
O-U-T spells Out.

Burne (1883), 572 [Shropshire] = Northall (1892), 344.

Eena, meena, mink (ming, mong). *See* **131**.

122   Eena, meena, mona, mina.
Jack the hena, hina, hona.
A, K, kick the ram.
Who will be the bravest man
To beat the horse,
To beat the drum,
To tell me when the enemy comes?
One, two, three, and out goes she!

   Cf. ending of **16**.

Steele, *Old Lore Misc.*, 2 (1909), 194 [Orphir, Orkney, 1853].
   "Eenie, meenie, mynie, moanie, / Sixty, steenie, stynie,

stony. / Gae away, gae away, kity galam, / Thou shalt be out, mistress mam."

Bolton (1888), 106 [Massachusetts].

John Nicholson (1890), 154. Begins "Eeny, meny, miny, mo, / Catalina si-ne so, / Kay-o-way, Kitty-ca-lan / Thou shalt be my soldier man, / To ride my horse," etc., and ends "O.U.T. spells very fair, / Rottom, bottom, dish clout, / Out goes she."

Gregor (1891), 20 [Scotland]. "Eena, meena, mina, moe, / Jack, alack, asina, so, / E, K, kitlie, klam, / Thou shalt be my soldier man," etc.

Addy (1895), 147–148. Two variants. One (ending "Ah me, count 'em along. / You shall be the soldier's man," etc.) = Opie (1969), 44.

Flett, *Old Lore Misc.*, 3 (1910), 3 [Orkney]. "Eenie, meenie, mynie, moanie, / Sixty, steenie, stynie, stony, / Care awa, Kity cala, / Thou shalt be my master's ma, / To saddle my horse," etc.

Eena, meena, mona (mony), mite (my, mi, mack). See **139**.

Eena, mena, dippa, deena. See **140**.

Eena, mena, mina, mike. See **139**.

Eena, mena, mina, mo. See **141**.

Een-a-rie, twa-a-rie, . . . See **410**.

Eendy, beendy, bamba roe (bamber eendy). See **133**, **141**, **273**.

Eene deena vinah voh. See **119**.

123   Eener, deener, abber, dasher,
Ooner, eye-sher,
Om, pom, tosh.
Iggery-eye, iggery-eye,
Pop the vinegar in the pie,
Harum scarum, pop canarum,
Skin it.

Notes and Queries, 10th ser., 11 (June 5, 1909), 446 [Orkney].
    Begins "Ena, dena, dasha, doma."
Opie (1969), 41 [Orkney, 1909; London, 1910, 1916]. Three
    variants cited as embryo forms of "Eena meena macker
    racker" rhyme (**120**). Two consist of two lines only:
    "Haberdasher, isher, asher, / Om, pom, tosh" and "Ena,
    dena, dasha, doma, / Hong, pong, toss" (the latter = *Notes*
    and Queries above).

Eeneri twaeri tukkeri seven. See **410**.

124   Eeneri twaeri zistery zan,
    Bessie Bell cam tudderi tan;
    Leeram laarim, Queen o' Fair;
    Titbow, tatbow, tiddi widdi halta-go
    Fetch in my coo, dy coo, Jeanne's coo:
    Eetlim putlim, penny muttl highness.

> *Cf.* **410** *for first two lines.*

Nicolson (1920), 91 [Shetland].

Eenertee (Eenerty), feenertee (feenerty), fickertie
    (fickery, fickerty), feg (fae, faig). See **129**.

Eenerty, fickerty, faig. See **129**.

Eenery, twaaerty (twaaery, twaery, twoery), . . .
    See **410**.

Eeney, meeny, tipty te. See **140**.

Eeney, pheeny, figgery fegg. See **129**.

125   Eenie meenie, clean peenie,
    If you want a piece and jelly,
    Just walk out.

Maclagan (1901), 249 [Scotland].

Eenie Meenie Hickory Dick. See **128**.

Eenie meenie macaracha (macca racca; maka, raka). *See* **120**.

Eenie, meenie, manie mo,
Catch a nigger by the toe. *See* **133**.

Eenie meenie mannie mo,
Sit the baby on the po. *See* **137**.

Eenie, meenie, mina, mo. *See* **133**.

Eenie, meenie, minie, mo (moe). *See* **134**, **135**, **136**.

Eenie, meenie, miny, mo. *See* **133**.

Eenie, meenie, monie, mite (Mike). *See* **139**.

Eenie, meenie, mynee, moe. *See* **139**.

Eenie, meenie, mynie, moanie. *See* **122**.

Eenie, meenie, ottie i. *See* **130**.

Eenie, meenie, teppa seenie (tip de-dee, tipsy tee, tipsie teenie, tipsy toe). *See* **140**.

Eeni, meeni, mackeracka. *See* **120**.

Eeni, meeny, money, my. *See* **139**.

Eenitie, feenitie, ficer, ta. *See* **129**.

Eenity, feenity, fickery (fickety), faig (fay, feg, fig). *See* **129**.

Eenity, feenity, my black hen. *See* **213**.

Eenity, finity fickerty, fegg. *See* **129**.

Eenity, meenity, . . . *See* **129**.

Eenity, peenity, my black hen. *See* **213**.

Eenity, peenity, pickety, iven. *See* **410**.

Eenity teenity feenity fay. *See* **129**.

Eenneri, anneri, sirterie, sannerie. *See* **145**.

Eenrie, twaarie, . . . *See* **410**.

Eenta, feenta, ficketie-feg. *See* **129**.

Een, teen (tean), tether (tuther), fether (feather, mether) fip (fitz, pip, pimp). *See* **500**.

Eentery, meentery, . . . *See* **287**.

Eentie teentie heathery beathery. *See* **500**.

Eentie teentie terry erry ram tam tosh. *See* **127**.

126
Eentie, teentie, tippernny bun,
The cat gud oat to get some fun,
To get some fun played on a drum (It got some fun on Toddy's grun).
Eentie, teentie, tipenny bun.

Opie (1969), 46–47 [Scotland, since 1855]. Three variants, beginning "Eenty teenty haligalum," "Eenty teenty tuppenny bun," and "Eenty-peenty, halligo lum."
Gregor (1881), 170 [northwest Scotland].
Gregor (1891), 19 [Scotland]. Five variants, beginning "Eenty, teenty," "Zeenty, teenty," "Zinty tinty," and "Ynky, pinky, hallogolum."
Maclagan (1901), 248 [Argyleshire] = Opie (1947), 55. "As Eenty Feenty Halligolum / The cat went out to get some fun. / He got some fun and tore his skin / As Eenty Feenty Halligolin."
Maclagan, *Folk-Lore*, 16 (1905), 452. Begins "Zinty, pinkty, halligolum." Third line: "It got some fun and back it come."
Kelly, *Misc. of Rymour Club*, 1 (1911), 5 [New Zealand]. Begins "Eenty-peenty, halligo lum."

Reid, *Misc. of Rymour Club*, 1 (1911), 103 [Edinburgh].

Marwick (1949), 72 [Orkney]. Begins "Eenty, peenty, halli-go-lum."

Ritchie (1965), 46, 47, [Edinburgh]. Two variants, beginning "Eentie teentie tuppenny bun" and "Inkie pinkie hala balum."

Eentie teentie tithery mithery bamfileerie. *See* **500**.

Eentil, teentil, eddy, galong. *See* **164**.

Een tw lacary seven. *See* **410**.

Eenty feenty fickery fell. *See* **129**.

Eenty, meenty, diggity, fig. *See* **129**.

Eenty, meenty, monty, my. *See* **139**.

Eenty, menty, tibby, fig. *See* **129**.

Eenty, peenty, halli-go-lum. *See* **126**.

Eenty, peenty, pickety, pae. *See* **129**.

Eenty, teenty, feggeine fell. *See* **212**.

Eenty, teenty fickery (figgery, figgerty, figury) fell. *See* **129**.

Eenty teenty haligalum (tuppeny bun). *See* **126**.

Eenty teenty, heathery bell (ithery bithery). *See* **500**.

127　Eenty, teenty, orry, ram, tam, toosh,
　　　Ging in alow the bed, an catch a wee fat moose.
　　　Cut it up in slices, and fry it in a pan.
　　　Mind and keep the gravy for the wee fat man.

Ritchie (1965), 39, 45 [Edinburgh]. Two variants, beginning "Eentie teentie terry erry ram tosh" and "Eat me, teat me, terry berry, ram tam toosh."
Opie (1969), 38 [Aberdeen and Edinburgh, Scotland].

Eenty, teenty, tethery, methery. *See* **500**.

Eenty, teenty, tickerty teven. *See* **410**.

Eenty, teenty, tippenny Ann. *See* **290**.

Eenty, teenty, tippenny bun. *See* **204**.

Eenty, teenty, tuppenny bun. *See* **580**.

Eeny, come Meeny, come down to your dinner. *See* **307**.

Eeny, meeny, choo cha leeny. *See* **140**.

Eeny, meeny, dilly, deany. *See* **140**.

128   Eeny, meeny, dippery Dick,
Deelia, dollia, Dominick,
Hypa, potcha, dominotcha,
Tee, taw, tick.

See **129** *for an explanation of this entry as a rhyme subcategory.*

Bolton (1888), 107–108, 110 [New York, Massachusetts]. Five variants. Other beginnings are "Ana, mana, dippery Dick," "Eeny, meeny, ipry Dick," "Haley, baley, tithaby, tick," "Hailey, bailey, tillamy Dick," "Ena, mena figgitty, fick," and "Zeeny, meeny, fickety, fick."
Hoke, *JAF*, 5 (1892), 120 [North Carolina]. Begins "Henery, Menery, Deepery Dick."
Chamberlain, *JAF*, 8 (1895), 252–253 [Ontario]. Begins "Eeny, meeny, dippery, Dick."
Waugh, *JAF*, 31 (1918), 42 [Ontario, 1909]. Begins "Eeny, meeny, hippery dic."
Gardner, *JAF*, 31 (1918), 528–529. Five variants; one begins

"Intery, mintery, hippity Dick"; another begins "Eena, meena, hickory, Dick."

Brewster (1952), 168 [North Carolina, 1923, 1926–1928]. Begins "Ana, mana, dippery dick."

Whitney and Bullock (1925), 135 [Maryland]. Begins "Aihie, mailie, tribily, trick."

Maryott, *SFQ*, 1, no. 4 (1937), 40 [Nebraska].

Cassidy, *PADS*, no. 29 (April 1958), 23–24 [Washington, North Dakota]. Two variants, beginning "Eenie Meenie Hickory Dick" and "Eeny, meeny, tooper tick."

Fowke (1969), 111 [Canada]. Three variants; one, "Eeny, meeny hipperdick, / Fee fi fo / Uckle buckle boo, / Out goes you. / Half a peach and half a plum, / Half a pound of chewing gum"; one, "Ealy mealy dibbly Dick, / Tine tone Tommy Nick, / Brock nock country brooch, / Tine tone tick."

Eeny, meeny dixie deeny. *See* **140**.

129 Eeny, meeny, figgledy, fig (faig, faep, feg, fell).
Delia, dolia, dominig,
Ozy, pozy doma-nozy,
Tee, tau, tut,
Uggeldy, buggedy, boo!
Out goes you.

*One nonsense rhyme is so ubiquitous and subject to such wide variation that it has been broken into three separately entered submembers: "Eeny, meeny, figgledy, fig" (given here), "Eeny, meeny, dippery Dick" (**128**), and "Eeny, meeny, tipsy, tee" (**140**). The rhyme so divided is clearly in the more inclusive "Eeny, meeny" series, but, as is typical of this series, it has many other phonetically similar beginnings. The factors which relate the various submembers of the rhyme are that the second line is usually "Delia, dolia, dominig" (ee, o, etc.) or some other close phonetic relative and that the third line is commonly something like "oker, poker, dominoker."*

The three submember divisions could easily have been expanded; they were chosen, somewhat arbitrarily, for reasons of economy. In general, the rhymes are entered in the three subcategories as follows:

"Eeny, meeny, dippery Dick": The last word of the first line is or rhymes with "Dick."

"Eeny, meeny, figgledy, fig": The last word of the first line begins with "f."

"Eeny, meeny, tipsy tee": The last word of the first line is or rhymes with "tee," "teeny," "toe," or "taily."

A few rhymes that meet none of these criteria appear under "Eeny, meeny, figgledy, fig."

Alternate third lines common in "Eeny, meeny, figgledy, fig" rhymes are variations of "Oats, floats, country notes" and "Irky, birky, story rock." See also **579**. As a jump-rope rhyme, see JRR, p. 89 ("Inty ninty tibbety fig").

Inglis (1894), 102 [Scotland, 1850's]. Begins "Eenerty, feenerty, fickerty, feg."

Napier, *Folk-Lore Record*, 4 (1881), 175. Begins "Zeenty, meeny, fickety, fick."

Gregor (1881), 173; (1891), 17–18 [Scotland]. Nineteen variants, beginning "Eenerty, feenerty, fickerty (fickery), fegg (faig)," "Eenerty, fickerty, faig," "Eenity, finity, fickety, fegg," "Inerty, finerty, fleckety, faig," "Innerty, finnerty, fickety fegg," "Iseenty, teenty, fickerty, faig," "Zeenty, teenty, fickety, faig," "Enity, fenity, ficty, fegg," "Eenerty, feenerty, fikerty, fae," "Inity, finity, fickerty, fae," "Eenity, feenity, fickety (ficer), fay (ta)," "Zeenty, feenty, fickety, fae," "Senty, tenty, ticity, fae," "Eenty, peenty, pickety, pae," "Eenty, teenty, figgerty, fell," and "Zeenty, teenty, tickety, tegg."

Bolton (1888), 103, 107–108, 123 [Nova Scotia; Connecticut; Virginia; Rhode Island; California; Cumberland, England; Scotland]. Ten variants; one from Napier, *Folk-Lore Record*, 4 (1881), one from *Folklore Journal*, 1 (1883). Beginnings are "Inty, minty, tippety, fis," "Heely, peely, tipty, fig," "Haley, maley, tippety, fig," "Ana, mana, tippety fig," "Ena, mena, figgitty, fick," "Zeeny, meeny, fickety, fick," "Eeney, pheeny, figgery fegg," and "Eenity, feenity, fickety, feg."

Folk-Lore Journal, 1 (1883), 385 [Cumberland, England] = Northall (1892), 344. Begins "Eeny, pheeny, figgery, fegg."

M'Bain (1887), 345 [Scotland]. Begins "Innertie, finnertie, fickertie, fegg."

Mills and Bishop, *The New Yorker* (November 13, 1937). 34 [Scotland, nineteenth century]. Two variants, beginning "Inty minty tibblety fig" (= Botkin [1944], 800) and "Eenerty feenerty fickerty fegg."

Opie (1969), 42–43, 51 [Philadelphia; Connecticut; New York City; Pasadena, California; Ruthin, England; Scotland; since late nineteenth century]. Eight variants (one from Bolton [1888], one from Evans [1956]), discussed in relation to other gibberish rhymes. Beginnings are "Inty, minty, tibbity, (tippety), fee (fig)," "Impty, dimpty, tibbity fig," "Zeenty, teenty, figery, fell," "Inty, tinty, figgery, fell," "Eenty, teeny, figury, fell," and "Zeeny, meeny, feeny, fig" (begins a "Sinty, tinty, huthery" rhyme [**500**]).

Bassett, *The Folk-Lorist*, 1 (1892–1893), 157 [Illinois]. Begins "Ena, mena, timety fig."

Clifton Johnson (1896), 166. Begins "Impty, mimpty, tibbity, fig."

Bolton, *JAF*, 10 (1897), 320 [Scotland]. Begins "Zeenty, teenty, fickety, fell."

Edward Nicholson (1897), 270 [Scotland]. Begins "Eenerty, feenerty, fickerty, feg."

Maclagan (1901), 250 [Argyleshire]. Begins "Zeenty feenty fanty fegg"; ends "I've a cherry, I've a chess, / I've a bonny blue glass / I've a dog among the corny / Cryin' Billy blow the horn."

Davis (1906), 209, 211 [Scotland]. Two variants, beginning "Eenity, feenity, fickety, fig" and "Delia Domna, Nona dig, / Oats floats, country notes."

Firth, *Old Lore Misc.*, 2 (1909), 135 [Orkney]. Begins "Eenta, feenta, ficketie-feg."

Maclennan (1909), 52 [Scotland]. Two variants, beginning "Eenerty, feenerty, fickerty, fae" and "Eenerty, feenerty, fickerty, faig."

Waugh, *JAF*, 31 (1918), 42, 45 [Ontario, 1909]. Three variants, beginning "Inty, minty, figgity, feg," "Enty, menty, figgity, fag," and "Sinty, vinity, vickety, vy."

Robertson, *NF*, 3, no. 2 (Summer 1960), 28–29 [Shelburne County, Nova Scotia, 1910 and 1960]. Three variants, beginning "Intry, mintry, dibbity, fig," "Eenty, meenty, diggity, fig," and "Enty, menty, tibby, fig."

Lyle, *Misc. of Rymour Club*, 1 (1911), 88 [East Lothian]. Begins "As eenta, feenta ficket a feg"; ends "Toosh out, toosh in; / Toosh about the ravel pin; / The ravel pin's owre dear; / Ten pounds every year."

G.W.R., *Old Lore Misc.*, 5 (1912), 6 [Kirkwall]. Two variants, beginning "Inty tinty fickery fell" and "Eenity teenity feenity fay."

Gardner, *JAF*, 31 (1918), 527, 528, 529 [Michigan]. Three variants; one begins "Empty, mempty, tick-a-to-fig"; one, "Inta, minta, dibbity, fig."

Botkin (1947), 905 [Vermont, 1930's]. Begins "Inty, minty, dibity fig."

Our Meigle Book (1932), 165 [Scotland]. Begins "Enity, feenity, fickity feg."

Maryott, *SFQ*, 1, no. 4 (1937), 43–44 [Nebraska]. Three variants: two begin "Inty, minty, dibbety (tippety) fig"; one begins "Inta, minta, diggity fig."

Withers (1946), n.p. Begins "Inty minty, tibblety fig."

Milne (1947), 58. Begins "Azeenty teenty figgery fell."

Roberts, *HF*, 8 (1949), 9 [Massachusetts]. Begins "Inty minty tippety fig."

Gullen (1950), 14. Begins "Eenity, feenity, fickety, feg."

Ogilvie (1952), 28 [Scotland]. Begins "Innerty, finnerty fickerty fig."

Randolph, *SFQ*, 17 (1953), 245 [Arkansas]. Begins "Inty minty seventy-six."

Evans (1956), 17. Begins "Impty, dimpty, tibbity, fig."

Cassidy, *PADS*, no. 29 (April 1958), 24 [Massachusetts, Michigan]. Two variants, beginning "Inty, minty, dibble de fig" and "Inty, minty, tibbity, fig."

Opie (1959), 378 [Forfar]. Begins "Innerty fenerty fickety fage."

Howard, *NYFQ*, 16 (1960), 137 [Australia, from Scotland via New Zealand]. Begins "Enty, tenty, fickery fig."

G. B. Adams, *Ulster Folklife*, 11 (1965), 94–95, 97 [Ireland and Scotland]. Five variants, beginning "Izeenty teenty figgery fell," "Eenerty feenerty fickery fey," "Eenty, feenty fickery fell," "Zeenty peenty figgery fell," and "Inty minty dibbity fig."

Those Dusty Bluebells (1965), 22 [Ayrshire]. Begins "Eenty teenty fickery fell."

McNaughtan, *Chapbook*, 4, no. 1 (1967?), 5 [Glasgow]. Begins "Eenty, teenty, figgery fell."

Fowke (1969), 111 [Canada]. Begins "Intry mintry dibbity fig."

Rodger (1969?), 19 [Scotland]. Begins "Eenertee, feenertee, fickertie, feg."

Brill, *GMW*, 24 (1972), 3. Begins "Inty, minty, tibity, fig."

Eeny, meeny hipperdick (hippity Dick, hippery dic). See 128.

Eeny, meeny, ipry Dick. See 128.

Eeny, meeny, maca (macca, macka, macker), racar (racca, racka, acker). See 120.

Eeny, meeny, many, moe. See 133.

130   Eeny, meeny, middy, mat,
Domido, domidat.
Santa, panta, pilla roos,
San, pan, toos.

Gregor (1891), 20 [Scotland]. Six variants, beginning "Eeny,
    meeny, mit a mat," "Zeeny, meeny, mina, ma," "Senny,
    menny, mitta ma," "Zinny, minny, mutta, ma," and
    "Zeeny, meeny, meta, ma," followed by close variations of
    "Dum ado, dum ada, / Zanty, panty, pull a roe, / Anty, tanty,
    tush, toe."
Edward Nicholson (1897), 219 [Glasgow, 1893]. Begins
    "Eeny, meeny, mitty, mat."
"Counting-Out Rhymes," *Misc. of Rymour Club*, 2, part 2
    (1913), 93 [Edinburgh]. "Eenie, meenie, ottie i, / Dummy
    doo, dummy di; / Anty, panty, peelie, roe, / An, tan, tush,
    toe."
Gardner, *JAF*, 31 (1918), 528 [Michigan].

Eeny meeny miney mo,
Katalawheela whila wo. See **119**.

Eeny meeny miney mo,
Stick the bairn on the po. See **137**.

Eeny meeny ming mong. See **131**.

131   Eeny, meeny, mink monk
Chink, chonk, chow
Oosa, noosa, nack-a-toosa
Oe, ni now.
Bread, butter, sugar, tea,
You are not he.

Bolton (1888), 110 [Wisconsin]. Begins "Eena, meena, mink."
Turner (1969), 12 [Canberra, 1955; Melbourne, 1968]. Two
    variants; one begins "Eeny meeny ming mong."
Evans (1956), 7.
Sutton-Smith (1959), 71 [New Zealand]. Two variants: "Esa
    vesa vack vesa, / Mink monk mow, / Esa vesa vack vesa, / Ve
    vi vow" and "Ina mina ping pong. / Ching chong, / Isa visa
    vacka tu. / Vi va veck."
Howard, *NYFQ*, 16 (1960), 134 [Australia]. Four variants; one
    begins "Eena meena."

Opie (1969), 45 [England, Australia, Rhodesia]. Four variants; one begins "Eena, meena, ming, mong"; another, "Ala mala ming mong."

Eeny meeny minney mo. See **119**.

Eeny, meeny, miny, man. See **132**.

Eeny, meeny, miny, maw. See **132**, **139**.

132   Eeny, meeny, miny, maw.
Erracle, terracle, tiny, taw.
One two, three,
Out goes s-h-e!

Bolton (1888), 105 [Doncaster, England].
Boyce and Bartlett (1946), 31.
Gullen (1950), 14. Begins "Eeny, meeny, miny, man."

Eeny, meeny, miny, min. See **134**.

Eeny, meeny, miny, mo,
Cas-a-lara, bina, bo (Catalina si-ne so). See **122**, **136**.

133   Eeny, meeny, miny, mo,
Catch a nigger (baby, rabbit) by the toe,
If he hollers, let him go.
Eeny, meeny, miny, mo.

See also **134**. *Also found as a jump-rope rhyme (JRR, p. 47).*
See Opie, Dictionary, pp. 156–157.

Knapp (1976), 4, 197–198 [United States from revolutionary times]. Discussed as racist rhyme since 1850. Mentions substituting names of animals or national enemies (Hitler, Tojo, Castro, Viet Cong) for "nigger."
Sutton-Smith (1959), 63 [New Zealand, 1870, 1880]. Two variants beginning "Eena deena dina doe (doh)"; one ends "Why did you let him go? / 'Cos he bit my finger so."
Robertson, NF, 3, no. 2 (Summer 1960), 28 [Shelburne County, Nova Scotia, since 1880's]. Two variants; one, from

1880's, adds "Hot potatoes on his chin, / 'Nuff to make the devil grin."

Babcock, *AA*, o.s., 1 (1888), 274 [District of Columbia]. Begins "Enee, menee, tipsy-toe."

Bolton (1888), 105–106 [throughout United States; Ireland; Edinburgh]. Six variants; one, "Eeny, meeny, miny, mum, / Catch a nigger by the thumb."

Opie (1969), 36 [England, current since at least 1890].

Gregor (1891), 19, 20, 31 [Scotland]. Four variants; one, "Catch your neighbor . . . / If he quarrels let him go"; one begins "Endy, bendy, bendy, bough, / Hold the tiger by the tow"; one, beginning "Eendy, beendy, bamba, roe, / Caught a chicken by the toe," begins an "Eeny, weeny, winey, wo" **(141)** rhyme.

Wheeler, *The Folk-Lorist*, 1 (1892–1893), 68 [Illinois].

Clifton Johnson (1896), 160. Begins "Ene, mene, mini, mo."

Edward Nicholson (1897), 308 [Scotland]. Begins "Eeny, meeny, many, moe."

Blakeborough (1898), 262 [Yorkshire]. Two variants, beginning "Ana, mana, mina, mo" and "Ena, mena, mina, mo."

Potter, "Eeny, Meeny, Miny, Mo," *Standard Dictionary* (1949), 339 [New England, upstate New York, northern United States, 1899; New York City, 1949]. Mentions trend to substituting "baby," "rooster," "black cat," or "rabbit" for "nigger."

Monroe, *AA*, n.s., 6 (1904), 47 [Massachussetts].

Maclagan, *Folk-Lore*, 16 (1905), 450. Begins "Eenie, meenie, manie, mo."

Davis (1906), 208. Two variants, beginning "Eena, deina, dina doe" and "Eeny, meeny, mony mo."

Notes and Queries, 10th ser., 11 (June 5, 1909), 466 [Orkney]. Begins "Rick, stick, stickity ho!"

Perrow, *JAF*, 26 (1913), 142 [Mississippi, 1909].

G.W.R., *Old Lore Misc.*, 5 (1912), 6 [Kirkwall, Scotland].

Anderson, *Evening Ledger* (May 17, 1916). Rhyme mentioned.

Douglas (1916), 44 [London]. Begins "Ener Dena Dinah Doe."

Soifer, *Story Parade*, 6, no. 7 (July 1941), 15 [Brooklyn, 1916].

Waugh, *JAF*, 31 (1918), 42 [Ontario]. Begins "Eny meny miny mo."

Wintemberg, *JAF*, 31 (1918), 150, 157 [New Dundee and Roebuck, Ontario].

Smiley, *JAF*, 32 (1919), 377 [Virginia].

Watson (1921), 38 [Somerset, England].

Acker (1923), 17.

Bett (1924), 58. Begins "Eena, meena, mina, mo."

Whitney and Bullock (1925), 134 [Maryland].

"Uncle Sandy," *Word-Lore*, 1 (1926), 224.

Heck, *JAF*, 40 (1927), 36.

Guy B. Johnson (1930), 165 [St. Helena Island, North Carolina]. Two variants: one, "Ketch a neighbor"; the other begins "Ink stink, tobacco stink."

Henry (1934), 238 [Indiana].

Turner (1969), 11–12 [Melbourne, ca. 1935; current throughout Australia]. Two variants; one begins "Eena deena dinah do."

Withers (1946), n.p. [from Brooklyn College students, 1935–1946].

Maryott, *SFQ*, 1, no. 4 (1937), 54, 55 [Nebraska]. Two variants; one begins "Filson, folson, Nicholas Dan, / Catch a nigger if you can."

Mills and Bishop, *The New Yorker* (November 13, 1937), 34 [Scotland]. Two lines only: "Endy bendy bamba roe, / Caught a chicken by the toe."

Brewster, *SFQ*, 3 (1939), 179.

Wood and Goddard (1940), 570.

"Folk Rhymes and Jingles" (1944), 4 [Maryland].

Bryant, *NYFQ*, 2 (1946), 291. Alternate second line: "Catch a Jap by the toe."

Emrich and Korson (1947), 122.

Yoffie, *JAF*, 60 (1947), 30 [Missouri].

Withers, *NYFQ*, 3 (1947), 214. "Eenie, meenie, miny, mo, / Catch a Jap (rabbit, tiger, rooster) by the toe."

Hansen, *WF*, 7 (1948), 52.

Withers (1948), 83.

Hines, *Daedalian Quarterly*, 17, no. 1 (Fall 1949), 41 [Texas].

Harry Harris, *Evening Bulletin* (May 30, 1949), 10.

Roberts, *HF*, 8 (1949), 8 [Indiana, Tennessee, New Jersey, Montreal, Pennsylvania, Maine].

Gullen (1950), 14.

Musick and Randolph, *JAF*, 63 (1950), 430–431 [Missouri].

Brewster (1952), 162–163 [North Carolina].

Evans (1956), 8.

Bley (1957), 96.

Bluebells My Cockle Shells (1961), n.p. [Ayrshire].

Koch (1961), 117 [Kansas].

Grayson (1962), 73. "Catch a tiger."

Leventhal and Cray, *WF*, 22 (1963), 240–241 [California]. Four variants; one begins "Mary had a little lamb."

Ritchie (1965), 45 [Edinburgh and Adelaide]. Two variants, beginning "Eenie meenie mina mo" and "Eeny, meeny, myny, mo"; one has "Catch a wombat" in second line.

Goldstein (1971), 169, 174 [Philadelphia, 1966–1967]. Two
   variants, featuring "tiger" and "feller," the latter extended
   by the lines "My mother says you are out. / But I say you are
   it."
Castagna, *NYFQ*, 25 (1969), 228 [New Rochelle, New York].
   "Catch a tiger"; ends "My mother says to pick this very best
   one and you are not it."
Fowke (1969), 111 [Canada]. Two variants: "Catch a monkey"
   and "Catch a beatnik . . . / If he hollers 'Daddy-O,' / Play it
   cool and let him go."
Enid Porter (1969), 209 [Cambridgeshire].
Rodger (1969?), 19 [Scotland].
Cooper (1972), 82. "I caught a lizard."
Milberg (1976), 24. "Catch a tiger."
Howard (1977), 212 [Texas].

134 Eeny, meeny, miny, mo,
Catch a nigger (darky) by the toe.
If he hollers, make him pay,
Fifty dollars every day.

With numerous conventional endings. See also **133**.

Potter, "Eeny, Meeny, Miny, Mo," *Standard Dictionary*
   (1949), 339 [Nebraska; Illinois, Iowa, and Connecticut,
   1880's]. Three variants (one "Eeny, meeny, miny, mum, /
   Catch a nigger by the thumb, / If he hollers send him hum, /
   Eeny, meeny, miny, mum") reflecting controversy over
   1850 Fugitive Slave Law = Knapp (1976), 197.
Bolton (1888), 105 [Iowa, Illinois, Nebraska] = Daiken (1949),
   10. Two variants, one ending "Every time the nigger hol-
   lers, / Make him pay you fifty dollars."
Perrow, *JAF*, 26 (1913), 142 [Mississippi, 1909].
Gardner, *JAF*, 31 (1918), 526 [Michigan].
Whitney and Bullock (1925), 34 [Maryland].
Hudson (1928), 116 [Mississippi].
Henry (1934), 238 [Indiana].
Maryott, *SFQ*, 1, no. 4 (1937), 54 [Nebraska].
Brewster, *SFQ*, 3 (1939), 179.
McAtee (1946), 22 [Indiana].
Yoffie, *JAF*, 60 (1947), 30 [Missouri].
Withers (1948), 83.
Hines, *Daedalian Quarterly*, 17, no. 1 (Fall 1949), 41 [Texas].
   Begins "Eenie, meenie, minie, mo."
Roberts, *HF*, 8 (1949), 8 [Tennessee].

Brewster (1952), 162–163 [North Carolina]. Begins "Eeny, meeny, miny, min, / Catch a nigger by the chin."
Evans (1956), 8.
Howard, *NYFQ*, 16 (1960), 135 [Australia, from United States].
Millard, *NYFQ*, 16 (1960), 148.
Koch (1961), 118 [Kansas].
Leventhal and Cray, *WF*, 22 (1963), 239–240 [California]. Five variants.
Brill, *GMW*, 24 (1972), 3. Begins "Eany, meany, miny, mow, / Catch a thief . . ."

135   Eeny, meeny, miny, mo,
Catch old Tojo by the toe.
If he hollers make him say,
I surrender, U.S.A.

Also found as a jump-rope rhyme; see JRR, p. 47 ("Eeny, meeny, miney mo. / Catch Castro by the toe.").

Soifer, *Story Parade*, 6, no. 7 (July 1941), 16 [Brooklyn, 1916]. "Catch the Kaiser . . ."
Potter, "Eeny, Meeny, Miny, Mo," *Standard Dictionary* (1949), 339 [New York City, current during World War II].
"Folk Rhymes and Jingles" (1944), 4 [Maryland]. "Catch a Jap."
Hines, *Daedalian Quarterly*, 17, no. 1 (Fall 1949), 41–42 [Texas]. Begins "Eenie, meenie, minie moe, / Catch a Jap by the ear."
Brewster (1952), 163 [North Carolina]. "Catch a nigger."

136   Eeny, meeny, miny, mo,
Cracka feeny, finy, fo,
Aber nuger, papa tuger,
Ruck buck, banjo.

Many nonsense variations of last two lines.

Bolton (1888), 106 [Louisiana, Indiana, Colorado, Tennessee, Missouri]. Five variants, including "Eny, meny," "Eena, meena," and "Eanae, meanae" beginnings.
Potter, "Eeny, Meeny, Miny, Mo," *Standard Dictionary* (1949), 340. From Bolton (1888).
Perrow, *JAF*, 26 (1913), 142 [Mississippi, 1909]. Begins "Eny meny miny mo!"
Gardner, *JAF*, 31 (1918), 527 [Michigan]. Four variants; one with "Pennsylvany, viny, vo!" as second line.

Wintemberg and Wintemberg, *JAF*, 31 (1918), 122 [Ontario]. Second line "Cas-a-lara, bina, bo." Ends with "Eggs, butter, cheese, bread" rhyme (**152**).

Udal (1922), 393 [Dorset]. Begins "Ena, mena, mina, mo, / Keska, lena, lima, lo," ending with "Eggs, butter, cheese, bread" rhyme (**152**).

Brewster (1952), 162 [North Carolina, 1923].

Bett (1924), 58 [Cumberland, England]. "Eena, meena, mina, mo, / Bassa lena, lina, lo."

Whitney and Bullock (1925), 134 [Maryland].

Botkin (1947), 905 [Vermont, 1930's].

Knapp (1976), 9 (1930's).

Henry (1934), 240 [Kentucky].

Maryott, *SFQ*, 1, no. 4 (1937), 39 [Nebraska]. Two variants.

Brewster, *SFQ*, 3 (1939), 179.

Hines, *Daedalian Quarterly*, 17, no. 1 (Fall 1949), 41 [Texas]. Begins "Eenie, meenie, minie, moe, / Catch a feenie, finie, foe."

Cassidy, *PADS*, no. 29 (April 1958), 24 [Oklahoma]. Ends "O-U-T spells out. / Get out of here you dirty old dishrag you."

137   Eeny, meeny, miny, mo,
Sit the baby on the po.
When he's done
Wipe his bum,
Tell his mummy what he's done.

Opie (1969), 36 [England, current since nineteenth century].

Ritchie (1965), 45 [Edinburgh]. Begins "Eenie meenie mannie mo."

Turner (1969), 12 [Geelong, Australia, 1967, from Scots migrant informant]. "Stick the bairn on the po."

138   Eeny meeny miny mo
This foot got to go.

Evans (1956), 28. With playing instructions.

Eeny, meeny, miny, mum. *See* **133, 134**.

Eeny, meeny, mit a mat (mitty, mat). *See* **130**.

Eeny, meeny, moany (money, mony), mite (Mike, mi, my). See **139**.

Eeny, meeny, mony mo. See **133**.

139   Eeny, meeny, mony, my (mike, mite).
Barcelony (Pisca, lara; Butter, lather) bony sty
   (story, strike),
Ara-wara, brown bear,
Acka-wacka, we wo, wack.

*Of the numerous nonsense-syllable endings, most begin
with "Hare, ware," "Hara, wara," or some other close sound.
A further common ending is the "Eggs, butter, cheese, bread"
rhyme (152). See also Opie, Dictionary, pp. 156–157.*

Potter, "Eeny, Meeny, Miny, Mo," *Standard Dictionary*
   (1949), 339–340 [Tauton, Massachusetts, 1780; New York
   City, 1815; Philadelphia, 1818; Cornwall, ca. 1850]. Four
   variants, beginning "Eeny, meeny, mony, my (Mike),"
   "Ana, mana, mona, Mike," and "Eena, meena, mona, mite"
   (= Knapp [1976], 5).
Opie (1969), 43–44 [New York, 1815; Northamptonshire,
   1854; Philadelphia, 1855; Cornwall, 1882]. Discussed in
   relation to other gibberish rhymes. Four variants: one from
   Baker (1854), two from *Notes and Queries*, 1st ser., 11
   (February 10 and May 5, 1855), and one from Jago (1882).
   Beginnings are "Any, many, mony, my," "Hana, mana,
   mona, mike," "Eeny, meeny, moany, mite," and "Eena,
   meena, mona, my."
Bolton (1888), 48, 103–105, 110 [New Hampshire; Michigan;
   Vermont, 1834–1840; Massachusetts; Connecticut; Delaware; New York City; Philadelphia, 1818–1825; New York;
   England; Cornwall; Maine; Wisconsin; Michigan; Mary-
   land; Pennsylvania; Scotland; Ontario]. Discusses possible
   German origin. Thirty-three variants, beginning "Eeny,
   meeny," "Eeni, meeny," "Eenty, meenty," "Eny, meny,"
   "Ena, meena," "Eenie, meenie," "Inty, minty," "Enie,
   menie," "Ana, mana," "Eena, meena," "Āny, māny," and
   "Eatum, peatum, penny, pie." Two variants are from Jago
   (1882), one from *Notes and Queries*, 1st ser., 10 (November
   4, 1854).
Buspidnick (1906), 213 [Cornwall, 1850, 1870]. Three variants, beginning "Ena mena mona mi," "Ena mena mora
   mi" (from Thomas [1895]) and "Ena mena mona mout."

Baker (1854), 2, 333. Begins "Any, many, mony, my"; ends "Ink, pink, pen and ink, / I command you to be / O-U-T of this link."

Northall (1892), 342, 344, 345. Five variants: one from Baker (1854); two from *Notes and Queries*, 1st ser., 10 (November 4, 1854); 11 (May 5, 1855); one from *Folk-Lore Journal*, 5 (1887); and one from Burne (1893).

Notes and Queries, 1st ser., 10 (November 4, 1854), 370. Begins "Ena, mena, mona, mite."

Notes and Queries, 1st ser., 11 (February 10, 1855), 113 [United States] (begins "Eeny, meeny, moany, mite"); (May 5, 1855), 352 (begins "Hana, mana, mona, mike").

Mill Hill Magazine, 5 (October 1877) = Ellis, *Transactions of the Philological Society* (1877), 367. Three variants, beginning "Ena, mena, mona, mite," "Eny, meeny, moany, mite," and "Hana, mana, mona, mite."

Robertson, *NF*, 3, no. 2 (Summer 1960), 27–28 [Shelburne County, Nova Scotia, since 1880's]. Four variants, beginning "Aina, maina, mona, mike," "Mica, mona, mina, mike," "Eena, mena, mina, mike," and "Eenie, meenie, mynee, moe."

Jago (1882), 160–161 [Cornwall]. Two variants, beginning "Ena, mena, mona, mite" and "Ena, mena, mona, mi."

Burne (1883), 572 [Shropshire]. "Eeny, weeny, wŏŏnny, why, / Artle, startle, stoney, sty, / Ebb, web, blue, snake, / Eee, tot, spot, out goes she."

Newell (1883), 199–200 [Massachusetts, Connecticut, Pennsylvania]. Four variants, beginning "Eny, meny, mony, mine (mite, my)" and "Ena, mena, mona, my." Three of the variants = Botkin (1944), 772.

Stoudt (1915), 45–46 [Cornwall and current among Pennsylvania-German children, 1855]. Two variants, beginning "Eeny, meeny, money Mike" and "Ena, mena, bora, mi."

Folk-Lore Journal, 5 (1887), 48 [Cornwall]. Begins "Ene, mene, mona, mi."

F.B.T., *Devon and Cornwall Notes and Gleanings*, 2, no. 18 (June 15, 1889), 87.

Courtney (1890), 175. Begins "Ena, mene, mona, mi."

Chope (1891), 37 [Hartland, England]. Begins "Ena, mena."

Gregor (1891), 20 [Scotland]. Begins "Eena, meena, mona, mack.

Hewett (1892), 40 [Devon, England].

Thomas (1895), 1 [Cornwall].

Clifton Johnson (1896), 160. Three variants beginning "Ene, mene, moni, mi."

Davis (1906), 207–208, 213 [United States, Cornwall, England, New Hampshire, Michigan]. Five variants, beginning "Eena, meena, mony (mona), my (mite)" and "Eeny, meeny, mony, my (mi)."

Botkin (1947), 905 [New Hampshire, 1906, and Vermont, 1930's]. Two variants, beginning "Eenie meenie" and "Eena, meena" (from Davis [1906]).

Wallace, *Misc. of Rymour Club*, 2, part 4 (1915), 169 [Scotland]. Begins "Ena, mina, mina mo."

Anderson, *Evening Ledger* (May 17, 1916) [New York State, New Jersey]. Two variants, beginning "Enie, menie, monie, my" and "Ana, Mana, Mona, Mi."

Gardner, *JAF*, 31 (1918), 329 [Michigan]. Begins "Aina, maina."

Wintemberg, *JAF*, 31 (1918), 157 [Roebuck, Ontario].

Bett (1924), 58 [Devon, England]. Begins "Eena, meena, mona, mi, / Pasca, lora, vora, vi."

Whitney and Bullock (1925), 133 [Maryland]. Three variants; second lines begin "Battle leather," "Battle, latter," and "Askalona."

Bury, *Word Lore*, 2 (1927), 50 [Cornwall]. Begins "Eena, meena, mona, mi."

Old Cornwall, 1, no. 5 (April 1927), 34. Begins "Eena, mena, moona, mi."

Maryott, *SFQ*, 1, no. 4 (1937), 40 [Nebraska]. Three variants; one begins "Aina, maina."

Mills and Bishop, *The New Yorker* (November 13, 1937), 34. Last line: "Harricky barricky wee wo wack."

Rolland, *New Masses*, 27 (May 10, 1938), 109.

Withers (1946), n.p. Begins "Butter, levi, boni, story."

Musick and Randolph, *JAF*, 63 (1950), 428 [Missouri]. Begins "Eekery, eckery, mony mike."

Evans (1956), 14. Begins "Butter, leve, bone, story."

Cassidy, *PADS*, no. 29 (April 1958), 24 [New York].

Rawe (1971), 33. Begins "Ena, mena, mona me."

Eeny, meeny, myny, mo. *See* **133**.

140   Eeny, meeny, tipsy tee (teeny, toe, taily).
Delia, dahlia, dominee;
Hatcha, patcha, dominatcha.
Hi, pon, tuss. O-U-T!

See **129** for an explanation of this entry as a rhyme subcategory. Also found as a jump-rope rhyme (JRR, p. 48. [Eeny, meeny, tipsy teeny"]). See also Opie, Dictionary, p. 223.

Notes and Queries, 1st ser., 11 (February 10, 1855), 113
[United States]. Begins "Eeny, meeny, tipty, te."
Bolton (1888), 107–108 [District of Columbia, Rhode Island, Pennsylvania, Ohio, Delaware, North Carolina, Virginia, South Carolina, New York]. Thirteen variants; one from Notes and Queries, 1st ser., 11 (February 10, 1855). Beginnings include "Inty, minty," "A-le, ma-le, tipte-tee," "Ala, mala," "Allory, mallory," "Haley, maley," "Henry, menry, deeper dee," "Eny, meny," "Aila, maila," "Eenie, meenie," and "Elaka, nelaka, tipakenee."
Opie (1969), 42–43 [Britain and United States, since mid-nineteenth century]. Five variants; one each from Notes and Queries, 1st ser., 11 (February 10, 1855), and Bolton (1888). Other beginnings are "Inty, minty," "Eeny, meeny, tipty, te," "Aila, maila, tip-tee tee," and "Eenie, meenie."
Mill Hill Magazine, 5 (October 1877) = Ellis, Transactions of the Philological Society (1878), 367. Two lines only: "Eeney, meeny, tipty te / Teena Dinah, Domine."
Robertson, NF, 3, no. 2 (Summer 1960), 30 [Shelburne County, Nova Scotia; popular from 1885 to 1910]. Begins "Eena, mena, dippa, deena."
Davis (1906), 210 [Plymouth, Massachusetts] = Botkin (1947), 905. Begins "Inditie, Mentitie, Petitee, Dee."
Anderson, Evening Ledger (May 17, 1916) [Pennsylvania, New Jersey]. Two variants of "Ena, mena, tipsa, tena (teney)," one ending "Apple jack and John Sweeney; / Have a peach and a plum. / Have a stick of chewing gum."
Whitney and Bullock (1925), 135 [Maryland]. Seven variants, beginning "Eely, meely," "Haily, maily," and "Aily, maily, tipsy taily."
Brewster (1952), 163 [North Carolina, 1927]. Two variants; one begins "Henry, menry, depeer dee."
Guy B. Johnson (1930), 165 [St. Helena Island, North Carolina]. Begins "Eeny, meeny, dilly, deeny, / Hit um a lick an' John de guney."
Henry, JAF, 47 (1934), 338. Begins "Eney, meny, dixey, deeny," with "Johnny Queeny" in second line.
Withers (1946), n.p. [from Brooklyn College students, 1936–1945]. Second line: "Applejack, John Sweeney."
Brewster, SFQ, 3 (1939), 179–180. Two variants, beginning "Eenie, meenie, teppa seenie" and "Alamala tipsy tee."
Saxon et al. (1945), 445 [Louisiana]. Begins "Inny ke nicky nacky noe."

Hines, *Daedalian Quarterly*, 17, no. 1 (Fall 1949), 41 [Texas].
Begins "Eenie meenie, tipsie, teenie."

Potter, "Counting-Out Rimes," *Standard Dictionary* (1949),
255. Begins "Haley, maley, tipsy tee."

Potter, "Eeny, Meeny, Miny, Mo," *Standard Dictionary*
(1949), 340 [United States]. Mentions "Eachy, peachy, Don
Ameche" as variant third line current in 1949.

Evans (1956), 7–8. Two variants: one begins "Eeny meeny
dixie deeny"; one has "Apple Jack Paul Sweeney" as second line.

Leventhal and Cray, *WF*, 22 (1963), 241 [California].

Knapp (1976), 27. Begins "Eeny, meeny, choo cha leeny / I
buy gumbaleny."

Eeny, meeny, tipty, te. *See* **140**.

Eeny, meeny, tooper tick. *See* **128**.

Eeny, pheeny, figgery, fegg. *See* **129**.

Eeny, teeny, ether, fether, fip (other feather hip).
See **500**.

141 Eeny, weeny, winey, wo,
Where do all the Frenchmen go?
To the east and to the west
And into the Old Crow's nest.

> *See Opie Dictionary, pp.157–158, and Opie (1969), pp.
> 210–211, for many early references as a game rhyme. See
> also* **238**.

Charles Taylor (1820) [Scotland]. Begins "Hickory, pickery,
pease scon. / Where with this young man gang?"

Chambers (1841), 121 [Scotland]. Begins "My Lord Provo',
my Lord Provo', / Where shall this poor fellow go?" Gives
footnote reference to mention in Sir Walter Scott's *The
Bride of Lammermoor*.

Notes and Queries, 3rd ser., 5 (May 4, 1864), 395 [Devon-
shire]. Begins "Iroe, diroe, ducca, medo."

Northall (1892), 347. Two variants, one each from *Notes and
Queries*, 3rd ser., 5 (May 4, 1864), and Burne (1883).

Burne (1883), 572–573 [Shropshire]. Two variants; one begins "Iram, biram, brendom bo, / Where do the sailors go?"
and ends "To the land which they love best."

Newell (1883), 165 [Maine]. Begins "Charley, barley, buck
and rye, / What's the way the Frenchmen fly?" Newell
connects the rhyme with a game, but it is not so collected.

John Nicholson (1890), 153. "Meeny, meeny, miny mo, / I ax
ya wheear mun this man go? / Sum gans east, an' sum gans
west, / An' sum gans over high crake nest."

Gregor (1891), 31 [Scotland]. Two variants: one begins "Issing, issing, issory, / Where will this poor boy go?" and the
other begins "Eendy, beendy, bamba, roe,/Caught a chick-
en by the toe" and ends "Hopping in the garden,/Swim-
ming in the sea, / If you want a pretty girl, / Please take me."

Bolton, JAF, 10 (1897), 320 [Shropshire].

"Counting-Out Rhymes," Misc. of Rymour Club, 2, part 2
(1913), 94 [Forfar]. "Skip, skip, sko; / Where shall this
young man go?/To the east or to the west,/Or the hoddie's
crow's nest."

Bett (1924), 57 [Durham, England]. Begins "Eena, meena,
mina, mo" and ends "Apples in the garden, / Fishes in the
sea, / If you want a pretty girl / Please choose me."

Old Cornwall, 1, no. 8 (October 1928), 39. Two variants: one
begins "Eena, deena, dina, do," and ends "and some to last
year's blackbird's nest"; the other ends a "Onery, twoery,
tickery, teven" rhyme (**410**).

Shaw (1969), 46 [Liverpool]. Begins "Eena, mena, mina, mo, /
Jack a sena sina so" and ends "Hopping in the garden, /
Skipping in the sea, / If you want a pretty girl / Pray pick out
she" (cf. **122**).

Eeny, weeny, woony (wŏŏnny), why. See **139**.

Eeper-peeper, chimney sweeper. See **203**.

Eerey, orey, ikerey Ann. See **408**.

Eerie, aarie, ackertie, Ann. See **408**.

142   Eerie, aarie (Eery, aary),
Biscuit Mary,
Pim, pam, pot.

Gregor (1881), 171 [Scotland].
Gregor (1891), 23 [Scotland]. Five variants; two end "Fite,
fish, black troot, / Eery, ary, ye-re oot."

Eerie, aarie, eeertie, ann. See **403**.

Eerie, arrie, aikerty, Ann. See **408**.

Eerie, irey, ickery Ann. See **408**.

Eerie, oarie, . . . See **143**, **408**.

143   Eerie, oarie, ickerie (ickory) am,
Put the vinegar in the pan.
Eerum squeerum boxie leerum,
Cheericks up the castle,
Down the close.
There stands a bonny white horse.
It can gallop, it can trot,
It can tell who's at home,
Father, mother, dirty Tom.

    See **403** and **408** for first two lines.

Ritchie (1965), 46 [Edinburgh].

Eerie, oorie, . . . See **408**.

Eerie, orie, ickery am (Ann). See **408**.

144   Eerie, orie, o'er the dam,
Fill your poke and let us gang.
Black fish and white trout,
Eerie, orie, you are out.

Napier, *Folk-Lore Record*, 4 (1881), 175.
Bolton (1888), 115, 117 [Scotland]. Two variants.

Eeringes, oranges. See **440**.

Eery, aary (ary), . . . See **142**, **403**, **408**, **410**, **465**.

Eery, airy, . . . See **408**.

Eery, iry, hickory, hum. See **408**.

Eery, oory, . . . See **410**.

Eery, orrey, o'er the mill dam. See **144**.

Eery, ory, . . . See **408**.

Eese, aase (aese, oose, ose, ouse oze), . . . See **112**.

145   Eesie, aisie, igars, a-van,
            Popsie, vinegar, I began;
            Teet-tat, moose-fat, carra-riddle, bump-fiddle,
            Stand back, thoo are out.

> See also **146**, **403**.

> Inglis (1894), 102. "Eenneri, anneri, sirterie, sannerie, / Drops
> o' vinegar, noo begun; / Eet, aat, moose fat, / Carrie diddle-
> play the fiddle. / Tike Bo! Bizz!"
> Firth, *Old Lore Misc.*, 2 (1909), 135 [Orkney].

Eesy, osy. See **112**.

146   Eet, aat,
            Moose, faat,
            Tilly, riddle,
            Fizz.

> *Also found as ending to* **403**. *See also* **145**.

> Gregor (1891), 27 [Scotland]. Two variants. One, "Eet, at, /
> Maise, fat, / Tell a riddle, / Bum, funk, fizz." Alternate third
> line: "Tarry, eedle."

Eetam (Eetem), peetam (peetem). See **149**, **204**.

Eethy, othy, . . . See **147**.

Eetie ottie.
See **147**.

Eetie, peetie, penny pie. See **204**.

Eetim, peetim, . . . See **149**, **204**.

Eetle peetle.
See **147**.

Eetter otter.
See **147**.

147 Eettle ottle,
Black bottle
Eettle ottle, OUT!

> *Often followed by various additional lines. Opie (1969)
> gives a distributional history. See also Opie, Dictionary, p.
> 222.*

Opie (1969), 32–34 [England, Scotland, Ireland; since 1890].
   Thirty-four variants. Most consist of three lines, the last
   repeating the first plus "out": "Iggy oggy, / Black froggy";
   "Iddy oddy, / Dog's (Cock's) body"; "Iddle oddle, / Black
   poddle (bobble, bubble)"; Ickle ockle, / Black (Ink, Chocolate) bottle"; "Ickle ockle, / Chockle bockle (chockle)"; "Iggle oggle, / Blue (Black) bottle"; "Eettle ottle, / Black bottle"; "Eetter otter, / Potter bottle, / Out jumps the cork";
   "Eetie ottie, / Horses are naughty"; "Ingle angle, / Silver
   (Golden) bangle"; "Hibble hobble, black bobble"; "Eatle
   autle, blue bottle." Extended endings given include: "My
   dog's deid"; "If you want a piece and jam (lump of jelly), /
   Please step (walk) out"; "If you want a pretty maid, / please
   choose me"; "If you see a policeman, / Punch him on the
   snout"; "If you want another bangle, / Please walk out";
   "Turn the dirty dish cloth / In-side-out"; "Tea and sugar's
   my delight, / Tea and sugar's out"; "Shining on the mantlepiece, / Just like a threepenny piece"; and "If you had
   been where I had been, / You would not have been out."
Gregor (1891), 27 [Scotland]. Five variants; one "Eetle peetle,
   / Black beetle, / You are out"; one ends "My dog's dead, / My
   cat gid awa till its bed wi' a sair head, / It cannot snap a
   biscuit, it cannot smoke a pipe, / Little Johnnie Middleton's
   breeks is too tight" (cf. "Ease, ose" rhyme [**112**]).
Edward Nicholson (1897), 307 [Scotland]. Begins "Eethy,
   othy."
Sutton-Smith (1959), 63, 71 [New Zealand, 1900, 1910, 1915].
   Four variants, all beginning "Ickle, ockle."
Maclagan (1901), 249 [Argyleshire]. Begins "Eddle oddle."
Notes and Queries, 10th ser., 11 (June 5, 1909), 446 [Orkney].
   Two variants; one beginning "Eeckie, ocky, black bokie,"

ends "If you had been to black bokie / You would not have been put out."

G.W.R., *Old Lore Misc.*, 4 (1911), 165 [Kirkwall]. Ends "Tea and sugar is my delight, / Tea and sugar is out."

Reid, *Misc. of Rymour Club* (1911), 103 [Edinburgh]. Ends "Shining on the mantlepiece / Like a silver threepenny piece; / Eetle, ottle" etc.

Robertson, *NF*, 3, no. 2 (Summer 1960), 29 [Shelburne County, Nova Scotia, since 1920's]. Begins "Ittle, ottle, black (blue) bottle."

Our Meigle Book (1932), 166 [Scotland].

Turner (1969), 12–13 [Melbourne, 1945 and 1967]. Two variants, one beginning "Ibble abble black bubble."

Gullen (1950), 15.

Howard, *NYFQ*, 16 (1960), 138 [Australia; earlier than 1954, no longer current]. Begins "Ickle, ockle."

MacColl and Seeger, Folkways 3565 (1962) [Durham, England]. Ends "If you want a canny lass, / Please choose me."

Ritchie (1965), 46–47 [Edinburgh]. Three variant endings: "Shining on the mantlepiece / Like a silver threepenny piece"; "Tea and sugar is my delight (And OUT spells 'out'!"; and "If ye want a piece of jam / Please step out."

Fowke (1969), 109 [Canada]. ". . . blue bottle."

Rodger (1969?), 20 [Scotland]. Ends "If you want a piece on jam / Just call out."

Stork, *Lore and Language*, no. 1 (July 1969), 3 [Sheffield]. Three "Ickle ockle" variants featuring "chocolate," "blue," and "black" bottle.

148 Eetum for peetum,
The King came t' meet him,
And dang John Hamilton doon the brae.

Gregor (1881), 171 [Scotland].

Gregor (1891), 10, 20 [Scotland]. Five variants; one begins "Heetum for peetum." Alternate last lines: "And broke his muckle big toe" and "And brok's mither's muckle toe."

Eetum, peetum, penny pie. *See* **204**.

149 Eetum, peetum, penny pump (plump),
A' the ladies in a lump,

Sax or saiven in a clew,
A' made wi' candy glue.

See also **204**.

Gregor (1881), 169 [Scotland] = Opie (1969), 49.
Gregor (1891), 16 [Scotland]. Three variants.
Maclagan, *Folk-Lore*, 16 (1905), 450. "Hockie, pockie, penny
    a lump, / That's the stuff to make you jump."
T.M., *Old Lore Misc.*, 4 (1911), 5 [Shetland]. Ends "First shee
    cust, an' dan shee drew, / An' it must be you."
Nicolson (1920), 90 [Shetland]. Ends "First she köst, an' dan
    she drew / An' it must be you."

Eety, peaty, penny, pie. *See* **204**.

Eevil, eevil, eevil-ine. *See* **465**.

Eexie, peeksie, pearie, plum. *See* **110**.

Eeze (Eezie), oze (ozie). *See* **112**.

150   Egden, begden, car pan derber,
Sola, riga, ossa, cherber,
Chea, cah, suboova,
Mishky, disky, edget, vishkey.

Bolton (1888), 110 [New Hampshire].

151   Eggs and ham,
Out you scram.

Opie (1969), 31 [Lydney, England].

152   Eggs, butter, cheese, bread,
Stick, stock, stone dead.
Stick him up, stick him down,
Stick him in the old man's crown.

Used as an ending for many rhymes, especially **139**. *See
also* **509**. *The following sources are only those which give
the rhyme as complete in itself.*

Bolton (1888), 110–111 [England; Connecticut, 1835; New Hampshire, 1860; Delaware; Cambridge, Massachusetts; and Saratoga, New York]. Three variants; one from Halliwell (1842); one, "Butter, eggs, cheese, bread, / Hit a nigger on the head; / If he hollers, hit him dead; / Butter, eggs, cheese, bread," = Knapp (1976), 191; cf. **133, 134**.

Halliwell (1842), 116.

Notes and Queries, 1st ser., 10 (November 4, 1854), 370 [Norfolk, England]. First two lines only.

Burne (1883), 572 [Shropshire]. First two lines only.

Newell (1883), 201 [Philadelphia]. Begins "Stick, stock, stone dead."

Courtney (1890), 175 [West Cornwall]. First two lines only.

Clifton Johnson (1896), 161.

Maclagan, *Folk-Lore*, 16 (1905), 453. Begins "Stick, stock, stone dead."

Davis (1906), 210, 212 [Plymouth, Massachusetts; United States]. Two variants. One, ending "Hang him up, lay him down, / On his father's living ground," = Botkin (1947), 905.

Acker (1923), 18. Begins "Stick, stock, stone dead."

Withers (1946), n.p. Two variants, one ends "Acker backer, soda cracker" rhyme (**10**).

Opie (1947), 56.

Musick, *HF*, 7 (1948), 13 [West Virginia]. Begins "Stick, stock, stone dead."

153   Egg shells
Inside out.

Opie (1969), 31 [Lancaster, England, 1920's].

Eina, mina (peina) . . . *See* **500**.

Einey, deeney, deiney, diss (duss). *See* **119**.

Ein (Eins), zwei, drei. *See* **429**.

Eis, aas, oos, ink. *See* **112**.

Elaka, nelaka, tipakenee. *See* **140**.

Elder belder, limber lock. *See* **287**.

154 Elephant trunk,
Out you bunk.

Opie (1969), 31 [Market Rasen, England].

Eli, meli, tiffi, tig. See **403**.

155 Ella mella deek or tella
She begora ootbahora
Riggy rum
Toogy spun
Snip snap
Snoota oota.

Evans (1956), 17.

156 Ely dely dipsy dely ili oli,
Dominali otchi batchi dominatchi,
I been chose.

Maryott, *SFQ*, 1, no. 4 (1937), 45 [Nebraska].

Empty, mempty, tick-a-to-fig. See **129**.

Ena, dena, dasha, doma. See **123**.

Ena, dena, dina, dust. See **119**.

Ena, meena, mona, Mike (mite). See **139**.

Ena, mena, bora, mi. See **139**.

Ena, mena, figgitty, fick. See **128**, **129**.

Ena, mena, mina, mo. See **133**, **136**.

Ena, mena, mona (mora), mite (mi, mout, my). See **139**.

Ena, mena, timety fig. See **129**.

Ena, mena, tipsa, tena (teney). *See* **140**.

Ena, mina, mina, mo. *See* **139**.

157   Ena, Minie, Martha, mo
To the Rover's they will go.
Drinking stout with all their might
Ena, Minnie, Martha, mo.

>*Refers to three "Coronation Street" (television show)
characters, Ena Sharples, Minnie Caldwell, and Martha
Longhurst.*

Ritchie (1965), 46 [Edinburgh].

Ena, tena, . . . *See* **500**.

158   Enden deena
Tucka lucka teena,
Sucka lucka ticky tacky
Enden boom.

Turner (1969), 13 [Melbourne, 1967].

159   Enderly, benderly, sickerly, sol,
Heebsha, deepsha, heller knoll.

Stoudt (1915), 53 [Pennsylvania German].

Endy bendy bamba roe. *See* **133**, **141**.

Endy, bendy,
Bamber, endy. *See* **273**.

Endy, bendy, bendy, bough. *See* **133**.

160   Endy tendy, ticker a bun (a-been),
I sent a letter to the Queen.
The Queen o' Jerusalem sent it (said) to me,
Ocus, pocus, one, two, three.

Gregor (1881), 170 [northeast Scotland].
Gregor (1891), 22 [Scotland]. Two variants: one has "The Queen o' Morocco" in third line; one begins "Inty tinty, tickery, been."

Enee, menee, tipsy-toe. *See* **133**.

Ene, mene, mini, mo. *See* **133**.

Ene, mene, mona (moni), mi. *See* **139**.

Ener Dena Dinah Doe. *See* **133**.

Enery, twoery, tickery, seven. *See* **410**.

Ene, tene . . . fether, fip. *See* **500**.

Eney, meny, dixie, deeny. *See* **140**.

161   Engine, engine, number nine,
Running (Riding) on the Chicago line.
How she's polished, how she shines,
Engine, engine, number nine.

Common alternate ending:

If the train should jump the track
Do you want your money back?

> *With a number of other third and fourth lines and stock endings. Also found as jump-rope rhyme; see JRR, p. 48.*

Newell (1883), 203 [Pennsylvania]. Begins "Engine No. 9."
Bolton (1888), 111 [Massachusetts, District of Columbia, Pennsylvania, New York]. Three variants, all beginning "Engine number nine." Second lines: "Half wood and half pine," "Eighteen hundred and seventy-nine," and "Ring the bell when it's time."
Opie (1969), 38, 58, 59 [United States (since 1890), England, Scotland, Ireland, Australia]. Five variants; one each from Bolton (1888) and Brewster (1952). One asks: "How many gallons does it take, / Five, six, seven, or eight?"
Waugh, *JAF*, 31 (1918), 43–44 [Ontario, 1909]. Three variant endings: "Running east and running west, / Running to the

cuckoo's nest. / O-u-t spells out"; "At the lake at half-past
eight. / Back once more at half-past four. / O-u-t spells out
goes she"; and "Please tell me the time" (player gives time,
with that number counted to decide who is out).

Gardner, *JAF*, 31 (1918), 531–532. Five variants.

Wintemberg, *JAF*, 31 (1918), 150 [Washington, Ontario].

Brewster (1952), 168 [North Carolina, 1925].

Whitney and Bullock (1925), 138 [Maryland].

Hudson (1928), 116 [Mississippi].

Withers (1946), n.p. [from Brooklyn College students, 1936–
1945].

Maryott, *SFQ*, 1, no. 4 (1937), 56 [Nebraska]. Four variants.

Brewster, *SFQ*, 3 (1939), 180.

Rae and Robb, *Christian Science Monitor Magazine* (March
21, 1942), 8. Ends "The gate flew in, the gate flew out, / And
that is how the fire went out" (cf. **179**).

"Folk Rhymes" (1944), 4 [Maryland].

McAtee (1946), 22 [Indiana]. "Chicago time."

Emrich and Korson (1947), 120.

Harry Harris, *Evening Bulletin* (May 30, 1949), 10.

Roberts, *HF*, 8 (1949), 8 [Indiana].

Musick and Randolph, *JAF*, 63 (1950), 429 [Missouri].

Evans (1946), 18–19. Three variants, one ends "I am silver, I
am fine. / When I stare along the track / People stand and
stare right back."

Turner (1969), 13 [Melbourne, 1957].

Sutton-Smith (1959), 69 [New Zealand].

Robertson, *NF*, 3, no. 2 (Summer 1960), 31 [Shelburne
County, Nova Scotia].

MacColl and Seeger, Folkways 3565 (1962) [Durham,
England]. "Engine, engine on the line, / Wasting water all
the time."

Allen, *Macleans* (July 6, 1963), 44.

Leventhal and Cray, *WF*, 22 (1963), 241–242 [California].
Nine variants.

Ritchie (1965), 47 [Edinburgh]. Ends "Run along the bogey
line. / Out, scoot, you're out / Engine, engine, number
nine."

Castagna, *NYFQ*, 25 (1969), 227 [New Rochelle, New York].

Fowke (1969), 110–111 [Canada]. Three variants, with the
following third and fourth lines: "Running east, running
west, / Running through the cuckoo's nest"; "At the lake at
half-past eight, / Back once more at half-past four"; and "If
the train goes off the track, / Do you want your money
back?"

Brill, *GMW*, 20 (1972), 3.

Knapp (1976), 26.
Milberg (1976), 25.

Engine number nine. See **161**, **465**.

162   Engle bengle,
Casey Stengel.
April fool,
Lefty O'Doul.
Go to hell,
Dick Bartell.
O-U-T spells out
Out goes you.

> The references are all to baseball players.

Evans (1956), 9.

Enie, menie, monie, my (Mike). See **139**.

Enity, feenity (fenity), fickity (ficty), feg. See **129**.

Enniki, benniki, my black hen. See **213**.

Enter, menter, pewter, corn. See **287**.

Entra, mentra, cutra, cora. See **287**.

Entry kentry, . . . See **287**.

Entry, mentry (mintery), . . . See **287**.

Enty, menty, figgity, fag. See **129**.

Enty, menty, tibby, fig. See **129**.

Enty, tenty, fickery fig. See **129**.

Enty, tenty, my black hen. See **213**.

Eny, meeny, maca, racka. See **120**.

Eny, meeny, moany mite. See **139**.

Eny meny miny mo. See **133**, **136**.

Eny, meny, mony, mine (mite, my). See **139**.

Eny, meny, tipsy, tee. See **140**.

Erie, Irie, Ickery, Ann. See **408**.

Eringes (Eringies), oranges (orangies). See **440**.

163   Errie, orrie, round the table,
Eat as much as you are able;
If you're able to eat the table,
Errie, orrie, out!

Opie (1969), 28 [England].

Ery, iry, . . . See **408**, **410**.

Ery, ory, ickery, Anne. See **403**.

Esa vesa vack vesa. See **131**.

164   Eseentse, teenste, tinnery, nunnery,
Hallelijah hallabaluny,
I saw the King of the hazle pazle
Jumping over Jersalem dyke
Playing on his pee wee pipe.

See also **248**, **500**.

Opie (1969), 46 [1820]. "As I sat on my sooty kin / I saw the
king of Irel pirel/Playing on Jerusalem pipes" and "Saw the
King of easel diesel/Jumping over Jerusalem wall" as
endings to "Sinty, tinty, huthery" rhymes (**506**).
Gregor (1891), 31 [Dundee, Scotland]. "Eentil, teentil, eddy,
galong, / Mortal, portal, peel, a gun, / France oot, France in, /
Saw ye the laird o' Easel-peasel / Jumpin' ower Jeroozlum
steeple, / Eery, ory, you are oot."

Findlay, *Misc. of Rymour Club*, 1 (1911), 55 [Scotland].
"Ninty, tinty, halogulum; / Mortal, portal, piel a gum, / I
saw the laird o' Eastle-Wastle, / Jumpin' owre Jerus'lem
Castle."

Gullen (1950), 15.

Howard, *NYFQ*, 16 (1960), 138 [Australia; reported by an
older woman who learned it from a Scottish grandmother
in New Zealand]. "I saw the King, / Rile, pile, jumping over
Jerusalum's dike, / Playing on his wee pied pipe" as ending
to "Sinty, tinty, huthery" rhyme (**500**).

Bluebells My Cockle Shells (1961), n.p. [Ayrshire]. "Law of
the King of Easel Diesel, / Jumping over Jerusalem wall. /
Black fish, white trout, / Eerie oorie, you are out" as ending
to "Sinty, tinty, huthery" rhyme (**500**).

G. B. Adams, *Ulster Folklife*, 11 (1965), 96–97 [Scotland].
"Izeenty, teenty, higglety, pigglety / Pam, valova, lova,
Dick; / Ah bought a ticket and saw the Queen / A-
Reilly-Peilly jumping over Jerusalem style / Playing on his
wee-pee-poe-pied-purrit pipe."

Ese, ose. See **112**.

165   Eskimo, Eskimo, Eskimo pie,
Turn around and touch the sky.

Fowke (1969), 109 [Canada].

Etem, petem, penny pie. See **204**.

166   Evie-ovie, turn the rope over;
Mother in the market, selling penny baskets;
Baby in the cradle, playing with a ladle.

*Usually found as a jump-rope rhyme; see JRR, p. 203
("Wavy, wavy, turn the rope over").*

Reid, *Misc. of Rymour Club*, 2, part 2 (1913), 70 [Scotland].

Evi, ivy, erickvy, Ann. See **408**.

167   Exy, dexy, silver texy
Exy, dexy, out.

Bolton (1888), 108 [Connecticut].

Eze, oze. See **112.**

F

168 Farmer, farmer, can I cross your coloured water
Or golden field today?
Not unless you have the colour blue,
And if you have it you can cross.

Those Dusty Bluebells (1965), 23 [Ayrshire].

169 The Farmer in the den,
Hi-ho, my cherry, ho.
The farmer takes a wife.
Hi-oh, my cherry, oh.
The wife takes a child, *etc.*
The child takes a nurse, *etc.*
The nurse takes a dog, *etc.*

Usually a singing game.

Bolton (1888), 119 [Virginia].

170 Farthing jelly biscuit;
You are out.

Reid, *Misc. of Rymour Club*, 2, part 2 (1913), 70 [Scotland].
Opie (1969), 31–32 [Luncarty, Helensburgh, and Bute,
England]. "Wee jelly biscuit is out."

171 Father Christmas lost his whiskers.
How many did he lose?
One, two, three, *etc.*

Howard, *NYFQ*, 16 (1960), 139 [Australia, 1954–1955].
Opie (1969), 58 [St. Peter Port and Wakefield, England]. "Father Christmas / Grew some whiskers, / How many inches

long?" Ends "And if you do not want to play / Just take your toy and run away / With a jolly good smack across your face. / Just like this."

172   Father's hope and mother's joy.
The darling little nigger boy.
O-U-T spells out.

Bolton (1888), 118 [Vermont, 1840].

173   February, March, April, May,
Who's to be it on this fine day?
One, 2, 3,
Oh, 'tis you, I see.

Bolton (1888), 119 [Iowa].

174   Fee, fy, fo, fum,
Higeldy, pigeldy, oh, what fun.
Here we go, there we go;
Hanko, banko, ke, kaw, buck.

Bolton (1888), 110 [Pennsylvania].

175   Fe, fi, fo, fum,
I smell the blood of an Englishman,
Be he live, or be he dead,
I'll grind his bones to make me bread.

Most commonly found in association with the folktale "Jack and the Beanstalk."

Bolton (1888), 112 [Ontario, Canada]. Line 2: "I" omitted; "an English mum." Lines 3 and 4: "Fum, fee, fo, fout, / One, two, three and you are out."
Davis (1906), 210, 212 [Plymouth, Massachusetts, 1906] = Botkin (1947), 905.
Whitney and Bullock (1925), 139 [Maryland].
Maryott, SFQ, 1, no. 4 (1937), 53 [Nebraska].

176   F for finis
I for inis
N for nocklebone,

I for Isaac,
S for Silas Silverspoon.

Bolton (1888), 119 [Litchfield, Connecticut].
Withers (1946), n.p.

177   Filson, folson, Nicholas Dan. *See* **133**.

178   "Fire! Fire!" says Obadiah.
"Where? Where?" says Stephen Clare.
"Behind the rocks," says Doctor Fox.
"Put it out," says Jimmy Trewin.
"That's a lie," says Jacky Treffry.

Also found as a jump-rope rhyme; see JRR, p. 50 ("'Fire, fire,' says Mr. McGuire").

Bolton, *JAF*, 10 (1897), 320 [Falmouth, England].

179   Fireman, fireman, number eight,
Struck his head against a gate,
The gate flew in, the gate flew out,
And that's the way the fire went out.

Also found as a jump-rope rhyme; see JRR, p. 50.

Gardner, *JAF*, 31 (1918), 532 [Michigan].
Withers (1946), n.p.
Emrich and Korson (1947), 118.
Margaret Taylor (1956), 78.

180   The First lieutenant, he was so neat.
He stopped the battle to wash his feet.

Bolton (1888), 112 [New York]. Begins "Our first Lieutenant."
Withers (1946), n.p.

First tae count the king's name. *See* **84**.

181   First to count to Hullee, one, two, three,
Out goes the bonnie lassie o' Dundee.

Gregor (1891), 30 [Scotland].

Fishes, fishes, in the brook. *See* **327**.

Fish, fish. *See* **67**.

182   Five, 10, 15, 20,
Sugar-plums are not plenty.

Bolton (1888), 94 [Massachusetts].

183   Four diddle-diddle-danders,
Two stiff-stiff-standers,
Two lookers, and a switch-about.
An old cow and you're it!

Originally a riddle; see Archer Taylor, English Riddles, no.
1478.

Withers (1946), n.p. [from Brooklyn College students, 1936–
1945].

Frank, Frank, turned the crank. *See* **304**.

A Frog walked into a public house. *See* **355**.

184   Fun, fun,
Son of a gun,
Eighteen hundred and ninety-one.

Evans (1956), 19.

185   Fussle Beardie hid a coo
Black an fite aboot the moo.
Wizna that a dainty coo.
Belongt to Fussle Beardie.

See Opie, Dictionary, p. 117.

Gregor (1881), 174 [Scotland]. Two variants; one begins
". . . hid a horse. / It hault the cairtie through the moss, /
Broke the cairtie, hangt the horse," followed by lines 3 and
4 above.
Gregor (1891), 26 [Scotland].

G

186 Gableo, gable end,
Rancy, fancy as a man,
Willie halpie, all 'e can,
On your gable end.

Maryott, *SFQ*, 1, no. 4 (1937), 45 [Nebraska].

187 Game, game, ba', ba',
Twenty lassies in a raw.
No' a boy among them a',
Game, game, ba', ba'.

Reid, *Misc. of Rymour Club*, 2, part 2 (1913), 71 [Scotland].

Gargy, Pargy, how's your wife. *See* **361**.

Gimmery, twaery, . . . *See* **410**.

188 Ginger, Ginger had some puppies.
How many puppies did she have?
One, two, three, four, five.

Maryott, *SFQ*, 1, no. 4 (1937), [Nebraska], 50.

189 Gipsy, gi, a-gibber, a-hay,
Hory, pory, dory,
Hoiky, poiky, soiky, moiky,
I enego, wilomi, dory.

Gregor (1891), 30 [Orkney, Scotland].

190 Gipsy, gipsy, lived in a tent,
Couldn't afford to pay the rent,
When the rent man came next day,
Gipsy, gipsy, ran away.

Also found as a ball-bouncing and jump-rope rhyme; see JRR, p. 57.

Rutherford (1971), 53 [Ushaw Moor, England, 1967]. Begins "Mrs. Dumb lived in a room, / Couldn't afford to pay the bum."
Opie (1969), 29 [Aberdeen].

Good Queen Caroline. See **465**.

191 Grandfather had some wheat and rye.
He put it out in the barn to dry.
Out came the mice to have some fun.
Up jumped pussy cat and made them all run.

Robertson, NF, 3, no. 2 (Summer 1960), 32 [Shelburne County, Nova Scotia, 1910].
Fowke (1969), 110 [Canada].

192 Great A, little A,
Bouncing B,
The cat's in the cupboard
And out go we.

Usually a nursery rhyme; see Opie, Dictionary, p. 51.

Bolton (1888), 119. Two variants; one "A, B, C, bouncing B," from Washington D.C.
Whitney and Bullock (1925), [Maryland]. "A, B, C, / Bouncing B."

Great house, little house, pig sty, barn. See **473**.

193 Green kail, cabbage, out.

Reid, *Misc. of Rymour Club*, 2, part 2 (1913), 69 [Scotland].

H

Haberdasher, isher, asher. See **123**.

Hackabacker, chew tobacco. See **10**.

194   Ha, ha, ha,
He, he, he,
Who's that laughing?
I'll soon see.
It is Johnny over there.
He is out we all declare.
He's He.

Howard, *NYFQ*, 16 (1960), 142 [Australia, 1954–1955].

Hailey, bailey, tillamy Dick. *See* **128**.

Haily, maily, . . . *See* **140**.

Haina, daina, diena, duss. *See* **119**.

Hairy, Hairy, ricketty Ann. *See* **408**.

Haley, baley, tithaby, tick. *See* **128**.

Haley, bayley, tithaby, table. *See* **410**.

Haley, maley, tippety, fig. *See* **129**.

Haley, maley, tipsy tee. *See* **140**.

195   Hallelujah make a dumpling.
Hallelujah bring it ben.
Hallelujah make a big one
Hallelujah amen.

Maclagan, *Folk-Lore*, 16 (1905), 453.

Hana dana tina das. *See* **119**.

Hana, mana, mona, mike (mite). *See* **139**.

196   Handy-dandy-riddledy ro,
Which will you have, high or low?

See Opie, Dictionary, pp. 197–198.

Bolton, *JAF*, 10 (1897), 320 [Cornwall]. "Handy, pandy, whiskey, wandy. / Which hand will you have, / Top or bottom?" With playing instructions.
Maryott, *SFQ*, 1, no. 4 (1937), 50 [Nebraska].

Handy, pandy, whiskey, wandy. See **19, 196.**

197   Harley, Marley, pease, straw,
Ten pinches is the law,
Pinch him now, pinch him then,
Pinch him till he counts ten.

Also found as a jump-rope rhyme; see JRR, p. 59.

Whitney and Bullock (1925), 138 [Maryland]. Also the variant "Barney, Barney, buckwheat straw, / How many pinches make a law? / Pinch me now and pinch me then, / And pinch me when I laugh again."

198   Haulk 'em, baulk 'em, muni corkum,
Hellicum, bellicum, buz.

Folk-Lore Journal, 1 (1883), 384 [Derbyshire] = Bolton (1888), 110. Begins "Horcum borcum curious corkum" and ends with "Eggs, butter, cheese, bread" rhyme (**152**).
Northall (1892), 347.
Waugh, *JAF*, 31 (1918), 43 [Ontario]. Begins "Awkum, bawkum / Curious kawkum."

199   Have a cherry, have a plum.
Have a piece of chewing gum.

Usually found as an ending to other rhymes.

Whitney and Bullock (1925), 139.

Have a cigarette, sir. See **269.**

200   Hayfoot strawfoot,
Specklefoot crowfoot,
Some flew east, some flew west,
Some flew over the cuckoo's nest.

See also **287**, **567**.

Babcock, *AA*, o.s., 1 (1888), 274 [District of Columbia].
Bolton (1888), 118 [District of Columbia].
Whitney and Bullock (1925), 140 [Maryland].

201   Heater, beater, Peter, mine,
Hey Betty Martin, tiptoe fine,
Higgeldy, piggeldy, up the spout,
Tip him, turn him round about.

Bolton (1888), 114 [Poughkeepsie, New York].

202   Heela, heela, dipsa deela,
Heela, hola, dema nolo,
Hotsha, botsha, dema notsha,
Hie ben dotz.

Maryott, *SFQ*, 1, no. 4 (1937), 45 [Nebraska].

Heely, peely, tipty, fig. See **129**.

Heena, deena, dina, dust. See **119**.

203   Heeper, weeper, chimney-sweeper
Got a wife and couldn't keep her.
Got another, couldn't love her,
Heeper, weeper, chimney-sweeper.

*Cf. the nursery rhyme "Peter, Peter, pumpkin eater" (Opie
Dictionary, p. 346). Also found as a jump-rope rhyme; see
JRR, p. 46 ("Eaper, Weaper, Chimbley-sweeper").*

Mill Hill Magazine, 5 (1877) = Opie (1959), 21 [England and
   Wales]. Also "Eaver Weaver" beginning.
Bolton (1888), 116 [Newcastle, England; New York]. Two
   variants: one from *Mill Hill Magazine*, 5 (1877); one begin-
   ning "Peter, Peter."
Northall (1892), 345 [Warwickshire].
Monroe, *AA*, n.s., 6 (1904), 48 [Massachusetts]. Begins "Pe-
   ter, Peter."
"Counting-Out Rhymes," *Misc. of Rymour Club*, 2, part 2

(1913), 96 [Scotland]. Begins "Eeper-peeper, chimney
sweeper."
Watson (1921), 38 [Somerset, England]. Ends "Up the chimney he did shove her. / O-U-T spells 'Out'."

Heetum for peetum. See **148**.

204 Heetum, peetum, penny pie
Populorum, gingum, gie;
East, West, North, South
Kirby, Kendal, Cock him out.

With various other nonsense endings; see also **149**, **251**.
Also found as a finger game; see Halliwell (ca. 1860), 74.

Ellis, *Transactions of the Philological Society* (1878), 366
[Langwathby, England]. Two variants, beginning "Hytum,
pytum" and "Eetum, peetum."
Bolton (1888), 108, 110 [Cumberland, England; Scotland].
Three variants; one each from Ellis (1878) and Clara Doty
Bates, *Nursery Jingles*. Beginnings are "Eatum, peatum,"
"Keetum, peetum," and "Hytum, pytum."
Dickinson (1881).
Gregor (1881), 169, 171, 172 [northeast Scotland]. Five var-
iants; beginnings are "Heetum, petum," "Eetum, peetum,"
and "Item, peetum."
Opie (1969), 49–50. Eight variants; one from Dickinson
(1881), two from Gregor (1881 and 1891), one from Macla-
gan, *Folk-Lore*, 16 (1905); one from Birnie, *Misc. of Rymour
Club*, 1 (1911). Discussed in relation to other gibberish
rhymes and to Welsh numerals. Beginnings include
"Eetum, peetum," "Eatum, peatum," "Eetem, peetem,"
"Ikey pikey," "Heetum, peetum," and "Zeetum, peetum."
Gregor (1891), 15–16, 28 [Scotland]. Twenty-five variants,
many ending "Staan ye oot bye / For a bonny penny pie,"
"Ah, day, doo, die, / Staan ye oot bye," "Black fish, white
trout, / I choose you out," or with variants of "Ease, ose"
rhyme (**112**). Beginnings include "Eetum, peetum," "Eetim,
peetim," "Itim, peetim," "Eetem, peetem," "Heetum,
peetum," "Hetem, petem," "Eety, peaty," "Inky, pinky,"
and "Eenty, teenty, tippenny bun."
Black and Thomas (1901), 263 [Orkney, Shetland]. Three
variants, all beginning "Etem, petem."
Maclagan, *Folk-Lore*, 16 (1905), 450. Begins "Eatum,
peetum"; ends with an "Ease, ose" rhyme (**112**).

Firth, *Old Lore Misc.*, 2 (1909), 135. Begins "Eetam, peetam."

Maclennan (1909), 52 [Scotland]. Begins "Eetam, peetam."

Notes and Queries, 10th ser., 11 (June 5, 1909), 446. Beginnings are "Eetum, peetum" and "Eetie, peetie."

Williamson, *Old Lore Misc.*, 3 (1910), 67 [Shetland]. Begins "Eetam, peetam."

Birnie, *Misc. of Rymour Club*, 1 (1911), 90 [Huntley District, Scotland]. Begins "Zeetum, peetum."

T.M., *Old Lore Misc.*, 4 (1911), 5 [Shetland]. Two variants; both begin "Eetam, peetam."

G.W.R., *Old Lore Misc.*, 5 (1912), 6 [Kirkwall]. Begins "Eetie peetie."

Nicolson (1920), 90 [Shetland]. Begins "Eetim, peetim."

Our Meigle Book (1932), 166 [Scotland]. "Eatum, peatum, potum, pie, / Babylonie stickum, sty, / Dog's tail, hog's snout, / Eerie, orie, you are out."

Henery, Menery, Deepery Dick. See **128**.

205   Henly, penly, chickly, chaw,
He, pe, clenly, awe, buck.

Bolton (1888), 109 [west Pennsylvania].

Henry is a good fisherman. See **567**.

Henry, menry, deeper, dee. See **140**.

Henry, pennery, pit for gold. See **259**.

Hentry, mentry, coutry corn. See **567**.

206   Here comes a duke a-riding by,
So ransom, tansom, titty bo tee.
And what are you riding here for?
So ransom, tansom, titty bo tee.
I'm riding here to be married.
So ransom, tansom, titty bo tee.

Usually a singing game.

Bolton (1888), 118 [Virginia].

207 Here's a circle,
Here's a lake,
Here's where you make your big mistake,
Everybody get out.

Hines, *Daedalian Quarterly*, 17, no. 1 (Fall 1949), 42 [Texas].
First player to follow instructions and leave circle is "it."

208 Here's a Spanian just from Spain,
To court your daughter Mary Jane.
My daughter Jane is far too young
To be controlled by anyone.

*Usually a singing game, "Three Knights of Spain." Also
found as a jump-rope rhyme; see JRR, p. 190 ("There came
two Spaniards just from Spain").*

Bolton (1888), 120 [District of Columbia]. Two variants; one
begins "We are three brethren out of Spain."

209 Here's a wise man from the East,
Hit me, tip me turny;
He will make you hide your head
For shouting in Caperny.

Bolton (1888), 117 [New Hampshire].

Hetem, petem, penny, pie. *See* **204**.

Hewery, hiery, hackery, heaven. *See* **410**.

210 Hey Cocky doo, how d' you do,
Sailing about in your best o' blue,
An alpaca frock, a green silk shawl,
A white straw bonnet and a pink parasol.

"Counting-Out Rhymes," *Misc. of Rymour Club*, 2, part 2
(1913), 95 [Scotland].

Hiary, diary, dockery, deven. *See* **410**.

Hiary, Hoary, Hickery, Heben. *See* **410**.

Hibberty bibberty . . . *See* **212**.

Hibble hobble, black bobble. *See* **147**.

Hickassy, pickassy pice a pickassy. *See* **212**.

Hickerty, pickerty, my black hen. *See* **213**.

Hickery, dickery, six and seven. *See* **410**.

211   Hickery, hoary, hairy, Ann,
Busybody over span
Pare, pare, virgin mare,
Pit, pout, out one.

> *Cf.* **403, 408**.

Notes and Queries, 1st ser., 10 (November 4, 1854), 369 =
    Bolton (1888), 96 = Northall (1892), 349.
Old Cornwall, 1, no. 5 (April 1927), 41 [Penzance, Cornwall,
    1880; Guernsey]. Four variants, beginning "Icary, Arry,
    Ourey, Ah," "Hickory, Harry, Oria, Ah," "Hickory, Airy,
    Ory, Anne," and "Eckary, Airy, Ory, Anne."
Bolton, JAF, 10 (1897), 319 [Cornwall] = Opie (1969), 29.
    Begins "Ickery, ahry, oary, ah."
Davis (1906), 208.

Hickery, pickery pease scon. *See* **141**.

212   Hickety, pickety, i-silicity,
Pompalorum jig,
Every man who has no hair
Generally wears a wig.

> *Also found as a jump-rope rhyme; see* JRR, *p.* 76.
> *("Icklety-picklety, isia–lickerty").*

Bolton (1888), 109, appendix [England]. Two variants; one
    begins "Ictum, pictum, pyrum, jictum"; the other ends
    "Make a posset of good ale, / And I will have a swig."
Opie (1969), 37 [since nineteenth century].
Gaskell, Transactions, 116 (1964), 211 [Lancashire, 1900].
    Begins "Hickassy, pickassy pice a pickassy"; ends "For a

rotten cotton dish clout / Boys and girls are often turned out."

Reid, *Misc. of Rymour Club*, 1 (1911), 106 [Edinburgh]. Begins "Ickerty, pickerty, pie-sel-sel-ickerty."

Waugh, *JAF*, 31 (1918), 43 [Ontario]. Begins "Ikerty pickerty."

"Uncle Sandy," *Word Lore*, 1 (1926), 224. Begins "Eckety, speckity, spice so lickety."

Daiken (1949), 2. Begins "Hickety, pickety, pize-a-rickety"; third and fourth lines as in Bolton's ending.

Gullen (1950), 18. Begins "Eenty, teenty, feggeine fell."

Howard, *NYFQ*, 16 (1960), 136, 138 [Australia, 1954–1955 and older]. Three variants, beginning "Hickitty, pickitty," "Higgety, piggety," and "Ickety, pickety."

Sutton-Smith (1959), 71. Begins "Hibberty bibberty."

Those Dusty Bluebells (1965), 23 [Ayrshire]. "Inky pinky pencil-sharpener / Pomperary jig, / All the men that are at the ball / Ought to wear a wig, / Made of rotten cotton / Dish-cloth torn in two, / Inky-pinky pencil-sharpener, / Out goes you."

213 Hickety, pickety, my black hen.
She lays eggs for the gentlemen.

Finished in a variety of ways. Two of the most common endings are "Sometimes nine, sometimes ten, / Hickety, pickety," etc., and "Gentlemen come everyday / To see what my black hen doth lay," though the latter may not be attached to the rhyme as used for counting-out. See Opie, Dictionary, *pp. 201–202.*

Burne (1883), 573. Begins "Enniki, benniki."

Newell (1883), 202 [Georgia]. Begins "Mittie, Mattie had a hen."

Bolton (1888), 117 [Ireland, Georgia, Connecticut, England]. Four variants. Two begin "Mitty, matty" = Daiken (1949), 10.

Edward Nicholson (1897), 216 [Scotland]. Five variants: two beginning "Scinty, tinty" and "Zeenty, tennty," plus three from Bolton (1888).

Gregor (1891), 18–19 [Scotland]. Eight variants, beginning "Eenity, feenity," "Inity, finity," "Innerty, finnerty," "Eenity, peenity," "Inty, tinty," "Inky, pinky," "Higley, pigley," and "Higilty, pigilty." Endings are "Files (Whiles) ane, files (whiles) twa, / An files (whiles) a bonnie black craw" or "Sometimes nine and sometimes ten" ending.

"Counting-Out Rhymes," *Misc. of Rymour Club*, 2, part 2

(1913), 93 [Fifeshire and Dunfermline, Scotland]. Two variants, beginning "Enty, tenty" and "Inky, pinky." Endings are "Whiles ane, whiles twa, / Whiles a bonnie black craw" and "Counts one, two, three / Out goes bonnie lassie (laddie), / Out goes she (he)."

Smiley, *JAF*, 32 (1919), 377 [Virginia]. Begins "Chickery, chickery."

Bury, *Word Lore*, 2 (1927), 50 [Cornwall]. Begins "Icketty, Spicketty."

Gullen (1950), 104. Begins "Inky, pinky."

Opie (1969), 38 [Scotland]. Begins "Skinty, tinty, my black hen."

Hickety, pickety, pize-a-rickety. *See* **212**.

Hickey, pickey, zickey, zan. *See* **410**.

Hickitty, pickitty, . . . *See* **212**.

214 Hickity, pickity, rovie, dovie,
Dinky tell, ram tam toosh.
You are out.

Ritchie (1965), 47 [Edinburgh].

Hickory, Airy, Ory, Anne. *See* **211**.

Hickory, dickory, altimo (algry, more). *See* **248**.

215 Hickory, dickory, dare,
The pig flew in the air.
The man in brown
Who brought him down;
Hickory, dickory, dare.

See Opie, Dictionary, p. 147.

Bolton (1888), 115 [Connecticut].
Clifton Johnson (1896), 165. Begins "Dickery, dickery, dare."
Withers (1946), n.p.

216 Hickory, dickory, dock,
The mouse ran up the clock,
The clock struck one,
And down he come (ran),
Hickory, dickory, dock.

Cf. **287**. See Opie, Dictionary, pp. 106–107.

Ritchie (1965), 38 [Scotland, since 1810]. Begins "Ziccotty diccotty dock."

Blackwood's Edinburgh Magazine, 10 (August 1821), 36. Begins "Zickety, dickety, dock, / The mouse ran up the nock."

Bolton (1888), 115. Three variants: one from Blackwood's Edinburgh Magazine, 10 (August 1821); one from Halliwell (1842); one ending an "Intery, mintery, cutery, corn" rhyme (**287**).

Halliwell (1842), 123 = Ellis, Transactions of the Philological Society (1878), 369.

Gregor (1881), 173 [northeast Scotland]. Begins "The moose ran up the clock."

Burne (1883), 573 [Shropshire]. Begins "Ickity, pickety, pock."

Gregor (1891), 27 [Scotland]. Four variants, including "Dirckty, dirckty, dock" and "Zickety, dickety, dock," the latter preceded by a "Sinty, tinty, huthery" rhyme (**500**). A variant beginning "The moose ran up the clock" ends "Ickety, dickety, dog, dan." Some variants give "moose" for "mouse" and "knock" or "nock" for "clock."

Northall (1892), 346.

Monroe, AA, n.s., 6 (1904), 48 [Massachusetts].

Maclagan, Folk-Lore, 16 (1905), 450. Begins "Ikery, dickory, dock, / The mouse ran up the knock."

Robertson, NF, 3, no. 2 (Summer 1960), 32 [Shelburne County, Nova Scotia, 1910].

G.W.R., Old Lore Misc., 4 (1911), 166 [Kirkwall]. Two variants, one begins "Rickety, rickety, rock."

Stoudt (1915), 46. First two lines only.

Udal (1922), 393 [Dorset]. Begins "Dickory, dickory, dock."

Whitney and Bullock (1925), 131. Two variants, one begins "Three mice run up the clock."

Maryott, SFQ, 1, no. 4 (1937), 53 [Nebraska].

Hickory, Hackory, Hockory, Heaven. See **410**.

Hickory, Harry, Oria, Ah. See **211**.

Hickory, pickery, pease scon. See **141**.

217   Hicktum, ticktum, tandry-datum,
Pisum, posum, rosum dee,
Eggs, butter, cheese, bread,
Stick, stock, stone, dead.
O-U-T spells out.

Baker (1854), vol. 2, p. 333 = Northall (1892), 346.

218   Hiddledy, diddledy, dumpty,
The cat ran up the plum tree;
Half-a-crown to fetch her down,
Hiddledy, diddledy, dumpty.

See Opie, Dictionary, pp. 113–114.

Bolton (1888), 114 [Limerick, Ireland; New York] = Daiken
(1949), 110. Two variants, one beginning "Iddlety, diddlety."
Gullen (1950), 16.

Hiery, diery, limber lock. See **287**.

Higgamy, diggamy, . . . See **248**.

Higgery, hoggery, higgery, ham. See **408**.

Higgety, piggety, . . . See **212**.

219   Higgledy, piggledy,
Osh, cosh, boh.
One, two, three,
And out goes she.

Gardner, JAF, 31 (1918), 329 [Michigan].

High, spy, limber lock. See **287**.

Higilty, pigilty, my fat hen. See **213**.

220 Higley, pigley, Margery John,
Crickly, crackly, battle is won.
General Jackson out of the strife;
Hockiby, pockiby, weary of life.

Bolton (1888), 110 [New Hampshire].

Higley, pigley, my fat hen. See **213**.

221 Hi li, the big fat guy.
The guy with the fat goes out.

Leventhal and Cray, WF, 22 (1963), 239 [Canada].

222 Hink, sink, the puddings stink (the devil winks),
The fat begins to fry,
Nobody at home but jumping Joan,
Father, mother, and I.
Stick, stock, stone, dead,
Blind man can't see.
Every knave will have a stave.
You and I must be he.

Cf. **408**, **509**. See also Opie, Dictionary, pp. 208–209.

Ker (1840) = Bolton (1888), 111.
Halliwell (1842), 87.
Northall (1892), 346. Two variants: one from Halliwell (1842);
    one from Notes and Queries, 1st ser., 10 (November 4,
    1854).
Notes and Queries, 1st ser., 10 (November 4, 1854), 369.
Halliwell (ca. 1860), 61. Begins with a "Onery, twoery, tick-
    ery teven" rhyme (**410**).
Edward Nicholson (1897), 218 [Scotland].
Davis (1906), 212 [England].
Opie (1947), 56. Begins "Hinx, minx, the old witch winks."

Hintery (Hinty), mintery (minty), . . . See **287**.

Hinty, tinty, tethery, minty. See **500**.

Hinx, minx, the old witch winks. See **222**.

223 Hip, hip, hip,
The Kaiser has the grippe.
Why, why, why?
Because he has to die.
When, when, when?
At half past ten.

Soifer, *Story Parade*, 6, no. 7 (July 1941), 16 [Brooklyn, 1916].

Hippiney, pippiney, craney crow. *See* **82**.

Hippity, pippity, . . . *See* **244**.

224 Hiro, piro, rantan, tara,
Northville, Sackville, rodo, dingo, whack!

Bolton (1888), 108 [Ashland, New York].

225 Hocca proach,
Ochre, poker,
Outcha, poutcha,
Ockaproche,
Hulkey, mulkey,
Hotchy, potchy,
Hitcha, pitcha,
Horter, sporter,
Uncle Brokes
Honda, konda,
Ocheke, pochake.

Bolton (1888), 106.

Hockie, pockie, penny a lump. *See* **149**.

Hokey, pokey, winkey, wong. *See* **408**.

226 Hoky, poky, penny pie,
Stan ye oot by.

See also **204**.

Gregor (1891), 30 [Scotland].

227   Hoky, poky, winky wum,
How do you like your 'taters done?
Snip, snap, snorum,
High popolorum,
Kate go scratch it,
You are out!

See Opie, Dictionary, p. 211.

Gregor (1881), 172 and (1891), 31 [northeast Scotland]. Begins "Yokie, pokie, yankie, fun."
Bolton (1888), 110 [New Hampshire].
Clifton Johnson (1896), 164. "Hokey, pokey, winky, wong. / Chingery, chongery, Nicholas John" as beginning to a "Onery, twoery, ickery Ann, / Phillisy, phollisy, Nicholas John" rhyme (**408**).
Udal (1922), 392–393 [Dorset]. Two variants; one ends "King of the Cannibal Islands."
Withers (1946), n.p.

228   Hono, ryfy,
Cabul, lyty,
Do not I,
Tanti, busque,
Oker!

Bolton (1888), appendix [Maine].

229   Hoo-i Buffalo, hoo-i Bill,
Hoo-i Buffalo, Buffalo Bill.
Hoo-i Jesse, hoo-i James,
Hoo-i Jesse, Jesse James.

Bolton (1888), appendix [Indiana].
Emrich and Korson (1947), 118.

230   Hop, hop, hop to the butcher's shop,
With a gold ring on my finger.

Reid, Misc. of Rymour Club, 2, part 2 (1913), 69 [Scotland].

231   Hop, hop, hop, we're off to the shop,
To buy some nice new toys;

And Jack will come and buy a drum,
For he likes to make a noise.

"Counting-Out Rhymes," *Misc. of Rymour Club*, 2, part 2 (1913), 61 [Scotland].

Horcum borcum curious corkum. *See* **198**.

Horse, cart, thimble. *See* **75**.

Horsie cartie rumble oot. *See* **75**.

232 Houk in, houk oot,
Fin ye sing ye dinna hoot,
So I shise you oot.

"Counting-Out Rhymes," *Misc. of Rymour Club*, 2, part 2 (1913), 60 [Scotland].

233 A House to let,
Apply within,
People left for drinking gin.
Drinking gin and taking snuff,
Don't you think that's bad enough.

Generally collected as a jump-rope rhyme; see JRR, pp. 66–67.

Bolton, *JAF*, 10 (1897), 319 [Cape Town].
Reid, *Misc. of Rymour Club*, 2, part 2 (1913), 71 [Scotland].
Two variants, ending "Lady put out for drinking gin" and "Jennie goes out and I go in."

234 How far do you think
Old mother fell down the sink? *See* **395**.

235 Humble, bumble, Mister Fumble,
Three score an' ten,
Learn me to double a hundred
Over an' over again.

Gregor (1881), 175, and (1891), 26 [Scotland].

236   Hunt the squirrel through the woods,
I lost him, I found him;
I sent a letter to his son,
I lost him, I found him.

> *Usually associated with a "drop handkerchief" game.*

Davis (1906), 210.

237   Hurdle gurdle, durdle purdle, wi' a shak',
Wi' a shak he ran;
Tied till a cat's tail,
In an auld pan.

> "Counting-Out Rhymes," *Misc. of Rymour Club*, 2, part 2
> (1913), 61 [Scotland].

Hurley, burley, limber lock. See **287**.

238   Hurly, burly, tramp the trace,
The coo shet owre the market-place;
East or west? the crow's nest?
Where does the poor man go?

> *Cf.* **141**.

> "Counting-Our Rhymes," *Misc. of Rymour Club*, 2, part 2
> (1913), 93 [Dunfermline].

239   Hurrah for Hoover, he's the man,
Threw Al Smith in the garbage can.

> Maryott, *SFQ*, 1, no. 4 (1937), 58 [Nebraska].

240   Hushie ba, baby, dinna mak' a din,
And ye'll get a fiskie fin the boatie comes in.

> Maclagan, *Folk-Lore*, 16 (1905), 453. Ends "An' ye'll get a
> piece whan the baker comes in."
> "Counting-Out Rhymes," *Misc. of Rymour Club*, 2, part 2
> (1913), 62 [Scotland].

Hytum, pytum, peni, pye. See **204**.

241   Hytum, skytum,
Perridi, styxum,
Perriwerri, wyxum,
A bonum D.

> Halliwell (1849), 135 = *Notes and Queries*, 4th ser., 11 (April
> 19, 1873), 330 = Bolton (1888), 108 [England] = Northall
> (1892), 347.
> Ellis, *Transactions of the Philological Society* (1878), 365.
> Ends "Eenah, deenah, dinah, doh" rhyme (**119**).

I

242   I am a little maiden, free from sin or strife,
But when I am big I will be a happy wife;
And so will you all, except one, two, three, and
   out goes she.

> "Counting-Out Rhymes," *Misc. of Rymour Club*, 2, part 2
> (1913), 62 [Scotland].

243   I am going down town
To smoke my pipe,
And won't be back till Monday night;
And if you let any of my children go,
I'll whip you black and blue
With my old rubber shoe.

> Gardner, *JAF*, 31 (1918), 532 [Michigan].

Ibbidy, bibbidy, bibbidy, sash (gibbety goat). *See*
   244.

Ibbity, bibbity, shindo. *See* **252**.

244   Ibbity bibbity sibbity sab,
Ibbity bibbity kanaba (canal boat),

Ibbity bibbity bibbity boo,
And out goes you.

With many other nonsense endings. Also found as a jump-rope rhyme; see JRR, p. 73.

Robertson, *NF*, 3, no. 2 (Summer 1960), 31 [Shelburne County, Nova Scotia, 1880's]. Ends "Dictionary down the ferry, / Out goes y-o-u."

Bolton (1888), 4, 109 [Connecticut, Massachusetts, California]. Four variants.

Opie (1969), 45–46 [United States, since 1888; northeast Scotland, since ca. 1910]. Two variants: one from Margaret Taylor (1956); one, "Ipetty, sipetty, ippetty sap, / Ippetty, sipetty, kinella kinack, / Kinella up, kinella down, / Kinella round the monkey o' town."

Clifton Johnson (1896), 166. "Ibbity, bibbity, sinity, salve, / Ibbity, bibbity, mellow."

Anderson, *Evening Ledger* (May 17, 1916) [Pennsylvania, New Jersey]. Ends "Dixie, daery, down the ferry, / In nineteen hundred and———."

Soifer, *Story Parade*, 6, no. 7 (July 1941) 17 [Brooklyn 1916]. Begins "Ibbidy, bibbidy, bibbidy, sash" and ends "Dictionary / Down the ferry, / Hum drum, American gun, / Eighteen hundred ninety one."

Gardner, *JAF*, 31 (1918), 529–530 [Michigan]. Two variants.

Bennett, *Children*, 12 (1927), 21. Third line: "Dictionary, down the ferry."

Withers (1946), n.p. [from Brooklyn College students, 1936–1945]. Two variants: one, ". . . canal boat, / By the river, down the river"; one with "Dictionary / Down the ferry" as third line.

Maryott, *SFQ*, 1, no. 4 (1937), 45 [Nebraska]. Four variants; one ends "Dictionary down the ferry, / Turn, turn, American gun, / Eighteen hundred and ninety-one."

Mills and Bishop, *The New Yorker* (November 13, 1937), 34 [New York City and New England]. Two variants; one, "Ibbity bibbity gibbety goat," ends "Dictionary / Down the Ferry / Out goes you" = Botkin (1944), 800.

Rae and Robb, *Christian Science Monitor Magazine* (March 21, 1942), 8. "Ibbity, bibbity, zibbity, zam. / Ibbity, bibbity, knabe. / Knabe in, knabe out, / Knabe round the water spout."

"Folk Rhymes" (1944), 4 [Maryland].

Emrich and Korson (1947), 117. Second and third lines: "Canaba in, canaba out, / Canaba over the water spout." With playing instructions.

Roberts, *HF*, 8 (1949), 9 [New Jersey].

Randolph, *SFQ*, 17 (1953), 245.

Evans (1956), 10–11. Four variants; one ending "Kanolla in / Kanolla out / Kanolla over the water spout"; one with "Dictionary / Down the ferry"; one ending "By the river, / Down the river / Out goes YOU."

Margaret Taylor (1956), 78. Ends "Dictionary / Down the ferry, / Fun, fun, / American gum, / Eighteen hundred / Ninety-one."

Howard, *NYFQ*, 16 (1960), 138 [Australia, from Scotland via New Zealand]. Begins "Hippity, pippity."

Millard, *NYFQ*, 16 (1960), 147 [New York].

Ibbity, bibbity, sinity, salve (zibbety zam). *See* **244**.

Ibble abble black bubble. *See* **147**.

245 **I**bse, ibse, ibse, ah,
Ibse, ibse, zebo.

> *Cf.* **301**.

> Opie (1969), 46 [Scotland]. Two variants, one beginning "Ibsy, bibsy, ibsy I."

Ibsy, bibsy, ibsy I. *See* **245**.

Icary, Array, Ourey, Ah. *See* **211**.

I-ca wad-ca gee-ca my-ca livin'-ca. *See* **299**.

246 **I**ce cream sold out.

> Opie (1969), 31.

247 **I** charge my daughters every one,
To keep good house while I am gone.
You, and you, but especially Sue (you),
Or else I'll beat you black and blue.

> Bolton (1888), 120 [Ohio].
> Gardner, *JAF*, 31 (1918), 532 [Michigan].

Icka backa soda cracker. See **10**.

Ickama, dickama, . . . See **248**.

248   Ickerma, dickerma, allega mo,
         Dick slew allega shuu,
         Hulka pulka Peter's gunn.

> Turner (1969), 13 [Tasmania, ca. 1865 and 1890]. Two
> variants: "Indy (Ingy), tindy (tingy), allego, Mary, / One
> two (Ax too) allego slum, / Orgy porgy peela gum"; one
> ends "Oox joox juddle-um, pipes," the other "Francis itty
> gritty goojelum gorjelum pipes."
> Newell (1883), 200 [Massachusetts] = Botkin (1944), 772.
> Begins "Ikkany, dukkany."
> Bolton (1888), 96, 109 [Massachusetts, Maryland, California,
> Virginia, West Virginia, Wisconsin]. Five variants, begin-
> ning "Ikkany, dukkany," "Ickama, dickama," "Higgamy,
> diggamy," "Hickory, dickory, altimo," and "One-a-
> manury, awkry, Ann; / Mulberry wax and tarry tan; / Hick-
> ory, dickory, algry, more," / etc.
> Opie (1969), 47, 52. Three variants: two from Bolton (1888);
> one, "Indi tindi alego Mary," [Australia, ca. 1895].
> Bolton, JAF, 10 (1897), 319 [New Town, Tasmania]. "Indy,
> tindy, allego, Mary, / Ax, too, allego, slum. / Orgie, porgie,
> peeler gum. / Francis itty, gritty, itty, / Gralum, joodlum,
> pipes."
> Edward Nicholson (1897), 308 [Scotland]. Begins "Zeanty,
> teenty, heligo, lum."
> Whitney and Bullock (1925), 136 [Maryland]. Three variants:
> one begins "Ickkany, dukkany"; one begins "Dicky,
> Dicky."
> Withers (1946), n.p. Begins "Ikkamy, dukkamy."
> Howard, NYFQ, 16 (1960), 138 [Australia, 1954–1955, but
> from older persons]. Begins "Indy, tinky."
> MacColl and Seeger, Folkways 3565 (1962) [Durham,
> England]. Begins "Iggledy, piggledy, allegaloo.'

Ickerty, pickerty, pie-sel-sel-ickerty. See **212**.

249   Ickery, ackery, ary, an
         Mulberry Tass and Tary Tam.

> Cf. **408**.

Bolton (1888), 96. Two variants, beginning "Ury, urry, angry Ann" and "One-a-manury, awkry, Ann." One ends with an "Ickerma, dickerma, allega mo" rhyme (**247**); the other ends with "Ink, stink, stiddle my stew" rhyme (**278**).

Hoke, *JAF*, 5 (1892), 120 [North Carolina].

Ickery, ahry, oary, ah. See **211**.

Icketty, Spicketty, my black hen. *See* **213**.

250   Ickety rickety rah rah rah,
Donna macka shicka shocka
Rom pom push.

Turner (1969), 13 [Melbourne, 1969].

251   Ickham, pickham
Penny Wickham
Cockalorum jay,
Eggs, butter, cheese, bread,
Hick, stick, stone dead!

Cf. **204**.

Jerrold (1908), 73.

252   Ickidy, bickidy, belinda,
The sheeny vas vashing the vinda.
The vinda got broke;
The sheeny got choke;
Ickidy, bickidy, belinda.

Maryott, *SFQ*, 1, no. 4 (1937), 41 [Nebraska]. Begins "Ony, crozony, crozinda."

Brewster, *SFQ*, 3 (1939), 180–181.

Withers (1946), n.p. Begins "Ibbity, bibbity, shindo; / My mother was washing the window."

Ickity, pickety, pock. *See* **216**.

Ickkany, dukkany, . . . See **248**.

Ickledee, pickledee, elleka-mah. See **276**.

Ickle ockle,
Black (Ink, chocolate) bottle. See **147**.

Ickle ockle,
Chockle bockle (chockle). See **147**.

253   Icks, ocks, donkey's cocks,
India-rubber balls.
If you want to join the scouts,
Join St. Paul's.

Rutherford (1971), 51 [Sunderland, England, 1930's].

254   Icky, picky, Polly,
Father bought a dolly.
Dolly cried, Father sighed.
Icky, picky, Polly.

    Cf. **282**.

Leventhal and Cray, WF, 22 (1963), 239.

I climbed up the apple tree. See **42**.

Ictum, pictum, pyrum, jictum. See **212**.

Iddle oddle,
Black poddle (bobble, bubble). See **147**.

Iddlety, diddlety dumpty. See **218**.

Iddy oddy,
Dog's (Cock's) body. See **147**.

255   I declare as a rule
Man's a fool.
When it's hot he wants it cool,
When it's cool he wants it hot,

Always wanting what he's not.
I declare as a rule
Man's a fool.

Bolton (1888), 118 [Connecticut].

256   I doot, I doot,
My fire is out,
And my little dog's not at home;
I'll saddle my cat, and I'll bridle my dog;
And send my little boy home,
Home, home again, home!

See Opie, Dictionary, pp. 280–281.

Chambers (1841), 121 [Scotland].
Gregor (1891), 32 [Scotland].

I-ery, you-ery, dickery seven. See **410**.

257   If you do not want to play
Just take your hoop and run away.

Common rhyme ending.

Turner (1969), 16 [Melbourne, 1967]. Begins "Out, girls,
out," ends "Just pack your books and run away."
Opie (1969), 35. Three variants. Alternate endings: "You can
'sling you hook' away" and "Go away with a jolly good
slap across your face like that."

258   If you had been where I'd been
You'd have seen the fairy queen;
If you'd been where I've been
You'd have been out.

Probably a descendant of the Jacobite song "Killiecrankie."

Reid, Misc. of Rymour Club, 2, part 2 (1913), 69 [Scotland].
Second and final line: "You wouldn't have been put out."
Opie (1969), 36 [England].

If your father chews tobacker. See **10**.

259   Igamy, ogamy, box of gold,
A louse in my head was seven years old.
I inched him and pinched him
To make his back smart,
And if I catch him
I'll tear—out—his—heart.

Bolton (1888), 115 [Maryland].
Davis (1906), 210 [Plymouth, Massachusetts] = Botkin
(1947), 905. Begins "Henry, pennery, pit for gold / Had a
louse in his head."
Whitney and Bullock (1925), 136 [Maryland]. Begins "Iggany, oggany, box of gold, / I had a louse seven years old, /
Seven and seven to that, / I thought the old fellow would
never get fat," etc.
Emrich and Korson (1947), 120.

Igdum, digdum, didum, dest. *See* **119**.

Iggany, oggany, box of gold. *See* **259**.

Iggledy, piggledy, allegaloo. *See* **248**.

Iggle oggle,
Blue (Black) bottle. *See* **147**.

Iggy oggy,
Black froggy. *See* **147**.

260   I had a dog, its name was Buff,
I sent it for a box o' snuff,
It broke the box, and skelt the snuff,
And that was a' my pennyworth.

See Opie, Dictionary, pp. 105–107.

Gregor (1891), 31 [Scotland].
Reid, *Misc. of Rymour Club*, 2, part 2 (1913), 70 [Scotland].

261   I had a little horse,
His name was Jack,

I put him in a barn,
And he jumped through a crack.

> *Usually an entertainment rhyme.*

Maryott, SFQ, 1, no. 4 (1937), 53 [Nebraska].

262   I had a little moppit
And I put it in my pocket,
And it shan't bite you [*repeat several times*].
But it shall bit you.

> *See Opie, Dictionary, pp.* 313.

Shaw (1969), 46 [Liverpool].

263   I had a mule named Jack.
I rode on his tail instead of his back.
His tail came off, and I fell off,
And that was the end of Jack.

> *Usually an entertainment rhyme. Also found as a jump-*
> *rope rhyme; see JRR, p. 82.*

Maryott, SFQ, 1, no. 4 (1937), 53 [Nebraska].

264   I had a sausage, a bonny, bonny sausage,
I put it in the oven for my tea.
I went down the cellar
To get salt and pepper,
And the sausage ran after me.

> *Parody of the song "I love a lassie." Also found as a jump-*
> *rope rhyme; see JRR, p. 81.*

Opie (1959), 92.

265   I have a grandmother down in Leith;
She has four-and-twenty teeth.
One fell out, and one fell in;
I choose you for that one in.

> *Notes and Queries*, 10th ser., 11 (June 5, 1909), 446 [Orkney].

266   I have a little nutmeg tree,
And nothing would it bear
But a silver nutmeg
And a golden pear.

> *Usually a nursery rhyme; see Opie, Dictionary, pp. 330–331. Also found as a jump-rope rhyme (see JRR, p. 81).*
>
> Bolton (1888), 113 [Derbyshire].

267   I've as mony bawbees a I can spend ava,
And gin ye need a shillin', man, it's I could gi'e ye
   twa.

> "Rhymes of General and Local Interest," *Misc. of Rymour Club*, 2, part 3 (1914), 113 [Scotland].

Ikerty pickerty,
Pisa a rickety. *See* **212**.

Ikery, dickory dock. *See* **216**.

Ikey pikey penny pie. *See* **204**.

Ikka bokka soda cracker. *See* **10**.

Ikkany (Ikkamy), dukkany (dukkamy), . . . *See*
   248.

268   Ikke blicky, combatty, see see.

> Maryott, *SFQ*, 1, no. 4 (1937), 44.

Ikkery, ekkery catamaran. *See* **408**.

269   I know a doctor,
He knows me.
He invited me to tea.
"Have a cigarette, sir?"
"No, sir."
"Why, sir?"

"Because I've a cold, sir."
"How many blankets do you need?"
"Three."
One, two, three, and out you must go.

Usually a ball-bouncing rhyme. Also found as a jump-rope rhyme; see JRR, p. 60 ("Hello, sir, hello, sir").

Opie (1969), 37, 59 [England, current since before World War I]. Three variants. Version above, with alternate endings "How many tablets do you need?" and "How many weeks did you stay in bed?" One, beginning "I know a washer-woman," ends "Because I have a cold, ma'm. / Out goes she." The third variant begins "Have a cigarette, sir" and ends "Let me hear you cough, sir. / Very bad indeed, sir. / You ought to be in bed, sir. / O-U-T spells out."

MacColl and Behan, Folkways 8501 (1958) [Glasgow, 1957]. "Are you going to coff, sir?" / No sir! Why, sir? / Because I have a cold, sir. / Where did you catch the cold, sir?"

I know a washerwoman. *See* **269**.

270   **I** know something I shan't tell,
Three little niggers in a peanut shell;
One can sing and one can dance,
And one can make a pair of pants.
O-U-T spells out goes she.

Bolton (1888), 113 [Connecticut].
Gardner, *JAF*, 31 (1918), 532 [Michigan]. Ends "One was black, one was blacker, / One was the color of chawin' tobacker." = Knapp (1976), 191–192.
Boyce and Bartlett (1946), 29.
Withers (1946), n.p.

271   **I** lit a candle
And it went out.

Knapp (1976), 27.

272   **I** love to jump,
I love to shout,
Y-O-U are out.

Robertson, *NF*, 3, no. 2 (Summer 1960), 33 [Shelburne County, Nova Scotia, 1910].

Impty, dimpty (mimpty), tibbity fig. *See* **129**.

Ina, dina, dinalo, dash. *See* **119**.

Ina, mina, maca, raca. *See* **120**.

Ina mina ping pong. *See* **131**.

In comes cat. *See* **443**.

Indian counting. *See* **500**.

Inditie, Mentitie, Petitee, Dee. *See* **140**.

Indi tindi alego Mary. *See* **248**.

Indy (Ingy), tindy (tingy, tinky), allego Mary. *See* **248**.

Inerty, finerty, fleckerty, faig. *See* **129**.

Iney, meney, macker, acker. *See* **120**.

273   Ingie, bingie, bamberingie,
Over, diver, dickit!
One, two three—
You—are—out!

Gregor (1891), 21 [Scotland]. Two variants, beginning "Eendy, beendy" and "Endy, bendy."
J.P.F., *Misc. of Rymour Club*, 2, part 5 (1917), 186 [Scotland].

Ingle, angle,
Silver (Golden) bangle. *See* **147**.

274   Ing, ping, piparsling,
Nelja, pelja, suga, luga,

Santa, piva, hiva, diva,
Dapa, krets.

Bolton, *JAF*, 10 (1897), 319 [Strömöe, Faröe Islands].

Ingry oory, accry davy. *See* **410**.

275   In hoc Domine quod
Duck's foot plump in the mud.

Bolton (1888), appendix [Massachusetts].

Inity, finity, fickerty, fae. *See* **129**.

Inity, finity, my black hen. *See* **213**.

Inka, bink (dink), . . . *See* **277**.

Inka, ponka, pinka, pa. *See* **276**.

Inka vanka vinegar. *See* **276**.

276   Inkey, pinkey ellakamar,
X, Q, santa mar,
Santa mar, ellacafa,
Sham.

See also **101**.

Opie (1969), 51–52 [southern Britain, since 1895]. Six variants; other beginnings are "Inky, pinky, ellakama," "Inka
vanka vinegar," "Inka, ponka, pinka, pa," "Ickledee,
pickledee, elleka-mah," and "Ecklie, picklie, eleka fa."

Inkie, bink, . . . *See* **277**.

Inkie pinkie hala balum. *See* **126**.

Ink, mink, . . . *See* **277**.

Ink, pink, papers, ink. *See* **277**.

277 Ink, pink, pen and ink (pepper stink, penny stink,
    penny wink),
I smell a dirty stink (bottle full of rotten ink)
And I think
It comes from Y-O-U.

Generally a taunt.

Halliwell (1849), 134. "Ink, pink, pen and ink; / A study, a
    stive, a stove, and a sink" as ending to "Onery, twoery,
    tickery, teven" rhyme (**410**).

Opie (1959), 48 [Halliwell (1849) version; also current in the
    United States].

Robertson, *NF*, 3, no. 2 (Summer 1960), 29 [Shelburne
    County, Nova Scotia, since 1880]. Two variants, one begin-
    ning "Pink wink, you stink" and "Ink, mink, who stinks, /
    Like any old mink. / O-U-T spells out and out you must go."

Gregor (1881), 169 [Scotland]. Begins ". . . penny stink."

Folk-Lore Journal, 1 (1883), 384 [Derbyshire].

Burne (1883), 572 [Shropshire]. "Ink, pink, pen and ink, / I
    stole, study, stink / O.U.T. spells out."

Northall (1892), 347. Two variants, one each from *Folk-Lore
    Journal*, 1 (1883), and Burne (1883).

Bolton (1888), 111 [Scotland; Massachusetts; New York City;
    Ontario, Canada]. Six variants, some beginning "Ink mink."

Gregor (1891), 29, 32 [Scotland]. Variants beginning
    ". . . penny stink" and "I think, I think" (the latter = Knapp
    [1976], 211).

Maclagan (1901), 249 [Scotland]. "Ink, pink pepperstink, half
    a glass of brandy. / One for you and one for me and one for
    Uncle Sandy."

Davis (1906), 212 [Plymouth, Massachusetts; Scotland]. Two
    variants: "Ink, pink, papers, ink, / Am pam push" and "Ink,
    mink, pepperstink, / Sarko, Larko, Bump" (the latter =
    Botkin [1947], 906).

Withers (1946), n.p. [Cedar County, Missouri, 1907–1913].
    Begins "Ink, a-bink, a bottle of ink."

Gardner, *JAF*, 31 (1918), 230 [New York]. "Rosy, posy, piny,
    pink / O bless me, how you do stink!"

Waugh, *JAF*, 31 (1918), 43 [Ontario]. "Ink pink penny wink, /
    Oh, how you do stink."

Wintemberg, *JAF*, 31 (1918), 150 [New Dundee Ontario].
    Same as Waugh version.

Opie (1969), 36 [England, since ca. 1920]. Two variants, one
    begins "Ip, dip, pen and ink."

Whitney and Bullock (1925), 138 [Maryland]. Ends "Sty,
    stow, steady, stink."

Turner (1969), 13–14 [Australia, since ca. 1935]. Two variants, one beginning "Inky pinky smell a dinky."

Maryott, SFQ, 1, no. 4 (1937), 44 [Nebraska].

Withers (1948), 85. Begins "Ink-a-bink."

Bley (1957), 96. "Inka bink, (Pull out the cork and take a drink."

Howard, NYFQ, 16 (1960), 136 [Australia].

Leventhal and Cray, WF, 22 (1963), 242 [California]. Two variants, beginning "Ink the bink, the bottle of ink" and "Inkie, bink."

Ritchie (1965), 47 [Edinburgh]. Begins "I think, I think."

Goldstein (1971), 174 [Philadelphia, 1966–1967]. Begins "Inka binka."

Castagna, NYFQ, 25 (1969), 227 [New Rochelle, New York]. "Ink-a-dink, a bottle of ink / The cork fell out and you stink. / Not because you're dirty, not because you're clean, / Just because you kissed a girl behind a magazine."

Fowke (1969), 110 [Canada]. Two variants: "Ink, mink, who stinks / Like any old mink? / O-U-T spells out / And out you must go" and Castagna version.

Knapp (1976), 212. "Inka blinka, bottle of ink / Cork fell out, and you stink."

Milberg (1976), 25. Begins "Ink a bink"; ends "Not because you're dirty; / Not because you're clean; / Just because you kissed a (boy or) girl / Behind a magazine."

278 Ink, stink, stiddle my stew,
Nobody stinks but bare lie you.

Bolton (1888), 96. Begins "Ury, urry, angry, Ann, / Mulberry wax and tyry tan."

McDowell, TFSB, 10, no. 3 (September 1944), 4.

Ink stink, tobacco stink. See **133**.

Ink the bink. See **277**.

Inky, minky, bottle of beer. See **357**.

279 Inky, pinky, alligator winky
Oxtail out.
I saw a butcher boy
Riding on a savaloy.
The savaloy busted,

And he fell in the mustard [*pronounced
   "mustid"*].
Inky, pinky, alligator winky
Oxtail out.

Howard, NYFQ, 16 (1960), 137 [Australia]. Two variants.

Inky, pinky, ellakama. See **276**.

Inky pinky fidgety fell. See **579**.

280   Inky pinky, forie, fum,
Cudjybo-peep, illury, cum,
Ongry fongry, forie fy,
King of the Tonga islands.

Bolton (1888), 110 [Kentucky].

Inky, pinky, my black hen. See **213**.

Inky, pinky, pea. See **430**.

Inky, pinky, peerie winkie. See **579**.

Inky-pinky pencil-sharpener. See **212**.

Inky, pinky, penny, pie. See **204**.

281   Inky pinky, piggidy, fell,
Ell dell, dro, mell.

G.W.R., *Old Lore Misc.*, 5 (1912), 53 [Kirkwall].

282   Inky, pinky, ponky,
Daddy's bought a donkey.
Donkey died, daddy cried,
Inky, pinky, ponky.

   Cf. **253**.

Opie (1969), 36 [England, current since ca. 1900].

Turner (1969), 14 [Australia, since ca. 1930].
Fowke (1969), 109 [Canada].

Inky pinky smell a dinky. *See* **277**.

Innerty (Innertie), finnerty (finnertie, fenerty),
    fickerty (fickertie, fickety), fegg (fig, fage). *See*
    129.

Innerty, finnerty, my black hen. *See* **213**.

283   Innery, unnery, eke u man eke,
    Hollaman, tollaman, erica man,
    Whiska, dinda, poker stinda,
    Holla, polla, you are out.

    Maclagan, *Folk-Lore*, 16 (1905), 450.

284   In nineteen forty-two, in 1942,
    Bentley sailed a canoe,
    He struck a rock, the clumsy clot.
    That was a good one, was it not?

    Opie (1959), 117 [Surbiton, England, 1950].

Inny ke nicky nacky noe. *See* **140**.

285   In pin, safety pin,
    In pin out.

    Opie (1969), 31.

286   I-N spells in,
    O-U-T spells out.

    Opie (1969), 31.

Inta, minta, dibbity (diggity), fig. *See* **129**.

287 Intery, mintery (Intry, mintry), cutery, corn,
Appleseed and briar thorn.
Wire, briar, limber lock.
Five (Three, Six) geese in a flock.
One flew east and one flew west
And one flew over the cuckoo's nest.

*A frequent alternate ending is "Sit and sing by a spring. /
O-U-T and in again." See also* **115, 200, 567.** *Used sometimes
as a jump-rope rhyme (see JRR, p. 88). See also Opie, Dictionary, p. 224.*

Bolton (1888), 3, 102–103 [Massachusetts, 1806; Connecticut, 1806 and 1880; Maine; Nebraska; Indiana; Rhode Island; Nova Scotia, 1815; New York City; New York; Maryland; Philadelphia; Michigan; Colorado; Florida; Ireland;
England]. Eleven variants, many coupled with "As I went
up the Brandy Hill" rhyme (**43**). Other beginnings are
"Entra, mentra, cutra, cora," "Hinty, minty, cuty corn,"
"Hintery, mintery," "Intrie, mintrie," "Intra, mintra," "Eddle, weddle, limber lock," and "Hurly, burley limber lock"
(from *Mill Hill Magazine*, 5 [1877]). One variant ends with
the ending from "Hickory, dickory dock" rhyme (**216**), one
ends with a "My old man and I fell out" rhyme (**383**), and
another ends "I sat, I sunkle, / Daylight spunkle, / Fellasy
dear, / To come to beer; / Invite you in to kill a fat / Little
white dog and a mountainy cat; / For that same reason pull
in your foot."
Notes and Queries, n.s., 16, no. 1 (May 1969), 172 [Quebec,
before 1875]. Ends "Twelve geese sitting in a flock. / Wind
your dish-cloth / Around their snout."
Mill Hill Magazine, 5 (1877). Begins "Hurley, burley, limber
lock."
Ellis, *Transactions of the Philological Society* (1878), 367
[New England].
Newell (1883), 3, 102–103 [Massachusetts] = Botkin (1944),
772.
Waugh, *JAF*, 31 (1918), 41–42 [Ontario, 1888, 1909]. Three
variants; one begins "Wire brier limber lock"; another,
"Onery, twoery, cutery corn."
F.B.T., *Devon and Cornwall Notes and Gleanings*, 2, no. 18
(June 15, 1889), 87 [Devonshire].
Northall (1892), 347.
Thomas (1895), 1 [Cornwall]. "Hiery, diery, limber lock, / One
a-mexey, two o'clock; / I sat, sing in the morning spring. /
Yellow, blue, black, green, / In nine; 'out'."

Clifton Johnson (1896), 162. Begins "Monkey, monkey, bottle of beer. / How many monkeys have we here? / One, two, three, out goes he. / Wire, brier," etc.

Monroe, *AA.*, n.s., 6 (1904), 48 [Massachusetts].

Davis (1906), 209, 210, 211. Three variants; one begins "Hinty, minty"; one ending "Set and sing by a spring, / My grandmother lives on the hill, / She has jewels, she has rings, / She has many pretty things, / O.U.T. spells out you go" (cf. **43**).

Anderson, *Evening Ledger* (May 17, 1916) [Kentucky, New Jersey]. Begins "Briar, wire, limber lock."

Gardner, *JAF*, 31 (1918), 526 [Michigan]. Two variants: one begins "Entry, mintry"; the other, "Entry, kentry."

Wintemberg, *JAF*, 31 (1918), 150 [New Dundee, Ontario].

Whitney and Bullock (1925), 135–136 [Maryland]. Four variants; one begins "Hintery, mintery"; one has the lines "Sit and sing till twelve o'clock, / Clock fall down, mouse ran 'round"; and another is "Lucky, minchy, cuchy cow, / Apple seed and berry thorn, / Briar, briar, limber lock, / Ten mice on a clock, / The clock fell down, / The mouse went around. / Tee tee, turn me out, / To get a bottle of wine."

Botkin (1947), 905 [Vermont, 1930's]. Begins "Entry, mentry"; last two lines omitted.

Ireland, *Recreation* (February 1937), 545.

Maryott, *SFQ*, 1, no. 4 (1937), 43, 44 [Nebraska]. Seven variants; two begin "Enter, menter, pewter, corn"; one begins "High, spy."

Mills, *Jack and Jill*, 2 (January 1940), 19.

Wood and Goddard (1940), 570.

Flowers, *TFSB*, 10, no. 3 (1944), 7 [Tennessee].

Withers (1946), n.p. Two variants, one with "As I went up the Brandy Hill" rhyme (**43**).

Emrich and Korson (1947), 116.

Potter, "Counting-Out Rimes," *Standard Dictionary* (1949), 255 [Nova Scotia; New England; Florida; Yorkshire, England]. Begins "Intra, mintra." Alternate fourth lines: "Three wires in a clock" and "Three mice on a rock."

Roberts, *HF*, 8 (1949), 8 [Tennessee]. Begins "Eentery, meentery."

Gullen (1950), 15. Begins "Elder, belder, limber, lock, / Three wives in a clock."

Randolph, *SFQ*, 17 (1953), 247 [Arkansas]. Two variants, beginning "Wire, brier"; one ends "the clock fell down, mouse ran around, / . . ."

Evans (1956), 6.

Turner (1969), 14–15 [Sydney, 1957].

Cassidy, *PADS*, no. 29 (April 1956), 25 [Nebraska]. Begins "Intry, wintry."

Covey, *GMW*, 12 (1960), 9 [Vermont].

Opie (1969), 43. First two lines only, cited as an American song by Eugene Field.

Fowke (1969), 110 [Canada]. Begins "Wire, brier, limber-lock."

Reisner, *Notes and Queries*, 16, no. 5 (May 1969), 171–172.

Intery, mintery, hippity Dick. See **128**.

Intra, mintra, . . . See **287**, **288**.

288 Intramintra middlety sing,
Della doller dew,
Ezzy pezzy dominezzy,
Out goes you.

Randolph, *SFQ*, 17 (1953), 245–246 [Ft. Smith, Arkansas].

Intrie, mintrie, . . . See **287**.

Intry, mintry, cutery, corn. See **287**.

Intry, mintry, dibbity, fig. See **129**.

Intry, tentry, tethery, methery. See **500**.

Intry, wintry, . . . See **287**.

Inty, minty . . . See **129**, **139**, **140**, **500**.

Inty minty dibbity (diddle de), fig. See **129**.

Inty, minty, figgity, feg. See **129**.

Inty, minty, munty, my. See **139**.

Inty minty seventy-six. See **129**.

Inty, minty, tibbity (tibblety, tippety, tipedy), fig (fee, fis). See **129.**

Inty, minty, tipsy, tee (toe). See **140.**

Inty tinty fickery (figgery) fell. See **129.**

Inty, tinty, my black hen. See **213.**

Inty tinty tethery methery. See **500.**

Inty, tinty, tickery, been. See **160.**

Iny, tiny . . . fethery, phips. See **500.**

Ip, dip, alaba da (dalabadi). See **101.**

289 Ip, dip, dip,
My blue ship,
Sailing on the water
Like a cup and saucer.
But you are not on it.

Opie (1969), 36 [England, current for fifty years]. Two variants: "Dip, dip, dip" and "Dash, dash, dash, / My blue sash."

Opie (1959), 378 [Pontypool, England]. With playing instructions.

Jennings (1968), 212 [Bransgore, Hants]. Begins "Dip dip dip."

Stork, *Lore and Language*, no. 1 (July 1969), 3 [Sheffield, England]. Two variants: "Ip, dip, dip" and "Ip, dip, dash."

Ip, dip, pen and ink. See **277.**

Ip, dip, sky blue. See **502.**

Ip, dip, tom-tit. See **538.**

Ipetty, sipetty, ippetty sap. See **244.**

Iram, biram, brendom bo. *See* **141**.

Irka, birka stoony rock. *See* **579**.

Iroe, diroe, ducca, medo. *See* **141**.

I-rum, bi-rum, brimberlock. *See* **115**.

Iry, ory (ury), hickory (ickery), Ann. *See* **408**.

290 I saw a doo flee our the dam,
Wi' silver wings an' golden ban,
She leukit east, she leukit west,
She leukit fahr t' light on best,
She lightit on a bank o' san';
T' see the cocks o' Cumberlan',
Fite puddin, black trout,
Ye're oot.

Gregor (1881), 170 [Scotland].
Gregor (1891), 31 [Scotland]. Three variants; one begins
   "Eenty, teenty, tippenny Ann."

291 I say your shoe is too dirty.
Please change it.

Howard, *NYFQ*, 16 (1960), 143 [Australia, 1954–1955]. Alternate version: "Your shoes need cleaning / With cherry
   blossom polish."
Turner (1969), 17 [Canberra (1955) and Melbourne (1957),
   Australia]. Begins "Your shoe is dirty."
Ritchie (1965), 49 [Edinburgh]. Begins "Your shoe is dirty."
Opie (1969), 55 [England]. Four variants: "Your shoes are
   dirty / Please change them"; "My mother says your shoes
   are dirty / Please change your feet"; "Your shoes need
   cleaning / With Cherry Blossom Boot Polish"; and "Your
   shoes are dirty, your shoes are clean, / Your shoes are not fit
   to be seen by the Queen, / Please change them."

Iseenty, teenty, fickerty faig. *See* **129**.

Iseenty, teenty, hethery, bethery. *See* **500**.

Ish, fish, codfish. *See* **67.**

292   Ishka biska tiska too
Once around and out goes you.

Evans (1956), 14.

293   Ish nee sunk
She go roo
Kish kosh koo
Ju ju-ju.

Evans (1956), 20.

294   Ishtish, tash tish
What color do you wish?

Withers (1946), n.p. [from Brooklyn College students, 1936–
1945]. With playing instructions.

Issing, issing, issory. *See* **141.**

Item, peetum, penny pie. *See* **204.**

I think, I think. *See* **277.**

Itim, peetim, penny, pie. *See* **204.**

295   It's afttimes I've been drunk, and afttimes I've
been fu',
But the drunkest time that ever I was,
I never set fire to my bussie o' woo.

"Counting-Out Rhymes," *Misc. of Rymour Club*, 2, part 2
(1913), 62 [Scotland].

296   It's quite fair that
You should go he.

Sutton-Smith (1959), 69 [New Zealand].

297   Itsa, bitsa, tootsa, la,
Falla-me linka, linka, la.
Falla-malu, falla-mila,
Falla-melinka, linka, la.

Withers (1946), n.p. [from Brooklyn College students, 1936–1945].

298   I-T spells it,
Thou art it.

Opie (1969), 30 [Blackburn, England].

Ittle, ottle, black (blue) bottle. See **147**.

Ivory, ovory, ickery, Ann. See **408**.

299   I wad gee a' my livin'
That my wife were as fite an as fair
As the swans that flee o'er the mill-dam.

The syllable ca *is added to the end of each word: "I-ca wad-ca gee-ca," etc.*

Gregor (1881), 172; (1891), 32 [Scotland].

I walked under an apple tree. See **42**.

I went to a Chinese laundry. See **120**.

300   I went to the river, I couldn't get across,
I paid ten shillings for an old blind horse;
I jumped on his back, he fell with a crack,
So I played the fiddle till the boat came back.

See Opie, Dictionary, *pp. 315–316.*

"Counting-Out Rhymes," *Misc. of Rymour Club*, 2, part 2 (1913), 95 [Dundee].

Izeenty teenty figgery fell. See **129**.

Izeenty, teenty, higglety, pigglety. See **164**.

301   Izzard, Izzard, Izzard I,
       Izzard, Izzard, Z.

>   *Cf.* **245**.

>   Opie (1969), 46 [Northamptonshire, 1854].
>   Northall (1892), 348.

J

302   Jack, be nimble!
       Jack, be quick!
       Jack jumped over the candlestick.

>   *See Opie, Dictionary, p. 227. Also found as a jump-rope
>   rhyme (JRR, p. 98).*

>   Waugh, *JAF*, 31 (1918), 46 [Ontario, 1909].

303   Jack, Jack, sat on a tack,
       And went to bed with a sore back.
       O-U-T, and out goes he.

>   *Usually a taunt.*

>   Withers (1946), n.p. [from Brooklyn College students, 1936–
>   1945].

Jack says to Jack. See **311**.

304   Jane, Jane, had a machane
       Jo, Jo, made it go;
       Frank, Frank, turn the crank;
       His mother came out and gave him a spank,
       And sent him over the garden bank.

>   *Usually a taunt. Also found as a jump-rope rhyme; see JRR,
>   p. 98.*

>   Bolton (1888), 117 [Connecticut].
>   Withers (1946), n.p. [from Brooklyn College students, 1936–
>   1945]. Begins "Frank, Frank."

305   Jean, Jean,
Dressed in green,
Went downtown
To eat ice cream.
How many dishes did she eat?
One, two, three, *etc.*

> *Usually a taunt.*

Withers (1946), n.p. [from Brooklyn College students, 1936–1945].

306   Jeema, jeema, juma, jo;
Jiekamy jackamy jory;
Hika, sika, pika, wo.
Jeema, jeema, jima, jo.

Bolton (1888), 106 [Somerset, England].

Jenny at the cottage door. See **421**.

307   Jenny, good spinner,
Come down to your dinner,
And taste the leg of a roasted frog!
I pray ye, good people,
Look over the kirk-steeple,
And see the cat play wi' the dog.

> *Cf.* **499**. *See also Opie, Dictionary, pp. 374–375.*

Chambers (1841), 121 [Scotland].
Bolton (1888), 118, appendix [New York, Indiana]. Two variants: "Old Dan Tucker, / Come home to supper" and "Penny, come Penny, come down to your dinner, / And taste the leg of the roast nigger" (= Knapp [1976], 190).
Gregor (1891), 26 [Scotland]. Two variants, beginning "Kettie Spinner" and "Kette, my spinner." Both end with "Doctor Foster's a very good man" rhymes (**103**), featuring "Johnnie Frog" or "Mr. Frog."
Whitney and Bullock (1925), 135 [Maryland]. Begins "Eeny, come Meeny, come down to your dinner, / To eat the hind leg of a hog."

308   Jenny Mack, my shirt is black,
What'll I do for Sunday?
Take if off and give it a wash
On Tuesday, Wednesday, Thursday,
Friday, Saturday, Sunday.

MacColl and Behan, Folkways 8501 (1958), [Dublin].

309   Jock's oot, Jock's in,
Jock's through a hecklepin.
Tak' a mell and knock him ower,
Een, twa, three, fower.

Rodger (1969?), 20 [Scotland].

Joe, Joe, lost his toe. See **351**.

Johnnie Frog is a very good man. See **103**.

310   Oh, Johnny Brown,
He went to town
Three score miles and ten;
He went at night
By candle light,
And never got home again.

*Usually the game "How many miles to Babylon"; see Opie,
Dictionary, pp. 63−64.*

Bolton (1888), appendix [Indiana].

311   John says to John,
"How much are your geese?"
John says to John,
"Twenty cents a-piece."
John says to John,
"That is too dear!"
John says to John,
"Get out of here!"

*Also found as a jump-rope rhyme; see JRR, p. 101
("Johnny, Johnny, what's the price of geese?")*

Bolton (1888), 116 [New York, Connecticut, Oregon]. Three
variants; one begins "Ching, chong, Chinee man."
Waugh, *JAF*, 31 (1918), 46 [Ontario, 1909]. Begins "Chinky
chinky Chinaman."
Gardner, *JAF*, 31 (1918), 530–531 [Michigan]. Two variants,
beginning "Chink, chink, Chinaman" and "Chick, chick,
chatterman."
Whitney and Bullock (1925), 138 [Maryland]. Begins "Jack
says to Jack."
Bennett, *Children*, 12 (1927), 21.
Withers (1946), n.p.

John Smith, a folla fine. See **59**.

312   Juba, Reeda, Caesar, Breeda,
Quawka, Dinah, Clamshell.

Bolton (1888), 114 [Rhode Island].

313   Jumbo, Jumbo, sitting on a match box
Eating bread and cheese.
Along came a rat and bit him on the back
And made poor Jumbo sneeze.

Howard, *NYFQ*, 16 (1960), 142 [Australia, 1954–1955].

K

Katy Mason broke a basin. See **362**.

Keemo, kimo. See **314**.

Keetum, peetum, peeny, pie. See **204**.

314   Kemo, kimo limdon Kimo,
Kemo, kimo karo,
Strin stran popinadle,

Lola bala rig dam,
Sing son kitty qitche kimo.

From the nineteenth-century minstrel song "Kemo Kimo."
See also **13**, **70**.

Bolton (1888), 121. "Keemo kimo / Dare-o ho / Mehi meho /
Rump stitch-a / Bump-er-tickle / Soap fat periwinkle /
Nimicat a nipcat / Sing-song Polly, / Kitchy kimeeyo."
Maryott, SFQ, 1, no. 4 (1937), 40 [Nebraska].

Kette, my spinner. *See* **307**.

Kettie Spinner. *See* **307**.

315   A Knife and a razor,
Spells Nebuchadnezzar;
A knife and a fork
Spells Nebuchadork.
A pair of slippers,
And an old pair of shoes,
Spells Nebuchadnezzar,
The king of the Jews.

Cf. **316**, **385**.

Bolton (1888), 114 [New York City].

316   Knife and fork,
Bottle and cork,
That's the way
To spell New York.

Generally a spelling riddle. Cf. **315**. *Also found as a jump-*
rope rhyme; see JRR, p. 106.

Bolton (1888), 114 [New York].
Whitney and Bullock (1925), 139 [Maryland].
Withers (1946), n.p. [from Brooklyn College students, 1936–
1945].

317   The Kookaburra sits on the old gum tree.
Merry merry king of the bush is he,
Catch the laughing kookaburra

Or you'll go out for three:
THREE.

Adaptation of the song "Kookaburra."

Ritchie (1965), 49 [Edinburgh via Adelaide].

L

318   Ladhar-pocan,
Ladhar-pocan,
Pocan seipinn
Seipinn Seonaid
Da mheur mheadhon.

Opie (1969), 56 [Scotland].

319   Lady, baby, gypsy, queen,
Elephant, monkey, tangerine.

Also used as a divination rhyme.

Rutherford (1971), 53 [Birtley, England, 1966].

320   Last night and the night before
Twenty-four robbers came to my door;
Some went east and some went west,
And some went toward the cuckoo's nest.

Usually a jump-rope rhyme; see JRR, p. 110.

Bolton (1888), 117 [Nevada]. Begins "All last night" and ends
"Wake up, wake up, ginger blue, / And don't be afraid of the
bugaboo."
Withers (1946), n.p. [from Brooklyn College students, 1936–
1945]. Ends "Wake up, wake up, ginger blue, / And don't be
afraid of the bugaboo."
Brewster, *SFQ*, 3 (1939), 181. Two variants.
Cassidy, *PADS*, no. 29 (April 1958), 25 [Louisiana]. Ends
"Shot 'em down with a forty-four. / All out!"

321   Leekie ma law, leekie ma la,
Who is the man to be crowned with stra'?

Notes and Queries, 10th ser., 11 (June 5, 1909), 446 [Orkney].

Lemons and oranges. See **440**.

322   Let us, oh, let us
Eat lettuce.

Howard, NYFQ, 16 (1960), 142 [Australia, 1954–1955].

323   Linnet, linnet,
Come this minute;
Here's a house with something in it
That was built for me I know.

Newell (1883), 202 [Pennsylvania].
Bolton (1888), 117 [Pennsylvania].
Justus (1957), 45 [Tennessee]. Second line: "Here's a nest
    with goose eggs in it."

324   Liss, tita, rise,
Bom, bel, gifis.
Rinka, stinka, bobolinka;
Flap, flail, fliss.

Bolton (1888), 110 [Massachusetts].

Little beggar. See **499**.

Little Black Doctor, how is your wife? See **361**.

325   Little boy driving cattle,
Don't you hear his money rattle?
One, 2, 3, out goes he.

Newell (1883), 203 [Massachusetts] = Botkin (1944), 773.
    Begins "Little man."
Bolton (1888), 116 [Massachusetts, Maine]. Two variants,
    both beginning "Little man."
Clifton Johnson (1896), 161.

Monroe, *AA*, n.s., 6 (1904), 48 [Massachusetts].
Acker (1923), 17.
Withers (1946), n.p. Begins "Three men driving cattle."
Musick, *HF*, 7 (1948), 13 [West Virginia].
Justus (1957), 44 [Tennessee].

326   Little dog sat on the porch,
And Bingo was his name.
B-I-N-G-O,
B-I-N-G-O,
B-I-N-G-O,
Bingo was his name.

  Usually part of a singing game.

Withers (1946), n.p.

Little fat policeman. See **460**.

Little fatty doctor, how's your wife? See **361**.

327   Little fishes in the brook,
Papa catch them with a hook;
Mamma fry them in a pan,
Bubby eats them like a man.

  Usually a nursery rhyme.

Bolton (1888), 113 [Colorado, Rhode Island].
Acker (1923), 18.
Withers (1946), n.p. Begins "Fishes, fishes, in the brook."
Musick, *HF*, 7 (1948), 13 [West Virginia].

Little Freddie at the door. See **421**.

A Little green snake. See **35**.

Little man driving cattle. See **325**.

328   Little Minnie
Washed her pinnie
In-side-out.

Opie (1969), 31.

Little Miss Pink. *See* **395**.

Little nigger
Come to dinner. *See* **499**.

Little old man and I fell out. *See* **383**.

Little Red taxi. *See* **469**.

329   Little Sallie Water (Walker),
        Sitting in the sun;
        Crying and a-weeping
        For a nice young man.
        Rise, Sallie, rise,
        Wipe out your eyes.

> *Cf.* **113**. *Commonly found as singing game; also a jump-rope rhyme (*JRR, *p.* 114).*

> Bolton (1888), 120 [New Hampshire].
> Gregor (1881), 174, and (1891), 26 [Scotland]. "Rise, Sally Walker, rise if you can, / Rise, Sally Walker, an follow your gueede man, / Come, choose to the East, / Come, choose to the West, / Come, choose to the very one I love best."

Little sinner. *See* **499**.

London County Council, L.C.C. *See* **66**.

330   Looby Lou,
        Looby Lou,
        When I'm finished
        Out goes you.

> *Cf. the singing game "Looby Loo."*

> Evans (1956), 22.

331   Looking through a window,
        A twenty-story window,

I slipped and sprained my eyebrow,
On the pavement, the pavement.

Maryott, *SFQ*, 1, no. 4 (1937), 61 [Nebraska].

332 Look upon the mantelpiece
There you see a ball of glass,
Shining like a pocket-piece,
O-U-T spells right out—
Out goes he.

Also used to end other rhymes.

Old Cornwall, 1, no. 5 (April 1927), 42 [England, 1880].

Look up, sky blue. See **412**.

333 The Lord made the mountain slippy as glass;
Down came the Devil sliding on his arse;
The elephant shit a monkey, the monkey shit a
    flea,
The flea shit a nanny-goat. Out goes he!

Rutherford (1971), 53 [Birtley, England, ca. 1915]. Sung to the
tune of "Ball o Kirriemuir."

Lucky, minchy, cuchy cow. See **287**.

334 Lucky Lockitt lost her pocket,
Katy Fisher found it.
Not a penny was there in it,
Only a ribbon round it.

Lady Fisher lost her pocket,
Lady Parker found it.
Lady Parker thanked her friend,
And said her cow was drownded.

Usually a nursery rhyme; see Opie, Dictionary, pp. 279–
280.

Bolton (1888), 118.

M

335   Mabel, Mabel, set the table,
Don't forget the sugar, salt,
And red hot pepper.

> Usually a jump-rope rhyme; see JRR, p. *115*.

> Maryott, *SFQ*, 1, no. 4 (1937), 56 [Nebraska].

336   Mademoiselle from Armentières, parlez-vous.
She hasn't been kissed for forty years, parlez-vous.
The Prince of Wales was put in jail
For riding a horse without a tail,
Inky-pinky parlez-vous.

> From the World War I soldier's song. Also used to chant, to
> play two-balls, and to jump rope (see JRR, p. 117).

> Opie (1959), 92 [western Scotland].

337   Maggie, Maggie, where is Jiggs?
Down in the cellar eating pigs.
How many pigs did he eat?

> Also found as a jump-rope rhyme; see JRR, p. 117.

> "Folk Rhymes" (1944), 4 [Maryland].

Maister (Master) Mundy, how's your wife? See
361.

338   Mamma's going to make me a dress,
What color does——like best?
"*Yellow*"
Y-E-L-L-O-W spells yellow,
And out goes you.

> *Cf.* **376**.

> Randolph, *SFQ*, 17 (1953), 248 [Searcy, Arkansas].

339 Mammy, Daddy, dish-clout,
O-U-T spells out.

Buspidnick (1906), 214 [Cornwall, 1870].

340 Marjorie, comparjorie,
The ido-go-sarijorie,
Tee-legged, toe-legged,
Bow-legged Marjorie.

*Usually a taunt. Also found as a jump-rope rhyme; see
JRR, p. 10 ("Annie cum banny").*

Maryott, SFQ, 1, no. 4 (1937), 51 [Nebraska]. Two variants;
one, "Mary, baum barry tee hadle go ferry, / Beelegged,
bilegged, bowlegged, Mary."

Mary at the cottage door (garden gate). See **421**.

Mary, baum barry tee hadle go ferry. See **340**.

Mary had a little lamb. See **133**.

Master Foster, very good man. See **103**.

341 Matthew, Mark, Luke, and John,
Saddle the cat and I'll get on,
Give me the switch and I'll be gone.
Out goes he.

*Parody of a popular children's prayer; see Opie, Diction-
ary, p. 305. Also found as a jump-rope rhyme (JRR, p. 121).*

Randolph, SFQ, 17 (1953), 248 [Arkansas].
MacColl and Seeger, Folkways 3565 (1962) [Durham,
England]. "Cuddy" instead of "cat"; ends "If it kicks,
pull its tail, / If it shits, hold a pail."

342 Me and my Grannie, and a great lot mair,
Kicket up a row gaun hame frae the fair;
By cam' the watchman, and cried, "What's
there?"—
Me and my Grannie, and a great lot mair.

"Rhymes of General and Local Interest," *Misc. of the Rymour Club*, 2, part 3 (1914), 113 [Scotland].

343   Me an' the minister's wife cast oot,
An guess ye what it was about?
Black puddin', dish-clout,
Eiri orie, your oot.

Cf. **383**.

Gregor (1891), 29 [Scotland].
Maclagan (1901), 249 [Scotland].
Our Meigle Book (1932), 166 [Scotland]. Begins "The minister's wife and I cuist out."

344   Me bindle, me bandle,
Me soo, me goo, me gay,
Me grandther, me sthradleum, dthradleum,
      dthrago, dthrafjean.

Bolton (1888), appendix [Ireland].

Meeny, meeny, miny mo. *See* **141**.

Melbourne City Council, one, two, three. *See* **66**.

Mica, mona, mina, mike. *See* **139**.

Mickey Mouse built a house. *See* **345, 366**.

345   Mickey Mouse (He) bought a house. *See* **346**.

Mickey Mouse built a house
Under an apple tree,
Mickey Mouse called his house
Number twenty-three.

Also found as a jump-rope rhyme; see JRR, p. 122.

Opie (1959), 111 [Dublin].

Mickey Mouse
In a public house. *See* **355**.

346 Mickey Mouse
Lived in a house.
What color was it?
"Red."
R-E-D spells red
And you are he.

Opie (1969), 59 [since 1936]. "Mickey Mouse bought a house.
/ What colour did he paint it?"
Howard, NYFQ, 16 (1960), 140 [Australia 1954–1955].
Ritchie (1965), 47 [Edinburgh]. Begins "Mickey Mouse / He
bought a house."

Mickey Mouse made (planned) a house. *See* **366**.

347 Mickey Mouse was in a house
Wondering what to do.
So he scratched his bun-tiddly-um,
Out goes you.

Opie (1959), 111 [Farnham, Surrey].

348 Miller, miller, dusty pole,
How many sacks have you stole?
Twenty-five and a peck.
Hang up the miller by his neck.

Withers (1946), n.p.

349 Mingledy, mingledy, clap, clap, clap,
How many fingers do I hold up?

Maryott, SFQ, 1, no. 4 (1937), 50 [Nebraska].

350 A Minister in his pulpit,
He couldn't say his prayers;
He giggled and he gaggled
Till he fell down the stairs:
The stairs gave a crack,
And he broke his humpie back,

And all the congregation
Gave a quack, quack, quack.

> *Usually an entertainment rhyme. Also found as a jump-rope rhyme; see JRR, p. 157 ("The parson in the pulpit").*

Reid, *Misc. of Rymour Club*, 1 (1911), 102 [Edinburgh].
G.W.R., *Old Lore Misc.*, 5 (1912), 6 [Kirkwall].

The **Minister's** wife and I cuist out. See **343**.

351 Miss Defoe broke her toe
On the way to Mexico.
Coming back she broke her back
Sliding down the railway track.

> *Usually a taunt. Also found as a jump-rope rhyme; see JRR, p. 16 ("Betty, Betty stumped her toe").*

Bolton, *JAF*, 10 (1897), 321 [western Pennsylvania]. "Joe, Joe, lost his toe / In the battle of Mexico."
Waugh, *JAF*, 31 (1918), 45 [Ontario, 1909].
Fowke (1969), 110 [Canada].

352 Miss Mary Mack, dressed in black,
Silver buttons on her back.
I love coffee, I love tea,
I love boys and the boys love me.

> *The first two lines are a riddle for "coffin" (see Archer Taylor, English Riddles, p. 234). Also found as jump-rope rhymes; see JRR, pp. 120 ("Mary Mack, dressed in black) and 85 ("I love coffee").*

Bolton (1888), 117 [Pennsylvania].

Mistress Mason broke her basin. See **362**.

Mittie Mattie (Mitty, Matty) had a hen. See **213**.

353 Monday's child is fair of face;
Tuesday's child is full of grace;
Wednesday's child is sour and sad;
Thursday's child is merry and glad;

Friday's child is full of sin;
Saturday's child is pure within;
The child that is born on the Sabbathday
To heaven its step shall tend away.

Usually a nursery rhyme; see Opie, Dictionary, *pp. 309–310.*

Newel (1883), 203 [Georgia].
Bolton (1888), 115 [Georgia, New England]. Two variants.

354   Monday, Tuesday, Wednesday,
Thursday, Friday, Saturday,
O-U-T spells out goes she.

Bolton (1888), 114 [Virginia]. Last line: "Out goes he."
Whitney and Bullock (1925), 139.

355   A Monkey came into my shop one day
And asked for a bottle of beer.
Where is your money?
In my pocket.
Where is your pocket?
I left it at home.
Well, please walk out.

Cf. **357, 580**. *Also found as a jump-rope rhyme; see JRR, p. 165 ("Rat-a-tat-tat, who is that?").*

Maclagan, *Folk-Lore,* 16 (1905), 453. Begins "Who is there? / Tom Blair. / What does he want? / A bottle of beer."
Sutton-Smith (1959), 65 [New Zealand, current 1910].
Opie (1959), 11, 111 [England: Swansea, 1939; Cleethorpes, 1952; Alton, 1950]. Three variants, beginning "A frog," "A pig," and "Mickey Mouse / In a public house / Drinking pints of beer."
Daiken (1963), 32 [Dublin]. Begins "A pig went into a public house."
Ritchie (1965), 48–49 [Edinburgh]. Begins "Who's there? / Tiny Tiny Bear. / What do you want? / A pint of beer."

356   Monkey in the match-box (band box)
Don't you hear him holler?

Take him to the station-house (jailhouse)
And make him pay a dollar.

Sometimes used to end **382**.

Bolton (1888), 112 [Connecticut, New York, Rhode Island].
Three variants, one beginning "Nigger in the woodshed."
Clifton Johnson (1896), 166. Three variants; two begin "Nig-
ger in (on) the woodpile."
Whitney and Bullock (1925), 139 [Maryland]. Begins "Nigger
in the woodshed."
Emrich and Korson (1947), 117.

Monkey, monkey, barley beer. *See* **357**.

357   Monkey, monkey, bottle of beer,
      How many monkeys are there here?
      One, two, three, out goes he.

Newell (1883), 202 [Massachusetts to Georgia] = Botkin
(1944), 773.
Bolton (1888), 112, 116 [Nebraska, Rhode Island, Virginia,
Minnesota, Pennsylvania, Iowa, Kansas, Missouri,
Mississippi, Connecticut, New York, Wisconsin, Illinois,
Vermont, North Carolina, New Jersey]. Ten variants, with
numerous minor changes; one ends "Tit comes one, this we
know, / For his mother told us so / . . ."
Clifton Johnson (1896), 162. Ends with "Wire, brier, limber
lock" ending of "Intery, mintery, cutery, corn" rhyme
(**287**).
Withers (1946), n.p. [Cedar County, Missouri, 1907–1913].
Waugh, *JAF*, 31 (1918), 44 [Ontario, 1909]. Two variants,
". . . making beer" and ". . . draw the beer," the latter end-
ing "2, 4, 6, 7, all good monkeys go to heaven. / O-u-t spells
out, so you are out, / And you are he."
Anderson, *Evening Ledger* (May 17, 1916) [Kentucky, New
Jersey].
Gardner, *JAF*, 31 (1918), 553 [Michigan].
Wintemberg, *JAF*, 31 (1918), 122–123, 150, 157 [Ontario].
Beginnings are "Monkey, monkey, barley beer" and
"Mumbly, mumbly, in the pot."
Brewster (1952), 164–165 [North Carolina, 1922–1923, 1928].
Two variants.
Acker (1923), 17. Begins "Monkey, monkey, looking so
queer."
Whitney and Bullock (1925), 138 [Maryland].

Gardner (1937), 229 [New York].

Ireland, *Recreation* (February 1937), 545.

Maryott, *SFQ*, 1, no. 4 (1937), 49 [Nebraska]. Two variants; one begins "Inky, minky."

Brewster, *SFQ*, 3 (1939), 180.

"Folk Rhymes" (1944), 4 [Maryland].

McAtee (1946), 22 [Indiana].

Emrich and Korson (1947), 122.

Musick, *HF*, 7 (1948), 13 [West Virginia].

Withers (1948), ". . . bottle of pop."

Potter, "Counting-Out Rimes," *Standard Dictionary* (1949), 255.

Musick and Randolph, *JAF*, 63 (1950), 427 [Missouri]. Three variants.

Ray Wood (1952), 88.

Randolph, *SFQ*, 17 (1953), 245 [Arkansas].

Cassidy, *PADS*, no. 29 (April 1958), 25 [Kansas].

Sutton-Smith (1959), 71 [New Zealand].

Sandberg (1963), 123 [North Carolina]. Ends with "One, two, three, four, five, six, seven, / All good children go to heaven" rhyme (**415**).

Fowke (1969), 111 [Canada]. Begins "Monkey, monkey, draw the beer."

Knapp (1976), 26. Begins "Monkey, monkey, bottle of pop / On which monkey do we stop?"

Monkey, monkey, draw the (making) beer (looking so queer). *See* **357**.

358   Monkey, monkey, sitting on a fence,
Trying to make a dollar out of fifteen cents.
One, two, three,
Out goes he.

Usually a taunt. Also found as a jump-rope rhyme; see JRR, p. 185 ("Tattletale, tattletale, settin' on a fence").

Withers (1946), n.p.

Monry, orey, . . . *See* **408**.

The Moose ran up the clock. *See* **216**.

Mother ketch a flea. *See* **429**.

359   Motor boat, motor boat, go so slow.
Motor boat, motor boat, go so fast.
Motor boat, motor boat, step on the gas.

> *Also found as a jump-rope rhyme; see JRR, p. 130.*

Leventhal and Cray, WF, 22 (1963), 239 [California]. Description of use.

Mr. Brown, how's your wife. See **361**.

Mr. Brown went to the store. See **376**.

Mr. Drum's (Dunn's) a very good man. See **103**.

Mr. Foster's a very good man. See **103**.

360   Mr. Foster went to Glo'ster
In a shower of rain.
Stepped in a puddle, up to his middle,
Never went there again.

> *Usually a nursery rhyme (see Opie, Dictionary, p. 173).*
> *Also found as a jump-rope rhyme (see JRR, p. 38: "Doctor Foster").*

Bolton (1888), 119 [Virginia].

Mr. Frog is a very good man. See **103**.

Mr. Macpherson, how's your wife? See **361**.

Mr. Macpherson's a very good man. See **103**.

Mr. Monday, how's your wife? See **361**.

361   "**Mr.** Munday (Mundie, Mungo, Murdock), how's
your wife?"
"Very sick and like to die."
"Can she eat any butcher meat?"
"Yes, more than I can buy.

Half a horse, half a coo,
Half three quarters o' a soo.
She mak's her pottage very thin;
A pound o' butter she puts in."
Fite puddin, black troot,
Ye're oot.

Opie (1959), 3 [England, since 1818]. Two variants, begin-
    ning "Doctor! Doctor!" and "Little fatty doctor."
Gregor (1881), 170, 173, 175 [northeast Scotland]. Three var-
    iants.
Edward Nicholson (1897), 309 [Scotland]. Three variants;
    two from Gregor (1881).
Gregor (1891), 24–25 [Scotland]. Eleven variants, beginning
    "Mr. Mundie," "Mr. Murdock," "Mr. Mungo," "Mr.
    Brown," "Mr. Macpherson."
Maclagan (1901), 249 [Scotland].
Maclennan (1909), 53 [Scotland]. Begins "Maister Mundy."
Home, *Misc. of Rymour Club*, 1 (1911), 113. Begins "Mr.
    Monday."
"Counting-Out Rhymes," *Misc. of Rymour Club*, 2, part 2
    (1913), 62 [Scotland].
Maryott, *SFQ*, 1, no. 4 (1937), 61 [Nebraska].
Udal (1922), 394 [Dorset]. Begins "Gargy, Pargy."
Gullen (1950), 16. Begins "Master Monday."
Shaw (1969), 47 [Liverpool]. "Little Black Doctor, how is
    your wife? / Very well, thank you, she's all right. / She
    won't eat salt-fish, / Or a stick of licquorice. / O-U-T spells
    out."

Mrs. Dumb lived in a room. *See* **190.**

362   Mrs. Mason broke her basin,
How much will it be?
Half-a-crown, says Mr. Brown,
Out goes she.

*See Opie, Dictionary, p. 302. Also found as a jump-rope
rhyme; see JRR, p. 143 ("Old Mother Mason").*

Burne (1883), 573 [Shropshire] = Northall (1892), 348 = Opie
    (1959), 12.
Reid, *Misc. of Rymour Club*, 1 (1911), 104 [Edinburgh]. Be-
    gins "Katy Mason."
Gullen (1950), 17. Begins "Mistress Mason."

Mr. Smith's a very good man. See **103**.

Mumbly, mumbly in the pot. See **357, 487**.

363   Muncho, poco, mala, bueno,
Zuni, Moqui, Navajo.

Bolton (1888), 112 [Arizona].

364   My blue slave, dressed in blue,
Died last night at half-past two.
What color was the blood?
"Red."
R-E-D spells red
And O-U-T spells out.

> *Cf.* **365**. *Usually a jump-rope rhyme; see JRR, p. 112 ("Little Miss Pinky, dressed in blue").*

Leventhal and Cray, WF, 22 (1963), 238 [California].

365   My doggie died last night.
What color was his blood?

> *Cf.* **364**.

Evans (1956), 23.
Milberg (1976), 24.

366   My father built a brand new house;
How many nails (bricks) did he put in it?

> *Cf.* **368**.

Clifton Johnson (1896), 162.
Waugh, JAF, 31 (1918), 47 [Ontario, 1909].
Gardner, JAF, 31 (1918), 534 [Michigan].
Whitney and Bullock (1925), 138 [Maryland].
Withers (1946), n.p. ". . . little red schoolhouse." With playing instructions.
Howard, NYFQ, 16 (1960), 140 [Australia, 1954–1955]. Begins "Mickey Mouse planned a house."
Evans (1956), 24. Begins "Mickey Mouse made a house."

Leventhal and Cray, *WF*, 22 (1963), 238 [California, 1959].
Begins "Mickey Mouse built a house."
Knapp (1976), 27. Begins "Mickey Mouse built a house."

367   My father had a fine fat pig,
Now I'll give you a touch of T-I-G.

Bolton (1888), 112 [Ireland] = Daiken (1949), 10.

My father had an old horse shoe. *See* **368**.

368   My father has a horse to shoe;
How many nails do you think will do?

Cf. **366**. *Also found as a jump-rope rhyme; see* JRR, *p.* 132.

Bolton (1888), 116 [Connecticut].
Clifton Johnson (1896), 162–163.
Reid, *Misc. of Rymour Club*, 1 (1911), 106 [Edinburgh]. With
playing instructions.
"Folk Rhymes" (1944), 4 [Maryland].
Withers (1946), n.p. With playing instructions.
Robertson, *NF*, 3, no. 2 (Summer 1960), 32 [Shelburne
County, Nova Scotia]. Begins "My father had an old horse
shoe."
Fowke (1969), 109 [Canada].

369   My girl, your girl,
Any girl at all;
I lost my girl
Going to the ball.

Bolton (1888), 114 [Wisconsin].

My grandfather's man and me coost out. *See* **383**.

370   My hert's in the Heilin's,
My claes in the pawn
And my wife's awa' to Paisley
Wi' anither wife's man.

Parody of the popular song "My Heart's in the Highlands."

– 150 –

"Rhymes of General and Local Interest," *Misc. of Rymour Club*, 2, part 3 (1914), 113 [Scotland].

371   My little cheety pussy likes sweet milk,
Fresh butter, salt butter, you are out.

Reid, *Misc. of Rymour Club*, 1 (1911), 106 [Edinburgh].

372   My little red ball
Went over the wall.
I told my mum.
She smacked my bum
Until it was red
And sent me to bed.

Jennings (1968), 212 [Brangrore, Hants].

My Lord Provo'. See **141**.

My mamma (mammy) told me. See **380**.

373   My mother and your mother
Had a fiddle.
My mother and your mother
Chopped it in the middle.
How many strings did it have?

Sutton-Smith (1959), 70 [New Zealand].

374   My mother and your mother
Were chopping up sticks.
My mother cut her finger tips.
What colour was the blood?
"Pink."
P-I-N-K spells pink,
So pink you must have on.

Cf. **375**.

Opie (1969), 60 [Swansea].

375   My mother and your mother
Were hanging out clothes.
My mother gave your mother
A punch in the nose.
What was the color of the blood?
"Blue."
B-L-U-E (or R-E-D).

> *Alternate ending: "Did it hurt? Yes! (or No) Y-E-S." Cf.* **374**.
> *Also found as a jump-rope rhyme; see JRR, pp. 133–134.*

Waugh, *JAF*, 31 (1918), 47 [Ontario, 1909].
Reid, *Misc. of Rymour Club*, 1 (1911), 107 [Edinburgh].
Opie (1969), 59 [widespread, Scotland favorite; cites Reid, *Misc. of Rymour Club*, 1 (1911)].
Anderson, *Evening Ledger* (May 17, 1916).
Gardner, *JAF*, 31 (1918), 533 [Michigan].
Bennett, *Children*, 12 (1927), 21. Begins "Your mother and my mother."
Brewster (1952), 167 [North Carolina, 1927]. Two variants.
Heck, *JAF*, 40 (1927), 37.
Withers (1946), n.p. [from Brooklyn College students, 1936–1945].
Maryott, *SFQ*, 1, no. 4 (1937), 55 [Nebraska].
Brewster, *SFQ*, 3 (1939), 181.
Rae and Robb, *Christian Science Monitor Magazine* (March 21, 1942), 8.
Emrich and Korson (1947), 118.
Withers (1948), 85.
Daiken (1963), 31 [Dublin].
Ritchie (1965), 39 [Edinburgh].
McNaughtan, *Chapbook*, 4, no. 1 (1967?), 5 [Glasgow].
Turner (1969), 14–15 [Geelong, Australia, 1967]. Begins "My mother gave your mother a bloody nose."
Brill, *GMW*, 24 (1972), 3.
Knapp (1976), 26.

376   My mother bought me a dress,
What color is it?
"Blue."
B-L-U-E spells blue,
So out you go for saying so.

> *Cf.* **338**.

Opie (1969), 58 [current since Edwardian days].

Wintemberg, *JAF*, 31 (1918), 157 [Roebuck, Ontario]. Begins "My mother sent me down the street to buy a new dress."

Brewster (1952), 167 [North Carolina]. Two variants; one begins "My mother went downtown to buy a new dress."

Sutton-Smith (1959), 70 [New Zealand]. Two variants; one, ". . . bought me a box of new ribbons."

Knapp (1976), 27. Begins "Mr. Brown went to the store to buy a bucket of paint."

My mother gave your mother a bloody nose. *See* **375**.

377 **My** mother made a chocolate cake.
How many eggs did she take?

> *Also found as a jump-rope rhyme; see JRR, p. 134.*

Gardner, *JAF*, 31 (1918), 534 [Michigan].
Opie (1969), 57. ". . . made a nice seedy cake. / Guess how many seeds were in the cake?"

378 **My** mother said I never should
Play with the gypsies in the wood.
If I did she would say,
"Naughty girl to disobey."

> *See Opie, Dictionary, pp. 315–316. Also found as a jump-rope rhyme; see JRR, pp. 134–135.*

Howard, *NYFQ*, 16 (1960), 142 (Australia, 1954–1955).

379 **My** mother says
I shan't be it.

> *Common rhyme ending.*

Whitney and Bullock (1925), 139 [Maryland].
Hines, *Daedalian Quarterly*, 17, no. 1 (Fall 1949), 42 [Texas]. "My mother says this one shall be it."

My mother says your shoes are dirty. *See* **291**.

My mother sent me down the street to buy a new dress. *See* **376**.

380 My mother told me to take this one.

Common rhyme ending.

Bolton (1888), 111 [Tennessee]. Begins "My mammy."
Bassett, *The Folk-Lorist*, 1 (1892–1893), 157.
Northall (1892), 348 = Gutch and Peacock (1908), 257. Ends
   "You are in and she is out / With a rotten dish clout / On her
   back."
Gardner, *JAF*, 31 (1918), 534 [Michigan].
Whitney and Bullock (1925), 139 [Maryland].
Hines, *Daedalian Quarterly*, 17, no. 1 (Fall 1949), 42 [Texas].
   Two variants beginning "My mama"; one ends "But I was
   naughty and took that one."

381 My mother washed me in milk
And set me on the table to dry.
D-R-Y spells dry,
And O-U-T spells out.

Maryott, *SFQ*, 1, no. 4 (1937), 61 [Nebraska].
Emrich and Korson (1947), 120.

My mother went downtown to buy a new dress.
See **376**.

382 My mother, your mother, lives across the way,
At 514 East Broadway,
And every night they have a fight,
And this is what they say:
Acka, backa, soda cracka,
Acka, backa, boo.
If your father chews tobacco,
Out goes you.

Cf. **10**. *Also a common jump-rope rhyme; see* JRR, p. 135.

Bolton (1888), 112 [Connecticut]. Ends with a "Monkey in the
   match-box" rhyme (**356**).
Gardner, *JAF*, 31 (1918), 533 [Michigan].
Bennet, *Children*, 12 (1927), 21.

Withers (1946), n.p. [from Brooklyn College students, 1936–1945].

Maryott, *SFQ*, 1, no. 4 (1937), 61 [Nebraska].

"Folk Rhymes" (1944), 4 [Maryland].

Emrich and Korson (1947), 117. Ends with a "Monkey in the match-box" rhyme variant (**356**).

Ray Wood (1952), 88. Begins "The people who live across the way."

383   My old man and I fell out,
And what do you think it was all about?
He had money and I had none
And that's the way the quarrel begun.
Go O-U-T—out!

Cf. **343**. See Opie, Dictionary, pp. 293–294.

Chambers (1841), 120 [Scotland]. Begins "My grandfather's man and me coost out."

Bolton (1888), 102 [Nova Scotia] = *Old Cornwall*, 1, no. 6 (October 1927), 44. Begins "Little old man . . ."; ends an "Intery, mintery, cutery corn" rhyme (**287**).

Old Cornwall, 1, no. 5 (April 1927), 34 [Penzance, Cornwall]. Begins "Little old man . . ." and ends "Impurpose to bring the matter about. / Bring them about as fast as you can, / And you turn out, you little old man."

Withers (1946), n.p.

My wee Jeanie. *See* **438**.

384   My wee man smokes a wee tobacco pipe.

Reid, *Misc. of Rymour Club*, 2, part 2 (1913), 71 [Scotland].

N

385   Nebuchadnezzar, king of the Jews.
Slipped off his slippers and slipped on his shoes.

Usually an entertainment rhyme. Cf. **315**. *Also found as a jump-rope rhyme; see JRR, p. 138.*

Bolton (1888), 116 [New York, New England]. Two variants;
the other ends "wore six pair of stockings, / And seven pair
of shoes."

Bolton, *JAF*, 10 (1897), 321 [western Pennsylvania]. "Pontius
Pilate, King of the Jews, / Sold his wife a pair of shoes. /
When the shoes began to wear / Pontius Pilate began to
swear."

Reid, *Misc. of Rymour Club*, 2, part 2 (1913), 70 [Scotland].
Begins "Nebuchadnezzar, the King o' the Jews" and continues as in Bolton (1897) version.

386   The Needle's eye it doth comply,
The thread that run's so true.
It has caught many a smiling lad
And now it has caught you.

Usually a singing game.

Cassidy, *PADS*, no. 29 (April 1958), 25 [Maine].

387   Neeny, neeny, nick nack,
Which hand will ye tak?
Tak the right or take the wrong,
I'll beguile ye if I can.

Cf. **569**.

Howard, *NYFQ*, 16 (1960), 138 [Australia; reported by an
older woman who had it from a Scottish grandmother in
New Zealand].

Nigger in (on) the woodshed (woodpile). *See* **356**.

Nigger, nigger, come to dinner. *See* **499**.

388   Nigger, nigger, never die,
Black face and shiny eye,
Kinky hair and crooked toes,
That's the way the nigger goes.

Usually taunt.

Bolton (1888), 112 [Pennsylvania] = Knapp (1976), 191.

Anderson, *Evening Ledger* (May 17, 1916) [Kentucky]. Two variants of two lines each; one second line is "Liver lip and shiny eye."

Gardner, *JAF*, 31 (1918), 534 [Michigan]. "Teapot nose and china eye."

Maryott, *SFQ*, 1, no. 4 (1937), 55 [Nebraska]. Begins "Niggy, niggy," with "crooked toe, tippy toe."

McAtee (1946), 22 [Indiana].

389   Nigger, Nigger,
Pull a trigger
Up and down the Ohio river;
Rigger, Jigger,
Nary snigger,
In a row we stand and shiver.

Usually a taunt.

Bolton (1888), 115 [Indiana] = Knapp (1976), 191.

390   Nigger up a tree,
One, 2, 3.
When will he come down?
Three, 2, 1.

Bolton (1888), 112 [Massachusetts].

Niggy, niggy, never die. *See* **388.**

Ninty, tinty, halogulum. *See* **164.**

391   Now I lay me down to sleep,
A bushel of apples at my feet.
If I should die before I wake,
You'll know I died of the bellyache.

Parody of a prayer.

Maryott, *SFQ*, 1, no. 4 (1937), 59 [Nebraska].

O

392   Oats, peas, beans, and barley corn,
'Tis you that's it on this fair morn.''

Beginning of a singing game.

Bolton (1888), 59 [Iowa].

Occa, bocca (Ocka, bocka), bona, cracka. See **10**.

Oggy, doggy. See **104**.

Ohe-y-bo two-y-bi. See **410**.

Oka, bocca, stona, crocka. See **10**.

Old Dan Tucker
Come home to supper. See **307**.

393   Old Father Christmas, guess what he did?
Upset the cradle,
Out fell the kid.
The kid began to bubble,
So he hit him with a shovel.
O-U-T spells out,
And out you must go for saying so.

Opie (1969), 37 [Halifax, England, ca. 1900].
Sutton-Smith (1959), 72 [New Zealand].

394   Old Father Niberty
Dander scribberty
Cat kill away.
Kill away cat with your long pair of guilders.
Huckabullroy, what call you this
But your gigglety moy.

Bolton, *JAF*, 10 (1897), 321 [New Hampshire, 1815].

395 Old Mother Ink
Fell down the sink.
How many miles
Did she fall?
"Three."
One, two, three.

Howard, NYFQ, 16 (1960), 140, 143 [Australia, 1954–1955].
   Two variants, beginning "Little Miss Pink" and "How far
   do you think / Old mother fell down the sink?"
Turner (1969), 14–15 [Australia, 1957, 1962, 1967, 1968].
   Three variants beginning "Little Miss Pink."
Sutton-Smith (1959), 69 [New Zealand].
Ritchie (1965), 40, 47 [Edinburgh]. Two variants, beginning
   "A bottle of ink" and "Little Miss Pink."
Opie (1969), 57.

396 Old Obadiah jumped in the fire,
Fire was so hot he jumped in the pot,
Pot was so black he jumped in a crack,
Crack was so high he jumped in the sky,
Sky was so blue he jumped in a canoe,
Canoe was so shallow he jumped in the tallow,
Tallow was so soft he jumped in the loft,
Loft was so rotten he jumped in the cotton.
Cotton was so white he stayed there all night.

Usually an entertainment rhyme. Also found as a jump-rope rhyme; see JRR, pp. 10–11 ("Anthy Maria jumped in the fire").

Brewster, SFQ, 3 (1939), 181.

397 Olicka bolicka,
Susan solicka,
Olicka bolicka,
Nob.
Opie (1969), 55 [Britain].

398 Oliver Cromwell lost his shoe,
In the battle of Waterloo.

Also found as a jump-rope rhyme; see JRR, p. 164 ("Queen Elizabeth lost her shoe").

Sutton-Smith (1959), 72 [New Zealand].

399 Once an apple met an apple;
Said the apple to the apple,
"Why the apple don't the apple
Get the apple *out* of here?"

Withers (1946), n.p. [from Brooklyn College students, 1936–1945].

Once I went up the heeple, steeple. *See* **39**.

One-a-manury, . . . *See* **248, 249, 410**.

One-amy, uery, hickory, seven. *See* **410**.

One a penny. *See* **406**.

One a zoll. *See* **403**.

400 One color, two color,
Three color, four,
Five color, six color,
Seven color, more.
What color is yours?

Cf. **406**.

Withers (1946), n.p. [from Brooklyn College students, 1936–1945]. With playing instructions.

401 One day I went a-fishing,
And I caught a little trout,
And I said, "You little beggar,
Does your mother know you're out?"

Gregor (1891), 31 [Scotland].

One dol, two dol. *See* **403**.

One-erie, two-erie, tickerie seven. *See* **410**.

One-ery, ew-ery, . . . *See* **410**.

One-ery, ō-ery (oo-ry, oo-ery), . . . *See* **408**, **410**.

One-ery, two-ery, bickary, bun. *See* **408**.

Oneery, twoery, dickery, dee (devon, devil, Davy). *See* **410**.

One-ery, twoery, eckeery Ann. *See* **408**.

One-ery, two-ery, hick-ary hum (hickery han). *See* **408**.

One-ery, two-ery, hickory, Ann. *See* **408**.

402   One-ery, two-ery, ickery E,
You and you, and you I see,
We'll soon begin to have a rout,
But we'll be in and you'll be out.

Bolton (1888), 115 [New York].
Emrich and Korson (1947), 21.

One-ery, two-ery, ickery on. *See* **408**.

One-ery, two-ery, six and seven. *See* **410**.

One-ery, two-ery, three-ery thumb. *See* **408**.

One-ery two-ery, tickery (ticcery) tee (seven). *See* **410**.

One-ery, two-ery, tick-er-y, ten;
Bobs of vinegar, gentlemen. *See* **21**.

One-ery, two-ery, ziccary, zan (zaw). *See* **410**.

One-ery, yon-ery, inkery, able. *See* **410**.

One-erzoll (ezzol), two erzoll (ezzol). *See* **403**.

One's all, two's all, three's all sand. *See* **403**.

One is all, two is all, / Zick is all zeven. *See* **410**.

403   One's all, two's all, zig, zall, zan,
Bobtail vinegar, tickery tall tan.
Harum, scarum, Virgin Mary,
Te taw tush.

*With a great many nonsense endings, many beginning with
"Harum, scarum" and ending with "buck" or "bunk" or
"out." See also* **21**, **145**, **211**. *Cf.* **408**.

Notes and Queries, 1st ser., 10 (November 4, 1854), 369 =
    Northall (1892), 349. Begins "Onery, twoery, ickery am."
Bolton (1888), 100–101, 109 [New Hampshire; Virginia; Del-
    aware; New York; Pennsylvania; Norfolk, England; Mas-
    sachusetts; Connecticut; Colorado; Indiana; North Carolina;
    South Carolina; Tennessee; Georgia]. Twenty-four variants,
    one from Notes and Queries, 1st ser., 10 (November 4,
    1854). Other beginnings are "One-erzoll," "One-zol,"
    "Onery," "One-zaw," "One-zall," "One sort," "One dol,"
    "One lady," "Onery, twoery, ickery, am," "Rumzo,
    romzo, hollow pot," "Eli, meli, tiffi, tig." One second
    line reads "Baptist minister, good Irish man."
Gregor (1881), 73. "Eerie, aarie, eeertie, ann, / Bobs in vinegar
    I began. / Eat, at, / Moose, rat, / I choose you oot for a pennie
    pie, / Pur."
Newell (1883), 198 [Massachusetts] = Botkin (1944), 771.
    Begins "One's all, zuzall, titeerall, tann."
Gregor (1891), 22–23. Two variants, beginning "Eery, ary,
    aickarty, Ann" and "Eery, aary, ecerty, Ann." Both have an
    "Eat, at, moose, fat (rat)" ending.
F. G. Adams, JAF, 5 (1892), 148. "Ery, ory, ickery, Anne, /
    Bobtailed vinegar barrel, / Tickle up a tan."
Clifton Johnson (1896), 163.
Davis (1906), 208, 209, 211 [New Hampshire, Delaware]. Four
    variants: two begin "One is all" (one with "Onery, twoery,
    tickery, teven" rhyme ending [**410**]); two begin "one-
    ezzol."
Botkin (1947), 905 [New Hampshire, 1906; Vermont, 1930's].
    Two variants: one beginning "One zaw, two zaw"; one
    from Davis (1906).

Waugh, *JAF*, 31 (1918), 44 [Ontario, 1909]. Two variants; one
    begins "One-zol."
Anderson, *Evening Ledger* (May 17, 1916) [South Carolina].
Gardner, *JAF*, 31 (1918), 525 [Michigan]. Begins "Ramsey in
    the pot; / One-sel . . ."
Udal (1922), 392 [Dorset]. "One a zoll."
Whitney and Bullock (1925), 132 [Maryland]. Six variants;
    one begins "One wall, two voll"; two begin "One zall."
Hudson (1928), 117 [Mississippi]. Begins "One zoy, two zoy,
    zicka zoy zan."
Gardner (1937), 230 [New York]. Begins "Ring around a sugar
    bowl, / One's out, . . ."
Maryott, *SFQ*, 1, no. 4 (1937), 41 [Nebraska]. Two variants;
    one begins "Rupso, oneso, twoso."
Rowell, *JAF*, 56 (1943), 206 [Virginia, from Pamunkey
    Indians]. Begins "Ones-zall / Twos-zall."
McDowell, *TFSB*, 10, no. 3 (September 1944), 4. Begins "One
    zol, zo zol, zig-a-zaw, zan."
Withers (1946), n.p.
Emrich and Korson (1947), 121. Two variants, beginning
    "One silk, two silk" and "Ring around a sugar bowl; / One's
    out, two's out . . ."
Potter, "Counting-Out Rimes," *Standard Dictionary* (1949),
    254–255. Two variants, beginning "One is all" and "One
    erzoll."
Brewster (1952), 164 [North Carolina]. Three variants, begin-
    ning "One-zall," "One-zol," and "One-erzoll."
Randolph, *SFQ*, 17 (1953), 247 [Arkansas]. "One's all, two's
    all, three's all sand, / Bake a cake for the baker's man."
Evans (1956), 12.
Grayson (1962), 74. Begins "One silk, two silk, three silk,
    zan."
Jones and Hawes (1972), 29. Begins "One saw, two saw, ziggy
    zaw zow."

One's all, zuzall, titerall tan. *See* **403.**

One lady, two ladies. *See* **403.**

404   One mimmy, u nimmy, yackamie yawn.

Millard, *NYFQ*, 16 (1960), 147 [New York]. First line only.

405   One o'clock, two o'clock, three o'clock, four
       o'clock,

Five o'clock, six o'clock, seven o'clock, eight
o'clock,
Nine o'clock, ten o'clock, eleven o'clock, twelve
o'clock,
All the numbers on the clock.

Rutherford (1971), 51 [Annitsford, England, 1966].

One pence on the water. *See* **454**.

406 One potato, two potato, three potato, four
Five potato, six potato, seven potato, more.

Cf. **400**. *Also found as a jump-rope rhyme; see* JRR, p. 149.

Robertson, NF, 3, no. 2 (Summer 1960), 30 [Shelburne
County, Nova Scotia, 1885 and ca. 1920]. Two variants; one
ends ". . . seven potatoes, lore; / Eight potatoes, nine
potatoes, ten potatoes, more."
Opie (1969), 54 [Britain and United States; throughout twen-
tieth century, particularly in the United States]. Alternate
ending: "seven potato, raw."
Anderson, *Evening Ledger* (May 17, 1916) [Pennsylvania,
New Jersey].
Heck, JAF, 40 (1927), 37.
Cranford, NCF, 1, no. 1 (June 1948), 14 [Davidson County,
North Carolina, ca. 1928].
Turner (1969), 15–16 [Australia, since ca. 1935]. Two var-
iants; one begins "One speed, two speed, . . ."
Withers (1946), n.p. [from Brooklyn College students, 1936–
1945; Missouri and Iowa, 1940]. With playing instructions.
Maryott, SFQ, 1, no. 4 (1937), 47 [Nebraska].
Brewster, SFQ, 3 (1939), 180.
"Folk Rhymes" (1944), 4 [Maryland].
Boyce and Bartlett (1946), 29.
Emrich and Korson (1947), 121.
Hansen, WF, 7 (1948), 52. Mentioned only.
Withers (1948), 84.
Harry Harris, *Evening Bulletin* (May 30, 1949), 10.
Hines, *Daedalian Quarterly*, 17, no. 1 (Fall 1949), 41 [Texas].
Roberts, HF, 8 (1949), 9 [Illinois, Indiana, Kentucky, Maine].
Gullen (1950), 32.
Randolph, SFQ, 17 (1953), 248 [Arkansas].
Evans (1956), 30–31. Two variants; one begins "One a
penny."
Bley (1957), 96.

Howard, *NYFQ*, 16 (1960), 133 [Australia]. Three variants; one substitutes "spud" for "potato," another substitutes "tate."

Bluebells My Cockle Shells (1961), n.p. [Ayrshire].

Koch (1961), 118. "One potato, two potatoes, three potatoes, OR."

Leventhal and Cray, *WF*, 22 (1963), 239 [California].

Sandburg (1963), 15 [Chicago].

Ritchie (1965), 41 [Edinburgh]. With playing instructions.

G. B. Adams, *Ulster Folklife*, 11 (1965), 91. Begins "One spud."

Goldstein (1971), 175–177 [Philadelphia, 1966–1967]. Discussed in relation to manipulative strategies used in counting-out.

Castagna, *NYFQ*, 25 (1969), 227 [New Rochelle, New York].

Fowke (1969), 109 [Canada].

Rodger (1969?), 19 [Scotland].

Brill, *GMW*, 24 (1972), 3.

Knapp (1976), 25. With playing instructions.

Milberg (1976), 24.

Onerey ory, . . . *See* **408**.

Onerie awrie (orie, ory), . . . *See* **408**.

407   **On**erie, twoerie,
Hahbo crackaro,
Henry Lary,
Guacahan Dandy,
Bullalie Collili
Forty-nine.

Davis (1906), 211.

Onerie, twoerie, tickerie, tivn. *See* **410**.

Onery, dickery, davery. *See* **410**.

Onery hurey hickory ham. *See* **408**.

Onery, oary (oery, oory, orery, orey, ory, overy), . . . *See* **408**.

Onery, two-ary, hick-ary hum. See **408**.

Onery, twoery, cutery corn. See **287**.

Onery, twoery, dickery Davy (daery, dee, deven, Davery). See **410**.

Onery, twoery, Hickery (hickory) Ann (hick'ry ham). See **408**.

Onery, two-ery, ickery, ack. See **408**.

Onery, two-ery ickery am. See **403**.

408 Onery, twoery, ickery, Ann,
Phillisy, phollisy, Nicholas John,
Queebe, quawby, Irish (Virgin) Mary (English navy),
Sinkum, sankum, Johnny-co, buck!

> Bolton felt this should be broken into two rhymes, one with the count of twenty-one, the other with the count of twenty-nine. We have not followed this division for reasons of bibliographical economy. The third line's frequent references to "Virgin Mary" relate this rhyme to **403**. Cf. also **211**. See Opie, Dictionary, pp. 335–336. As a jump-rope rhyme, see JRR, pp. 146–147.

Opie (1969), 53 [Dorsetshire, New England; since early nineteenth century]. Two variants, beginning "One-ery, oo-ry, ick-ry, an" and "Onery, uery, ickory, Ann" (from Newell [1883]).
Bolton (1888), 94–96 [England; Montreal, Canada; United States; Massachusetts; Pennsylvania; Ohio; Iowa; Texas; Missouri; Kansas; New England; New York; Connecticut, 1860; Rhode Island; Maine, 1840 and 1855; Indiana; Arkansas]. Twenty-five variants; from Clara Doty Bates, Nursery Jingles; Halliwell (ca. 1860); Cowan (1881); Ellis, Transactions of the Philological Society (1878); and many from Masonic ritual. Variant beginnings are "Winnery, ory, accory, han," "Iry, ury, ickery Ann," "Onery, youery," "Ery, iry," "Eery, iry, hickory, hum," "Wunnery, youery," "Eerey, orey, ikerey Ann," "Query, ory," "Winnery, orrey, hickory Ann," "One-wee, you-wee, ick-wee, aye," "One-

ery, ō-ery," "On-ery, two-ery, hick-ary hum (hickery
han)," "Onery, ory," "One-ery, two-ery, ickery on,"
"Onery, ury, ikery a," "Onery, two-ery, hickory Ann,"
"Onerey, ory," and "Onery, two-ery, ickery, ack."

A. A. Adams, *Word Lore*, 3 (1928), 51 [Devon and Cornwall,
ca. 1850]. Begins "Hairy, Hairy, ricketty Ann, / Pipestone
Vinegar, Uncle Jan," ends with a "Hink, sink, the puddings stink" rhyme (**222**).

Halliwell (1853), 167; (ca. 1860), 66 [Somersetshire]. Begins
"Onery, two-ary, hick-ary hum." Used for counting-out in
the game "Pee-wit."

Ellis, *Transactions of the Philological Society* (1878), 368–
369. Three variants: one each from Halliwell (1853) and
Mill Hill Magazine, 5 (June 1877), and one beginning
"Winnery ory accory han."

Northall (1892), 349. Three variants: one each from Halliwell
(1853), *Mill Hill Magazine*, 5 (June 1877), and Ellis, *Transactions of the Philological Society* (1878).

Notes and Queries, 1st ser., 11 (February 10, 1855), 113.
Begins "One-ery, Two-ery, Hickory, Ann."

Turner (1969), 12–13, 15–16 [central and western Victoria,
Australia, 1865 and current]. Two variants, beginning "Onery, overy, ickery am" and "Eerie, oarie, ickory am."

Stoudt (1915), 47 [throughout United States; current in
Lehigh County, Pennsylvania, 1875].

Mill Hill Magazine, 5 (June 1877). Begins "Onery, twoery
Hickery Ann."

Newell (1883), 197–198 [Pennsylvania; New England; Cin-
cinnati, 1880]. Three variants beginning "Onery uery"; one
variant = Botkin (1944), 771.

Cowan (1881), 337 [southwest Pennsylvania]. Begins "One-
wee, you-wee, ick-wee, aye."

Gregor (1881), 171–173 [northeast Scotland]. Two variants
beginning "Eerie, aarie, ackertie, Ann."

Robertson, *NF*, 3, no. 2 (Summer 1960), 31 [Shelburne
County, Nova Scotia, 1885]. Two variants, beginning
"Ivory, ovory, ickery, Ann" and "Iry, ory, hickory, Ann."

Gregor (1891), 22–23 [Scotland]. Twelve variants, beginning
"Eery (eerie), ary (aary, airy, orie, ory), ickerty (ackertie,
eckerty, ekarty, ikery), Ann (am)." One has "Bobs and
vinegar" in the second line (cf. **403**). Other endings are: "A
fish in the sea, a bird in the air, / A lady came jumping down
the stair"; "Back oot, back in, / Back throw the heely pin, /
Peter cam t' oor door / Playin at the pipes, / Cum a riddle,
fizz, oot"; and "Pick-me, nick-me, ship-me, sham, / Oram,
scoram, pick-me, nor-am, / She, sho, sham, shutters."

Chamberlain, *JAF*, 8 (1895), 252 [Ontario].

Clifton Johnson (1896), 164. Two variants, beginning "One-ery, u-ery" and "Hokey, pokey, winkey, wong."

Bolton, *JAF*, 10 (1897), 314, 319 [Scilly Islands]. Two variants, both beginning "One-ery, two-ery."

Blakeborough (1898), 261 [Yorkshire and United States]. Two variants; one begins "Eary, ory, hickory, on."

Dew (1898), 81 [Suffolk, England]. Begins "Higgery, hoggery, higgery, ham."

Davis (1906), 211, 212, 213 [Guernsey; England; Cambridge, Massachusetts]. Three variants, beginning "Onery, youery, eckery Anna," "Winnery, ory, accury han," and "One-ery, two-ery, eckeery Ann" (the latter = Botkin [1947], 906).

Perrow, *JAF*, 26 (1913), 142 [Virginia, 1909]. Begins "Wun a me noory, ikka me Ann."

Waugh, *JAF*, 31 (1918), 45–46 [Ontario, 1909]. Three variants, beginning "Eery, ory, ickery Ann," "Onery, varey, ickery Ann," and "Onery, orery, eckery Ann."

Potter, "Counting-Out Rimes," *Standard Dictionary* (1949), 255 [Indiana, 1910]. Begins "Onery, oery, ickery Ann."

"Counting-Out Rhymes," *Misc. of Rymour Club*, 2, part 2 (1913), 61, 95 [Scotland]. Two variants: one begins "Eerie, arrie, aikerty, Ann"; the other is "Eerie, orrie, eckerie, am, / Pick me, mick me, shick me sham; / Orum, scorum, pick-ma-norum, / Shee, sho, sham, shutter—You're out!"

Brewster (1952), 163–164 [North Carolina, 1914–1915, 1923]. Seven variants. Other beginnings are "Onery uery," "Onery hurey hickory ham," "Onery, twoery, hick'ry ham," "Onery oary," "Onery, oery," and "Overy, Ivory, Hickory Ann."

Anderson, *Evening Ledger* (May 17, 1916) [Kentucky].

Gardner, *JAF*, 31 (1918), 523–524 [Michigan]. Seven variants; one begins "Sybil, Sybil, Fred and Don," one, "Erie, Irie, Ickery, Ann," one "Wry, Iry, Ickery Jam."

Wintemberg, *JAF*, 31 (1918), 157 [Roebuck, Ontario]. Begins "Airy, eyery, ickory Ann."

Smiley, *JAF*, 32 (1919), 377 [Virginia]. Begins "One'-ry, or-ery."

Udal (1922), 392 [Dorset]. Two variants, beginning "Onery, youery" and "Onery, oory, ick-ry, an."

Whitney and Bullock (1925), 131 [Maryland].

"Uncle Sandy," *Word Lore*, 1 (1926), 224.

Maryott, *SFQ*, 1, no. 4 (1937), 42 [Nebraska]. Five variants; other beginnings are "Onry, onry, ickory Ann," "Eerie, orie, ickery Ann," "Evi, ivy, erickvy Ann," and "One-ery, two-ery, bickary, bun."

Mills and Bishop, *The New Yorker* (November 13, 1937), 34 = Botkin (1944), 800.

Ray Wood (1938), 17. Begins "Eerie, oarie, eckerie, Ann."

Rae and Robb, *Christian Science Monitor Magazine* (March
21, 1942), 8.

Ó Súilleabháin (1942), 681 [Ireland].

McDowell, *TFSB*, 10, no. 3 (September 1944), 4. Begins
"Onerie, orie, okrie, ann."

Withers (1946), n.p.

McAtee (1946), 22 [Indiana].

Emrich and Korson (1947), 118. Begins "Eerie, oorie."

Gullen (1950), 14. Begins "Eerie, orie, ickery, ann."

Musick and Randolph, *JAF*, 63 (1950), 428–429 [Missouri].
Three variants; one begins "Onery-orey, ickry Ann," one,
"Ikkery, ekkery catamaran, / Fillisy follisy mend a tin pan."

Randolph, *SFQ*, 17 (1953), 247 [Arkansas]. Four variants; one
begins "Ee-e-ry, o-e-ry, ick-e-ry, Ann," one, "Ee-ery, or-e-
ry, ick-e-ry, bum."

Evans (1956), 12. Two variants, beginning "Onerie ory" and
"Monry orey."

Cassidy, *PADS*, no. 29 (April 1958), 25 [Wisconsin and
Connecticut]. Two variants, beginning "Eerie, irey, ickery
Ann" and "Wunnery, unnery, ickery Ann."

Sutton-Smith (1959), 64 [New Zealand]. Begins "Onerie awrie."

Howard, *NYFQ*, 16 (1960), 138 [Australia, from Scotland via
New Zealand].

Millard, *NYFQ*, 16 (1960), 147 [New York].

Musick (1960), 60. "One-ery, two-ery, three-ery thumb /
Backsley, Billy, Nicholas, Bum, / Pot, pan, riddle man, /
Link, pink, sink."

Fowke (1969), 110 [Canada].

409   Onery, twoery, ickery Ann,
Threery, fourery, quick as you can.
O-U-T spells out.

Leon, *JAF*, 8 (1895), 256 [Rhode Island].

410   Onery, twoery, tickery, teven (tabery, tee, ten,
seven) (Dickery Davy),
Alabone, crackabone, ten and eleven.
Pin, pam, musky dam (Spit, spot, must be done),
Tweedleum, twadleum, twenty-one.

Cf. **119** *for last two lines. A common alternate ending is*
"Discum Dan (Wishcombe dandy), merry combine (come

time), / *Humbledee, humbledee, twenty-nine.*" See *Opie* Dictionary, pp. 336–337.

Newell (1883), 198 [Massachusetts, ca. 1800; Georgia; Connecticut]. Four variants, beginning "Onery, uery, hickory able," "One-amy, uery, hickory seven," "Onery, uery, ickory a," and "Onery, uery, ickery see" (the latter two = Botkin [1944], 771).

Notes and Queries, 1st ser., 10 (November 4, 1854), 369, 370 [Aberdeen, early nineteenth century]. Three variants, beginning "One-ery, two-ery, dickery deven (Davy)" and "Eenery, twaaery, / Tuckery, tayuen."

Grammar Gurton's Garland (1810), 31; (1866), 40. Begins "One-ery, two-ery, ziccary, zan"; ends with a "Hink, sink, the puddings stink" rhyme (**222**).

Opie (1969), 52–53 [England, Scotland; since early nineteenth century]. Discussed in relation to other gibberish rhymes. Three variants: one each from *Grammar Gurton's Garland* (1810), *Blackwood's Edinburgh Magazine*, 10 (August 1821), and Jamieson (1825).

Charles Taylor (1820). Begins "Anery, twaery, / Duckery seven."

Notes and Queries, 1st ser., 10 (September 9, 1854), 210. Two variants: one beginning "Hiary, diary, dockery, deven" and Charles Taylor (1820) variant.

Bolton (1888), 96–100, 108 [England, Scotland, Ireland, Guernsey, Indiana, Massachusetts, Maine, Georgia, Connecticut, New York City, Pennsylvania, New York, Virginia, Michigan, New Hampshire, Wisconsin, Tennessee, Ontario]. Fifty-two variants; some from Charles Taylor (1820); *Blackwood's Edinburgh Magazine*, 10 (August 1821); Ker (1840); *Notes and Queries*, 1st ser., 10 (1854) [including November 4 early-nineteenth-century Aberdeen variant] and 11 (1855); Halliwell (ca. 1860); *Mill Hill Magazine*, 5 (1877); Newell (1883); Clara Doty Bates, *Nursery Jingles*; and John Brown's *Marjorie Fleming*. Alternate beginnings are: "Hickery, dickery, six and seven," "Hiary, diary, dockery, deven," "I-ery, you-ery, dickery seven," "Wonery, twoery," "Anery, twaery," "Yen-rie twa-rie," "Eenery, twaa-ery, tuckery, tayven," "One-a-manury," "One-y-bo, two-y-bo, / Tick-y-bo, teben," "One-y, two-y, silly, solly, san," "One-ery, yon-ery, inkery, able," "One to two, ticky to tee," "Onery uery," "One-ery, ew-ery," and "Haley, bayley, tithaby, table." Variations within rhymes are discussed on page 96.

Blackwood's Edinburgh Magazine, 10 (August 1821), 36. Begins "Anery, twaery, tickery, seven."

Jamieson (1825). Begins "One-erie, two-erie, tickerie, seven."

Anderson, *Evening Ledger* (May 17, 1916) [Pennsylvania and New Jersey, since 1835]. Begins "Oneery, twoery, dickery, devon (devil)."

Ker (1840). Begins "One-ery, two-ery, ziccary, zaw."

Halliwell (1842), 86. Begins "One-ery, two-ery, ziccary, zan," ends with a "Hink, sink, the puddings stink" rhyme (**222**).

Ellis, *Transactions of the Philological Society* (1878), 368 [Scotland]. Three variants, from Halliwell (1842), *Notes and Queries*, 1st ser., 10 (August 12, 1854), and *Mill Hill Magazine*, 5 (June 1877).

Northall (1892), 345–346, 348–350. Nine variants, from Halliwell (1842; 1849); *Notes and Queries*, 1st ser., 10 (1854), and 11 (1855); and *Grammar Gurton's Garland* (1866).

Halliwell (1849), 134, 135.

Notes and Queries, 1st ser., 10 (August 12, 1854), 124. Begins "One-er-y, two-er-y, tick-er-y, seven."

Notes and Queries, 1st ser., 11 (March 3, 1855), 174. Begins "Onery, twoery, ziggery, zan."

Notes and Queries, 1st ser., 11 (March 17, 1855), 215. Begins "One-ery, two-ery, dickery, davy."

Halliwell (ca. 1860), 61, 230–231. Three variants; one ends with an "Ink, pink, pen and ink" rhyme (**277**).

Mill Hill Magazine, 5 (June 1877). [Ireland, south Scotland, north England]. Four variants, one beginning "Yen-rie, twa-rie, tickery seven."

Potter, "Counting-Out Rimes," *Standard Dictionary* (1949), 254, 255 [1880's; Indiana, 1910]. Two variants, beginning "One-ery, two-ery, six and seven" and "Onery, twoery, tickery, tabery," the latter ending "Humpty Dumpty is ninety-nine, / And one's a hundred." Mentions various changes in first, second, and third lines.

Gregor (1881), 172 [northeast Scotland]. Eight variants, beginning "Anerie, twaarie" and "Eenrie, twaarie."

Gregor (1891), 11–14 [Scotland]. Forty-four variants, beginning "Anery, twary (tary, twaery, twaaery, twaory), tickery (tuckery, saxery, tickry), teven (taiven, tyven, tiven, saiven, seiven, seven, ten)," "Eery, aary (oory), tickery (dockery), teven (seven)," "Eenery (Enery), twaery (twoery, twaaery), tickery (tackery, tuckery, tuckerty), teven (taven, taiven, seven, ten)," "Eenty, teenty, tickerty teven," "Onery, twoery (twory, tounery), tickery (dickery), seven (saiven, ten, Davy)" and "Eenity, peenity, pickety, iven."

Leon, *JAF*, 8 (1895), 256 [Rhode Island].

Old Cornwall, 1, no. 8 (October 1928), 29 [St. Just, Cornwall, 1895]. Begins "Hickory, Hackory, Hockory, Heaven"; additional lines are "where's all the French men gone? / Some gone East and some gone West; / and some gone over the Canary's nest."

Thomas (1895), 1 [Cornwall]. Begins "Hewery, hiery, hackery, heaven."

Clifton Johnson (1896), 164. Begins "E-ry, i-ry, ickery Ann."

Black and Thomas (1901), 263 [Shetland]. Begins "Eenery, twaery, ockery, seven."

Davis (1906), 208, 209 [Ireland]. Two variants; one begins "One is all, two is all, / Zick is all zeven" (cf. **403**).

Johnston, *Old Lore Misc.*, 1 (1908), 296 [Stromness, Orkney]. Begins "Onerie twoerie tickerie tivn."

Notes and Queries, 10th ser., 11 (June 5, 1909), 446 [Orkney]. Begins "One-ery, two-ery, ticcery, seven."

Williamson, *Old Lore Misc.*, 3 (1910), 67 [Shetland]. Begins "Een-a-rie, twa-a-rie, tuck-a-rie, seeven."

G.W.R., *Old Lore Misc.*, 4 (1911), 166; 5 (1912), 7 [Kirkwall]. Beginnings are "Een tw lacary seven" and "Anery twaery tickery seven."

Simpkins (1914), 187 [Fife].

Gardner, *JAF*, 31 (1918), 524–525 [Michigan]. Two variants, beginning "Hickery, dickery, six and seven" and "Gimmery, twaery."

Nicolson (1920), 90 [Shetland]. Begins "Eeneri twaeri tukkeri seven."

Udal (1922), 393 [Dorsetshire]. Begins "Onery, twory, Dickory Davy."

Acker (1923), 18. Begins "Onery, twoery, tickery tee."

Whitney and Bullock (1925), 131–139 [Maryland]. Two variants; one begins "Ohe-y-bo [*sic*] two-y-bi."

Elliott, *Word-Lore*, 1 (1926), 95 [Tyneside, England]. Begins "Wonnery, Tooery, Tickery, Sevorn."

Dobie (1927), 68. Begins "Hickey, pickey, zickey, zan."

Old Cornwall, 1, no. 5 (April 1927), 34. Begins "Hiary, Hoary, Hickery, Heben."

Ireland, *Recreation* (February 1937), 545. Begins "One-ery, two-ery, tickery tee."

Maryott, *SFQ*, 1, no. 4 (1937), 40–42 [Nebraska]. Five variants.

Wood and Goddard (1940), 570.

Boyce and Bartlett (1946), 32. Begins "Hickery, dickery, six and seven."

Withers (1946), n.p.

Emrich and Korson (1947), 119.

Daiken (1949), 2.

Gullen (1950), 15, 16, 17. Five variants; other beginnings are "Hickery dickery, six and seven," "Ingry oory, accry davy," and "Anery, twaery, duckery, seven."

Evans (1956) 13. Begins "Onery, twoery, zickery zan."
Katherine Harris, *Ulster Folklife,* (1958), 73. Begins "Onery, two-ery, dickery, davy."
Sutton-Smith (1959), 64 [New Zealand]. Three variants.
Howard, *NYFQ,* 16 (1960), 136 [Australia]. Begins "Onery, dickery, davery."
Katherine Harris, *Ulster Folklife* (1962), 39 [Ireland and Scotland]. Begins "Wannery Too, er, ey Dickery Dairy."
Lomax (1964), 57.
G. B. Adams, *Ulster Folklife,* 11 (1965), 92, 97. Five variants. Other beginnings are "Wannery, tooery, dickery, dairy," "Onery, twoery, dickery, daery (Davery)," and "One-ery, oo-ery, ig-ery, ay-ery."
Those Dusty Bluebells (1965), 23 [Ayrshire]. Begins "Ane twa dickery seeven."
Fowke (1969), 110 [Canada]. Begins "Onery twoery dickery dee."
Jones and Hawes (1972), 27. Begins "One-ry, two-ery, dickery seven."

Onery, twoery, zickery (ziggery) zan. *See* **410.**

Onery, twory, Dickory (dickery) Davy (dee, seven). *See* **410.**

Onery uery, . . . *See* **408, 410.**

Onery, ury, ikery a. *See* **408.**

Onery, varey, ickery Ann. *See* **408.**

Onery-youery, . . . *See* **408.**

One saw, two saw, ziggy zaw zow. *See* **403.**

One silk, two silk. *See* **403.**

One sort, two sort. *See* **403.**

One speed, two speed. *See* **406.**

One spud, two spuds. *See* **406.**

Ones-zall . . . See **403**.

One tate, two tates. *See* **406**.

One to two, ticky to tee. *See* **410**.

411 One, two, buckle my shoe.
Three, four, open the door.
Five, six, pick up sticks.
Seven, eight, lay them straight.
Nine, ten, a good fat hen.
Eleven, twelve, dig and delve.
Thirteen, fourteen, maids a-courting.
Fifteen, sixteen, maids in the kitchen (maids
a-kissing).
Seventeen, eighteen, maids a-waiting.
Nineteen, twenty, my plate's (stomach's) empty.

See Opie, *Dictionary*, pp. 333–334. *Also found as a jump-rope rhyme; see* JRR, p. 149.

Babcock, *AA*, o.s., 1 (1888), 272 [District of Columbia].
Bolton (1888), 7, 92 [England, West Virginia]. Three variants; one continues to "thirty makes a kerchy"; one ends "19, 20, weddings plenty."
Howard, *NYFQ*, 16 (1960), 139 [Australia; reported in use in 1890, found among school children in 1954–1955].
Chamberlain, *JAF*, 8 (1895), 253 [Ontario].
G.W.R., *Old Lore Misc.*, 4 (1911), 166 [Kirkwall]. "Eleven, twelve, ring the bell."
Johnstone, *Misc. of Rymour Club*, 1 (1911), 86 [Annandale, Scotland]. "Three, four, ne'er gae oure." Continues to "twenty-four."
Maryott, *SFQ*, 1, no. 4 (1937), 46 [Nebraska]. To "eight."
Hines, *Daedalian Quarterly*, 17, no. 1 (Fall 1949), 42 [Texas].
Millard, *NYFQ*, 16 (1960), 147 [New York state].

412 One, two, sky blue.
All out but you.

See also **470**, **502**.

Opie (1969), 30, 31 [United States and Britain; since Victorian days].
Bolton (1888), 92 [Tennessee].

Gregor (1891), 30 [Scotland].
Maclagan (1901), 249 [Scotland].
G.W.R., *Old Lore Misc.*, 4 (1911), 165 [Kirkwall].
Reid, *Misc. of Rymour Club*, 1 (1911), 105 [Edinburgh].
Maryott, *SFQ*, 1, no. 4 (1937), 46 [Nebraska].
"Folk Rhymes" (1944), 4 [Maryland].
Boyce and Bartlett (1946), 33.
Withers (1946), n.p.
Gullen (1950), 32.
Brewster (1952), 166 [North Carolina]. ". . . star blue."
Howard, *NYFQ*, 16 (1960), 143 [Australia, 1954–1955].
Sutton-Smith (1959), 69. Two variants; one begins "Look up."
Ritchie (1965), 39 [Edinburgh].
Rodger (1969 ?), 20 [Scotland].

One, two, star blue. See **412**.

One, two, three, a bumble bee. See **52**.

413 One, two, three a nation,
I received my salvation
On the day of declaration;
One, two, three a nation.

Usually a ball-bouncing rhyme.

Evans (1956), 16.

414 One, two, three, four, five,
I caught a hare (fish) alive.
Six, seven, eight, nine, ten,
I let him go again.
Why did you let it go?
Because it bit my finger so.

*See Opie, Dictionary, pp. 334–335. Also found as a
jump-rope rhyme; see JRR, pp. 150–151.*

Goddard, *Word-Lore*, 2(1927), 163 [Suffolk, 1870]. Additional line: "And made me cry, O ho! O ho!"
Bolton (1888), 93 [Missouri, Nebraska, Ohio, Pennsylvania]. Three variants.
Leland, *JAF*, 2 (1889), 115.
Robertson, *NF*, 3, no. 2 (Summer 1960), 29–30 [Shelburne County, Nova Scotia, early 1890's].

Gregor (1891), 32 [Scotland].
Withers (1946), n.p. [Cedar County, Missouri, 1907–1913].
Two variants; one "mouse," one "fish."
Maclagan (1901), 250 [Scotland].
G.W.R., *Old Lore Misc.*, 4, (1911), 165 [Kirkwall].
Reid, *Misc. of Rymour Club*, 1, (1911), 106 [Edinburg]. Ends
"Because it bit my muckly toe; / Eery, orry, wee doory, eery,
orry, out."
Gardner, *JAF*, 31 (1918), 522 [Michigan].
Wintemberg and Wintemberg, *JAF*, 31 (1918), 122 [Ontario].
Askew, *Word-Lore*, 2 (1927), 95 [Durham County, England].
Bury, *Word-Lore*, 2 (1927), 50 [Cornwall]. "Catching pil-
chards all alive."
Maryott, *SFQ*, 1, no. 4 (1937), 47 [Nebraska].
Wood and Goddard (1940), 569.
Emrich and Korson (1947), 116.
Withers (1948), 86.
Gullen (1950), 34.
Grayson (1962), 60, 64. Variant ending: "Which finger did it
bite? / The little finger or the right."
Turner (1969), 15–16 [Melbourne, 1962].
Sandburg (1963), 15 [Chicago].
Fowke (1969), 109 [Canada].
Rodger (1969?), 20 [Scotland].

415   One, two, three, four, five, six, seven,
All good children go to heaven.
One, two, three, four, five, six, seven, eight,
All bad children have to wait.

This rhyme has many other final lines. One of the most
common is "One flew east and one flew west." A number of
other variants talk of bad children going to Hell. A further
common ending is "Penny on the water, / Tuppence on the
sea, / Threepence on the railway, / Out goes she" (**454**).
Also found as a jump-rope rhyme; see JRR, pp. 151–152.

Opie (1969), 37 [current since 1880's].
Newell (1883), 202 [Massachusetts to Pennsylvania] = Botkin
(1944), 773. Two variants.
Babcock, *AA*, o.s., 1 (1888), 274 [District of Columbia].
Bolton (1888), 94 [Massachusetts; Pennsylvania; Maryland;
Missouri; Ohio; Connecticut; Doncastor, England]. Nine
variants.
Howard, *NYFQ*, 16 (1960), 139 [Australia, 1890 and 1954–
1955].

Robertson, *NF*, 3, no. 2 (Summer 1960), 30 [Shelburne County, Nova Scotia, 1890's and ca. 1915]. Two variants: one, "all good niggers"; one ending "One goes up and one goes down, / One goes way back and sits down."

Clifton Johnson (1896), 162. First two lines only.

Gaskell, *Transactions*, 116 (1964), 211 [Lancashire, 1900].

Maclagan (1901), 249 [Argyleshire].

Monroe, *AA*, n.s., 6 (1904), 47 [Massachusetts].

G.W.R., *Old Lore Misc.*, 4 (1911), 165 [Kirkwall]. Third line: "When they die, their sins forgiven."

Reid, *Misc. of Rymour Club*, 1 (1911), 105 [Edinburgh].

Anderson, *Evening Ledger* (May 17, 1916) [Pennsylvania, New Jersey]. Ends "Naughty children come too late."

Gardner, *JAF*, 31 (1918), 522–523 [Michigan]. Five variants.

Waugh, *JAF*, 31 (1918), 43 [Ontario]. Ends "If you swear you won't go there, / One, two, three, four, five, six, seven."

Wintemberg and Wintemberg, *JAF*, 31 (1918), 123 [Ontario].

Watson (1921), 38 [Somerset, England].

Whitney and Bullock (1925), 133 [Maryland]. Three variants.

Heck, *JAF*, 40 (1927), 36.

Turner (1969), 15–16 [western Victoria (ca. 1930) and Sydney (ca. 1945), Australia].

Maryott, *SFQ*, 1, no. 4 (1937), 46 [Nebraska].

Boyce and Bartlett (1946), 29, 33. Two variants.

Withers (1946), n.p.

Emrich and Korson (1947), 121.

Opie (1947), 56.

Yoffie, *JAF*, 60 (1947), 29 [Missouri].

Gullen (1950), 35. Three variants.

Brewster (1952), 165 [North Carolina]. Two variants.

Evans (1956), 15. Two variants.

MacColl and Behan, Folkways 8501 (1958) [Dublin].

Sutton-Smith (1959), 64.

Bluebells My Cockle Shells (1961), n.p. [Ayrshire]. Third line: "When they are, their sins forgiven."

Koch (1961), 118 [Kansas].

Grayson (1962), 71. Ends "All good children go to Devon. / When they get there they will shout / O-U-T spells 'out.'"

Sandburg (1963), 123 [North Carolina]. Ends "When they get there they will shout, / 'O-U-T,' and that spells out."

Those Dusty Bluebells (1965), 22 [Ayrshire]. With "Penny on the water" ending (**454**).

GMW, 20 (1968), 6.

Fowke (1969), 109 [Canada]. Third line: "Those that swear don't go there."

Rodger (1969 ?), 20 [Scotland]. Third line: "When they die, their sins forgiven."

416 One, two, three, four, five, six, seven,
A' that fisher dodds widna win t' haven.

Gregor (1881), 169 [Scotland].
Gregor (1891), 30 [Scotland].

417 One, two, three, four, five, six, seven,
Count the lovely arch of heaven.
Seven colors make a bow,
Sweetest, fairest thing I know.
See the rainbow in the heaven,
One, two, three, four, five, six, seven.

Clifton Johnson (1896), 163–164.

418 One, two, three, four, five, six, seven, eight, nine,
Ma pa runs a big ingine.

Bolton (1888), 94 [Massachusetts].

419 One, two, three, four, five, six, seven, eight, nine
Ingine,
Number nine.
What do you wish?
Beer or wine?
W-I-N-E.

Heck, *JAF*, 40 (1927), 36.

420 One, two, three, four, five,
Twenty bees in a hive;
Eight flew out,
And twelve flew about.

Bolton (1888), 93 [New Jersey].

One, two, three, four,
Lily at the kitchen door. *See* **421**.

421 One, two, three, four,
Mary's at the cottage door.

Five, six, seven, eight,
Eating cherries (berries, plums) off a plate.

The last two lines are often reversed. The rhyme is traced to Regency days in Opie, Dictionary, p. 334. Also found as a jump-rope rhyme; see JRR, p. 108 ("Lady, lady, at the gate").

Newell (1883), 201–202 [Massachusetts, 1820] = Botkin (1944), 773. Three variants; one has the final line "Mary at the garden gate"; one counts to "eight" in the first line.

Bolton (1888), 93 [England, Rhode Island, Philadelpia, Montreal, Quebec, Massachusetts]. Six variants; one from Newell (1883), two from *Mill Hill Magazine*, 5 (1877); one ends "In comes cat, in comes rat, / In comes a lady with a great big-see-saw hat."

Mill Hill Magazine, 5 (1877). Two variants; one begins "Two, four, six, eight"; one, "Little Freddie at the door / Picking cherries off the floor."

Gregor (1881), 173 [northeast Scotland].

Burne (1883), 573 [Shropshire].

Folk-Lore Journal, 1 (1883), 384 [Derbyshire].

Northall (1892), 350 [Derbyshire, Cumberland, Shropshire]. Three variants; one each from Burne (1883) and *Folk-Lore Journal*, 1 (1883).

Gregor (1891), 23 [Scotland]. Four variants; one begins "Ane, twa, three, four"; one ends "Down fell the summer seat, / I've a kistie, I've a creel, / I've a baggie fu' o' meal, / I've a doggie at the door, / One, two, three, four."

Clifton Johnson (1896), 165. Begins "Two, four, six, eight."

Edward Nicholson (1897), 125 [Scotland].

Dew (1898), 80 [Norfolk, England]. "Two, four, six, eight, / Mary at the garden gate."

Waugh, *JAF*, 31 (1918), 44–45 [Ontario, 1909]. Two variants; one begins "1, 2, 3, 4, / Lily at the kitchen door."

G.W.R., *Old Lore Misc.*, 4 (1911), 165 [Kirkwall].

Reid, *Misc. of Rymour Club*, 1 (1911), 107 [Edinburgh]. Ends "Doon fell the summer seat: / I've a kistie, I've a creel, / I've a barrelie fu' o' meal, / To serve my bairneis till 't be done, / Come teetle, come tottle, come 21."

Gardner, *JAF*, 31 (1918), 522 [Michigan]. Third line: "Giving cherries to the poor."

Watson (1921), 38 [Somerset]. Begins "Two, four, six, eight, / Mary at the cottage gate."

Udal (1922), 392 [Dorset]. Begins "Mary at the garden gate" (from *Somerset and Dorset Notes & Queries*, vol. 1, p. 174).

Whitney and Bullock (1925), 131 [Maryland]. Two variants.

Wood and Goddard (1940), 569.

Turner (1969), 15–16 [Sydney, Australia, ca. 1945]. Last line: "Mary at the cottage gate."
Withers (1946), n.p.
Gullen (1950), 34. Three variants.
Evans (1956), 15.
Justus (1957), 46 [Tennessee].
Sutton-Smith (1959), 64, 70, 71 [New Zealand]. Three variants; all begin "Two, four, six, eight, / Mary (Swinging) at the cottage gate."
Millard, NYFQ, 16 (1960), 147 [New York].
Grayson (1962), 74.
Fowke (1969), 109 [Canada]. ". . . kitchen door."
Opie (1969), 37. Begins "Two, four, six, eight, / Mary's at the cottage gate."
Shaw (1969), 46 [Liverpool]. Begins "Jenny at the cottage door."
Carey (1970), 77 [Maryland].
Brill, GMW, 24 (1972), 3. Begins "Two, four, six, eight"; ends "If I'm late don't wait. / Two, four, six, eight."

422 One, two, three, four,
Mother scrubbed the kitchen floor.
Floor dried, mother cried (died),
One two three four.

> Cf. **429**. Also found as a jump-rope rhyme; see JRR, p. 153 ("One, two, three, four, / Mother washed the floor").

Bolton (1888), 93 [Florida].
Whitney and Bullock (1925), 132 [Maryland].
Maryott, SFQ, 1, no. 4 (1937), 47 [Nebraska].
Withers (1946), n.p.
Ray Wood (1952), 13.
Evans (1956), 16.

423 One, two, three, four,
Tack a mill on ding 'im our.

Gregor (1881), 169; (1891), 30 [Scotland].

424 One, two, three!
Get out of my father's apple tree
Or you're IT.

Withers (1946), n.p.

425   One, two, three,
God bless me,
God never tells a lie,
One, two, three.

Turner (1969), 15–16 [Geelong, Australia, 1967, via
Scotland].

One, two, three,
Granny caught a flea. *See* **429**.

426   One, two, three,
I love coffee
And Billy loves tea;
How good you be.
One, two, three,
I love coffee,
And Billy loves tea.

See Opie, Dictionary, p. *334.*

Bolton (1888), 92 [England].

427   One, two, three, ladies and gents,
There it goes over a highboard fence.

Bolton (1888), 93 [Chicago].
Emrich and Korson (1947), 118.

428   One, two, three,
Mammy caught a flea;
Four, five, six,
Wasn't that a fix;
Seven, eight, nine,
'Cas it came to dine,
Ten, eleven, twelve,
All by itself.

Reid, *Misc. of Rymour Club*, 1 (1911), 107 [Edinburgh].

429   One, two, three,
Mother caught a flea.
Flea died, Mother cried,
One, two, three (Out goes she).

*Cf. **422**. Also found as a jump-rope rhyme; see JRR, p. 153.*

Babcock, *AA*, o.s., 1 (1888), 274 [District of Columbia].
"Nannie caught a flea."
Bolton (1888), 92 [Delaware, Rhode Island, Tennessee,
Maryland]. Two variants; one begins "Ein, zwei, drei."
Gregor (1891), 30 [Scotland]. "Granny caught a flea."
Northall (1892), 350.
Clifton Johnson (1896), 161.
Edward Nicholson (1897), 307 [Scotland].
Davis (1906), 212 [United States]. "Nanny caught a flea."
Stoudt (1915), 48 [from Pennsylvania Germans]. Begins
"Eins, zwei, drei."
Gardner, *JAF*, 31 (1918), 521 [Michigan].
Whitney and Bullock (1925), 133 [Maryland].
Heck, *JAF*, 40 (1927), 37.
Guy B. Johnson (1930), 166 [St. Helena Island, North Caro-
lina]. Begins "Mother ketch a flea."
Maryott, *SFQ*, 1, no. 4 (1937), 46–47 [Nebraska]. Two var-
iants; one begins "Eins, zwei, drei."
Brewster (1952), 166 [North Carolina, 1941]. Two variants;
one begins "A, B, C."
Withers (1946), n.p.
Emrich and Korson (1947), 121.
Gullen (1950), 34.
Randolph, *SFQ*, 17 (1953), 244 [Arkansas].
Sutton-Smith (1959), 64 [New Zealand].

430   One, two, three, Mother caught a flea,
Put it in a teapot and made a cup of tea.
When she put the sugar in, it went down flop,
And when she put the milk in, it came to the top.

*Also found as a jump-rope rhyme; see JRR, p. 36 ("O
Dear me, mother caught a flea").*

Opie (1969), 37, 38 [since late nineteenth century]. Two variants. One is "Oh, dear me, / Ma grannie catcht a flea, / She
roastit it and toastit it / An' took it till her tea." The other
begins "Oh, dreary me" and ends "The flea jumped out /
And bit mother's snout, / In come daddy / With his shirt
hanging out."

Howard, *NYFQ*, 16 (1960), 143 [Australia 1954–1955]. Two
variants; one begins "Inky, pinky, pea."

Daiken (1963), 32 [Dublin]. "One, two, three / Yer auld wan
caught a flea. / Salted it and peppered it / And put it in her
tea."

Ritchie (1965), 44 [Edinburgh]. "A, B, C, / My Grannie caught
a flea. / She salted it and peppered it / And took it for her
tea."

One, two, three,
Nannie (Nanny) caught a flea. *See* **429**.

431   One, two, three,
Out goes he.

*Often extended by "In the middle of the sea" or "With a
dirty dishrag on his knee." A common ending for many other
rhymes.*

Bolton (1888), 92 [Colorado, Pennsylvania]. Ends "In come
another / Out goes Jack's brother."

Edward Nicholson (1897), 307 [Scotland].

Davis (1906), 212.

Waugh, *JAF*, 31 (1918), 46 [Ontario, 1909].

Gardner, *JAF*, 31 (1918), 534 [Michigan].

Whitney and Bullock (1925), 133 [Maryland].

Brewster (1952), 166 [North Carolina, 1928].

Maryott, *SFQ*, 1, no. 4 (1937), 47 [Nebraska].

Brewster, *SFQ*, 3 (1939), 179.

McDowell, *TFSB*, 10, no. 3 (September 1944), 4.

Yoffie, *JAF*, 60 (1947), 28 [Missouri].

Hines, *Daedalian Quarterly*, 17, no. 1 (Fall 1949), 42 [Texas].

Randolph, *SFQ*, 17 (1953), 244–245 [Arkansas].

432   One, two, three,
The bumble bee,
The rooster crows,
And away he goes.

*Cf. the jump-rope "One, two, three, / Bumble, bumble
bee" (JRR, p. 150).*

Bolton (1888), 93 [Michigan, New York].

Gardner, *JAF*, 31 (1918), 522 [Michigan].

Wintemberg and Wintemberg, *JAF*, 31 (1918), 123 [Ontario].

Maryott, *SFQ*, 1, no. 4 (1937), 46 [Nebraska].
Withers (1946), n.p.
Evans (1956), 16.

433   One, two, three,
Tommy hurt his knee.
He couldn't slide and so he cried,
Out goes he!

Also found as a jump-rope rhyme; see JRR, p. 154.

Bolton (1888), 93 [Massachusetts].
Boyce and Bartlett (1946), 33.
Withers (1946), n.p.
Emrich and Korson (1947), 120.

434   One, two, three,
What can the matter be?
Three old maids tied up
To an apple tree!

Bolton (1888), 93 [Massachusetts].

One, two, three,
Yer auld wan caught a flea. *See* **430**.

One wall, two voll. *See* **403**.

One-wee, you-wee, ick-wee, aye. *See* **408**.

One-y-bo, two-y-bo,
Tick-y-bo teben. *See* **410**.

One-y, two-y, silly, solly, san. *See* **410**.

One zall (zol, zoy, zaw). *See* **403**.

435   On, gron, gray,
Kotza lomma zay.
Lomma zee, lomma zoe,
Lomma isha tisha santimo

Ongry kokry,
On gron gray.

Soifer, *Story Parade*, 6, no. 7 (July 1941), 17 [Brooklyn, 1916].

Onry, onry, ickory Ann. *See* **408**.

Ony, crozony, crozinda. *See* **252**.

Ooka, dooka soda cracker. *See* **10**.

Oola, doola doff. *See* **436**.

436   Oolan, doolan, duff
King Kong cuff
Ing fe ana mack a bana
Oolan, doolan, duff.

Howard, *NYFQ*, 16 (1960), 138 [Australia; from older people but not current among school children in 1954–1955].
Turner (1969), 15–16 [Melbourne, 1967]. "Oola doola doff, / Keep me anna coff, / Coff me anna / Orka banna, / Oola doola doff."

437   Oon, two, dree, vour,
Bells of Girt Toller (Great Toller),
Who can mëake pancëake
Thout fat or vlour?

Udal (1922), 393 [Dorsetshire, 1889].

438   Oor wee Jeanie
Had a nice clean peenie.
Guess what colour it was?
"*Blue.*"
B-L-U-E spells blue
And blue you must have on.

Bluebells My Cockle Shells (1961), n.p. [Ayrshire].
Ritchie (1965), 41 [Edinburgh]. Ends ". . . and if you have it on, you go out of this game with a slap on the face."
Those Dusty Bluebells (1965), 22 [Ayrshire].

Opie (1969), 60 [Scotland]. Begins "My wee Jeanie," ends
"The bonny bonny colour of blue / And if you have it on
you are out."

Oot Scoot, you're oot. *See* **63**.

439 Oozie, oozie, arns,
You without the harns,
Up and doon a' the toon,
Glowerin' at the starns;
Eeeksie, peeksie, turn aboot,
One, two, you are *oot.*

"Counting-Out Rhymes," *Misc. of Rymour Club*, 2, part 2
(1913), 94 [Perthshire].

440 Oranges, oranges, two (four) for a penny,
It takes a good scholar to count so many.
One, two, three
Out goes he.

*Second line often "My father got drunk from eating so
many."*

Opie (1969), 38 [since nineteenth century]. Ends "All went
down the donkey's belly; / The donkey's belly was full of
jelly, / Out goes you."
Chambers (1841), 121 [Scotland]. Begins "Lemons and
oranges."
Gregor (1881), 169 [northeast Scotland]. Two variants: one
begins "Eeringes, oranges"; one, "Eringies, orangies," the
latter including lines from "Roses are red" (**482**) and ending with a "Mr. Frog" variant of "Dr. Foster's a very good
man" (**103**).
Burne (1883), 573 [Shropshire].
Newell (1883), 201 [Pennsylvania]. Begins "Apples and
oranges."
Bolton (1888), 112 [England, New York]. Two variants; one
begins "Apples and oranges."
A.H.T., *Yorkshire Folklore Journal*, 1 (1888), 214. Second
line: "How do you think she gives so many?"
Gregor (1891), 26, 30 [Scotland]. Two variants, beginning
"Eeringes, oranges" and "Eringes, oranges." One ends

"The rose is red, the grass is green, / The days are gane / That I hae seen."

Maclagan (1901), 250 [Argyleshire].

G.W.R., *Old Lore Misc.*, 4 (1911), 166 [Kirkwall]. Three variants; one ends "Eeng tang musky dan, / Tweedlum toodlum twenty-one."

Lyle, *Misc. of Rymour Club*, 1 (1911), 173 [Scotland]. Begins "Apples and oranges"; ends "It's well ye get so man; / Ink, pink, pen and ink."

Fraser, *Misc. of Rymour Club*, 2, part 2 (1913), 80. Ends "Two and two are a tuppeny loaf, / Two and two are out."

Anderson, *Evening Ledger* (May 17, 1916) [South Carolina].

Whitney and Bullock (1925), 139 [Maryland].

Gullen (1950), 16. Begins "Lemons and oranges"; ends "The rose is red, the grass is green, / The days are past that I have seen."

MacColl and Seeger, Folkways 3565 (1962) [Durham, England].

Otchie, potchie, dominotchie. *See* **441**.

441   Ouchy, pouchy, diminouchy
Te taw tush,
Ugly bugly boo,
Out goes you.

> *Cf.* **129**.

Waugh, *JAF*, 31 (1918), 42 [Ontario, 1909]. Two variants; one ends "O-U-T spells out goes she, / Out in the middle of the dark blue sea."

Maryott, *SFQ*, 1, no. 4 (1937) [Nebraska]. "Otchie, potchie, dominotchie, / Tusk in, tusk out, / All around the river spout, / Have a peach, have a plum, / Have a box of chewing gum. / O-U-T spells out goes he."

Our first Lieutenant, he was so neat. *See* **180**.

Out, girls, out. *See* **257**.

442   Out goes a bonny lass, out goes she,
Out goes a bonny lass, one, two, three.

> *Rhyme ending.*

Opie (1969), 34 [Aberdeen, Scotland].

443   Out goes the rat,
Out goes the cat,
Out goes the lady
With the big green hat.
Y-O-U, spells you;
O-U-T, spells out!

> *Cf. the jump-rope rhyme "Mother, mother, I am ill" (JRR, pp. 126–128).*

> Bolton (1888), 93. "In comes cat, in comes rat, / In comes a *lady with a great big-see-saw hat" as ending to a "One, two, three, four, / Mary's at the cottage door"* rhyme (**421**).
> Withers (1948), 87.
> Carey (1970), 77 [Maryland].

444   O-U-T spells out,
And out goes you.

> *Common rhyme ending.*

> Opie (1969), 34, 35 [since 1860's]. Four variants. Three involve "dish cloths" or "clouts." One ends "Because the king and queen says so."
> Bolton (1888), 25, 99. Two variants, ending "With the old dish cloth / Out, boys out!" and "With a dis, dash, dirt or clout, / Out goes he."
> Waugh, *JAF*, 31 (1918), 46 [Ontario, 1909]. Ends "With a dirty dish-cloth in your mouth."
> Whitney and Bullock (1925), 140 [Maryland]. "O-U-T spells out goes she, / Right in the middle of the / Deep blue sea."
> Brewster, *SFQ*, 3 (1939), 179.
> Hines, *Daedalian Quarterly*, 17, no. 1 (Fall 1949), 42 [Texas]. Two variants; one ends "You dirty dishrag you."
> Potter, "Eeny, Meeny, Miny, Mo," *Standard Dictionary* (1949), 340. Ends "Right in the middle of / The dark blue sea."
> Sutton-Smith (1959), 69 [New Zealand].

445   And Out you go with a jolly good clout
Upon your ear-hole spout.

Common rhyme ending.

Opie (1969), 35.

Overy, Ivory, Hickory Ann. *See* **408**.

446   Owre don, owre Dee,
Owre the lea cam' ye to me?
Owre the lea cam' ye to me?
Skip the rigs o' Ballachree;
Ballachree and Jocky Snipe
Steal 't the tail frae my tyke;
Frae my tyke, and frae my ram,
Kent ye blind Tam.

"Counting-Out Rhymes," *Misc. of Rymour Club*, 2, part 2
  (1913), 60 [Scotland].
Board, *Word-Lore*, 2 (1927), 190 [Scotland]. Second and third
  lines omitted; ends "Willie Buck, Willie Boo" rhyme (**568**).

P

447   Paddy on the railway, picking up stones.
Up came the engine and broke Paddy's bones.
"Ah," said Paddy, "that's not fair."
"Puff," said the Engine, "I don't care."

*According to the Opies the rhyme stems from the old Scots
ditty "Pussy at the fireside suppin' up brose." Also found as a
jump-rope rhyme; see JRR, pp. 159–160 ("Piggy on the
railway").*

Opie (1969), 37 [current since beginning of century]. Six
  variants: "Paddy," "Piggy," "Polly," "Peggy," "Tommy,"
  and "Teddy."
Gullen (1950), 17.
Howard, *NYFQ*, 16 (1960), 139 [Australia, 1954–1955]. Two
  variants; one begins "Piggy on the railroad."
Sutton-Smith (1959), 65 [New Zealand].
Fowke (1969), 110 [Canada]. Begins "Piggy."
Knapp (1976), 27 [Montana, 1975]. Begins "Piggie."

448   Papa, mama, big dish clout;
O-U-T puts you out!

Common rhyme ending.

Bolton (1888), 111 [Massachusetts].

449   A Peanut sat on the railroad track
Its heart was all aflutter
Along came engine two sixteen,
Toot, toot, peanut butter.

Usually an entertainment rhyme.

Maryott, SFQ, 1, no. 4 (1937), 56 [Nebraska].
Sutton-Smith (1959), 12 [New Zealand]. Line 3: "The train
    came roaring around the bend."

Pear, apple, peach and plum. See **27**.

450   Pease brose again, mother,
Pease brose again,
Thinking I'm a blackbird,
Me your ane wean.

Maclagan, *Folk-Lore*, 16 (1905), 453.

451   Peas porridge hot.
Peas porridge cold.
Peas porridge in the pot,
Nine days old.
Some like it hot.
Some like it cold.
Some like it in the pot
Nine days old.

For its history as nursery rhyme, see Opie, Dictionary, p.
345.

Leventhal and Cray, WF, 22, (1963), 239 [California]. De-
    scribes method of use.

Peggy on the railway. See **447**.

452   Pennies, pennies in a fountain,
How many pennies make a mountain?

Knapp (1976), 27.

453   A **P**ennorth of chips
To grease your lips.
Out goes one,
Out goes two,
Out goes the little boy
Dressed in blue.

> *Cf. the jump-rope rhyme "I know a Scout" (JRR, p. 83).*

Opie (1969), 36 [England, current since the 1920's].
Rutherford (1971), 51 [Durham, England, 1966]. Begins "Dip.
/ A penny chip to grease my lip" and ends "Out goes
another one, and that is you."

A **P**enny chip. See **453**.

Penny, come Penny, come down to your dinner.
See **307**.

Penny on the railway. See **454**.

454   A **P**enny on the water,
Tuppence on the sea,
Threepence on the railway
And out goes she.

> *Often used to end other rhymes, especially* **415**. *Also
found as a jump-rope rhyme; see JRR, p. 159.*

Turner (1969), 16 [Sydney, 1945 and 1959]. Two variants;
one begins "Penny on the railway."
Howard, NYFQ, 16 (1960), 142 [Australia, 1954–1955]. Begins "One pence on the water."
Rodger (1969?), 21 [Scotland].

The **P**eople who live across the way. See **382**.

455 Peter Dumdick, when did you flit?
Yesterday morn when I got the kick.

Maclagan, *Folk-Lore*, 16 (1905), 453.

Peter Matrimity (Mutrimity Tram, McQuinity) . . .
See **567**.

456 Peter patter, oure the watter,
Barnfare, dinna yatter;
Puddin' wives in Paisley,
Gentlemen in Glesca.
Glesca and Patrick Mills,
Carneaverok and Carneaverok hills;
The smiddy and the smiddy hills,
The cankert buddy o' Clover hills;
King kid, king kell,
Auchendrauch in the fell,
The goolie and the Gawkie.

"Counting-Out Rhymes," *Misc. of Rymour Club*, 2, part 2 (1913), 95 [Greenock, Scotland].

Peter, Peter, pumpkin eater. See **203**.

457 Peter Riley eats fish
And catches eels.
Eels catch alligators,
Fanny eats raw potatoes.

Whitney and Bullock (1925), 138 [Maryland].

Piggy (Piggie) on the railway. See **447**.

458 Pig snout,
Walk out.

Usually an ending for other rhymes. Cf. **63**.

Waugh, *JAF*, 31 (1918), 46 [Ontario, 1909].
Opie (1969), 31 [since 1910].

Opie (1959), 4 [England, Scotland, Wales, current since
    1911].
Reid, *Misc. of Rymour Club*, 2, part 2 (1913), 69 [Scotland].
Wintemberg and Wintemberg, *JAF*, 31 (1918), 122 [Ontario].
Withers (1946), n.p.
Sutton-Smith (1959), 69 [New Zealand].

A **P**ig walked (went) into a public house. *See* **355**.

Pink, wink, you stink. *See* **277**.

Pin, pan, musky by dam. *See* **578**.

459   **P**lease missy, big missy, lend missy your imber
            bow,
        Amber bow, iron bow, Timothy, sacrephy,
            forbody,
        Lilicky, lalick, best part of whirlicky.

    Bolton (1888), 119 [New York].

460   **P**oliceman, policeman, don't take me,
        Take that man behind that tree;
        I took brass, he took gold,
        Policeman, policeman, don't take hold.

        *Also found as a jump-rope rhyme (JRR, p. 161) and as a
    taunt.*

    Bolton (1888), 112, 113 [New York, South Carolina]. Two
        variants, beginning "P'liceman" and "Watchman."
    Withers (1946), n.p. [Cedar County, Missouri, 1907–1913].
        Ends "He stole apples, I stole none; / Put him in the jail-
        house just for fun."
    Reid, *Misc. of Rymour Club*, 1 (1911), 106 [Edinburgh].
    Howard, *NYFQ*, 16 (1960), 139 [Australia, 1954–1955]. Be-
        gins "Little fat policeman."
    MacColl and Behan, Folkways 8501 (1958) [Scotland].

Polly on the railway. *See* **447**.

461   Polly wants a cracker,
Polly wants a ball,
Polly wants you to be
First (Second, *etc.*) of all.

Withers (1946), n.p. [from Brooklyn College students, 1936–
1945].

Pontius Pilate, King of the Jews. See 385.

462   A Poor little boy without any shoe;
One, 2, 3, and out goes you.

Also found as a jump-rope rhyme; see JRR, p. 162.

Bolton (1888), 111 [Massachusetts].
Withers (1946), n.p.
Emrich and Korson (1947), 119.

463   Prest an, pop an,
Cock on t' spire,
Holy Alice,
Dah mell fire.

Blakeborough (1898), 259 [Yorkshire].

464   Prinkushun, velvet cheer,
Christmas comes but once a year!
When it comes we turn the spit,
I brent my fingers, I feel it yet.
The cat's paw flew over the table,
The cat began to play the ladle.
In came Tush, ken ye me?
I'm the constable, can't ye agree?
Ha'penny pudd'n, ha'penny pie,
Stand ye out by!

See Opie, Dictionary, p. 396.

Bolton, JAF, 10 (1897), 320 [Scotland].

Q

465   Queen, queen, Caroline,
Dipped her hair in turpentine,
Turpentine made it shine.
Queen, queen Caroline.

> *Usually a taunt. Also found as a jump-rope rhyme; see JRR,
> p. 184 ("Sweet, sweet Caroline").*

Bolton (1888), 116 [Edinburgh, Scotland].
Gregor (1891), 11, 24 [Scotland]. Six variants; one begins
   "Eevil, eevil, eevil-ine"; one, "Eery, ary, areline."
Clifton Johnson (1896), 165. Begins "Engine number nine."
Waugh, *JAF*, 31 (1918), 46 [Ontario, 1909].
Reid, *Misc. of Rymour Club*, 1 (1911), 104 [Edinburgh]. Be-
   gins "Good Queen Caroline."
Ritchie (1965), 40, 47 [Edinburgh]. Two variants.

Query, ory, . . . See **408**.

R

466   Raggle taggle dish cloth torn in two,
Out goes you.

> *Rhyme ending.*

Opie (1969), 34.

Ramsey in the pot. See **403**.

467   Ra, ra,
Chuckeree, chuckeree,
Ony, pony,
Ningy, ningy, na,
Addy, caddy, wester,
Anty, poo,

Chutipan, chutipan,
China, chu.

Gregor (1891), 30 [Fraserburgh, Scotland].
Opie (1969), 39, 53. Three variants: one each from Gregor
    (1891) and Bolton, JAF, 10 (1897), and "Addi, addi, chick-
    ari, chickari, / Oonie, poonie, om pom alarie, / Ala wala
    whiskey, / Chinese chunk."
Bolton, JAF, 10 (1897), 321 [Pennsylvania]. "Rye, chy,
    chookereye, chookereye, / Choo, choo, ronee, ponee, / Icky,
    picky, nigh, / Caddy, paddy, vester, / Canlee, poo. / Itty pau,
    jutty pau, / Chinese Jew."
Opie (1947), 111. "Ah, ra, chickera, / Roly, poly, pickena, /
    Kinny, minny, festi, / Shanti-poo / Ickerman, chickerman,
    chinee-choo."
Ritchie (1965), 48 [Edinburgh]. "Ra ra joober-a, roenee,
    ponee, ping-a-ring-a-ra / It-a bit-a west-a canti pooh / It-a
    bit-a it-a chit-a Chinese Jew. / Eerie orie you are out."

Ra ra joober-a, roenee, ponee, ping-a-ring-a-ra.
See **407.**

468 Red and blue;
Dutch clear through.
Your father is a Dutchman
And so are you.

See also **472.**

Gardner, JAF, 31 (1918), 535 [Michigan].

469 Red Top taxi, one, two, three,
Red Top taxi, you're not he.

Howard, NYFQ, 16 (1960), 141 [Australia, 1954–1955].
Turner (1969), 16–17 [Australia, 1967]. Also "Black Top,"
    "Silver Top," and "Little Red taxi" beginnings.

470 Red, white, and blue,
All out but you.

See also **412.**

Newell (1883), 203 [Pennsylvania].
Bolton (1888), 111 [New England, Pennsylvania].

Opie (1969), 30, 31 [United States and Britain, since at least 1888].
Clifton Johnson (1896), 161.
Monroe, *AA*, n.s., 6 (1904), 47 [Massachusetts].
G.W.R., *Old Lore Misc.*, 5 (1912), 7 [Kirkwall].
Anderson, *Evening Bulletin* (May 17, 1916) [Pennsylvania, New Jersey].
Waugh, *JAF*, 31 (1918), 43 [Ontario].
Whitney and Bullock (1925), 139 [Maryland].
Gardner (1937), 229 [New York].
Maryott, *SFQ*, 1, no. 4 (1937), 62 [Nebraska].
Withers (1946), n.p.
Gullen (1950), 17.
Howard, *NYFQ*, 16 (1960), 142 [Australia, 1954–1955]. "Dip, red, white, blue, / Who's he? Not you."
Turner (1969), 11 [Adelaide, Australia, 1957]. "Dip, red, white, blue, / Who's he? Not you."

471 Red, white, and blue,
The cat's got the flu,
The baby has the whooping cough
And out goes you.

> *Also found as a jump-rope rhyme; see JRR, p. 167 ("Red, white, and blue / My mother caught the flu)."*

Opie (1969), 36 [England].

472 Red, white, and blue.
Your father is a Jew (Dago);
Your mother is a red-head (cabbage head);
So are you.

> *Cf.* **468**. *Usually a taunt. Also found as a jump-rope rhyme (JRR, p. 168).*

Gardner, *JAF*, 31 (1918), 534 [Michigan].
Brewster (1952), 168 [North Carolina, ca. 1924].

Rene, tene, tother, feather, fib. See **500.**

473 Richman, poorman, beggarman, thief,
Lawyer, doctor, merchant, chief.

Usually a divination rhyme; see Opie, Dictionary, pp. 404–405. Also a jump-rope rhyme (JRR, p. 168).

Monroe, AA, n.s., 6 (1904), 47 [Massachusetts].
Davis (1906), 213. "Great house, little house, pig sty, barn. / Rich man, poor man, beggar man."
Ritchie (1965), 48 [Edinburgh]. "Tinker, tailor, soldier, sailor, / Rich man, poor man, beggarman, thief."

474   Rich, Rich, fell in the ditch,
And never got back till half-past six.
My mother told me you are it.

Usually a taunt or connected with the dialogue game "Old Mommy Witch." Also found as a jump-rope rhyme; see JRR, p. 143 ("Old Mother Rich").

Withers (1946), n.p. [from Brooklyn College students, 1936–1945].

475   Rickety rickety rickety rye,
Two fat cheeks and one black eye,
Rickety rickety rickety rout,
Whoever I touch next is out.

Musick and Randolph, JAF, 63 (1950), 428 [Missouri].

Rickety, rickety, rock. See **216**.

Rick, stick, stickity ho! See **133**.

476   A Riddle,
A riddle,
A hole in the middle.
Somebody stuck his finger in.

Usually found as an obscene riddle.

Evans (1956), 27. With playing instructions.

Rimety, trimety, he's a good man. See **567**.

477 Rimly, rimly, rimbut,
Onesser, twoser;
Rimly, timley, tan;
Tee, taw, butt.

Bolton (1888), appendix [New York].

478 Ring a ring of roses,
A pocket full of posies.
One, two, three,
Out goes he.

*Usually a singing game. See Opie, Dictionary, pp. 364 –
365.*

Bolton (1888), 15 [Connecticut].

Ring around a sugar bowl. *See* **403**.

479 Rip sacksay,
One sack, two sack,
Three sack say.
Halaback, attaback,
Wee, wo, why, wack.

Bolton (1888), 110 [New York].

Rise, Sally Walker. *See* **329**.

480 Rob Law's lum seeks
Roon about the chimney cheeks.

Gregor (1881), 174; (1891), 30 [Scotland].

481 Roly, poly shot a bear,
And he shot him right in there.

Maryott, SFQ, 1, no. 4 (1937), 50 [Nebraska]. With playing
instructions.

482 Roses are red,
Violets are blue,
When I choose,
It will be you.

Usually an autograph-album rhyme. Also found as a jump-rope rhyme; see JRR, p. 171.

Maryott, SFQ, 1, no. 4 (1937), 62 [Nebraska].
Emrich and Korson (1947), 120.

483 Roses come, roses go,
Violets begin to blow.
Neither you nor I do know
Why they come or why they go.

Bolton (1888), 119 [New Hampshire].

Rosy, posy, piny, pink. *See* **277**.

484 A Rough shirt
And a standing collar
Will choke a nigger till he holler.

Whitney and Bullock (1925), 139 [Maryland].

485 Round about, round about, applety pie,
Daddy loves ale, and so do I;
Up, mammy, up,
Fill us a cup,
And daddy and me'll sup it all up.

See Opie, Dictionary, pp. 375–376.

Bolton (1888), 114 [Yorkshire, England].

Round and round the butter dish. *See* **16**.

486 Rub-a-dub, dub,
Three men in a tub.
The butcher, the baker,

The candlestick maker,
All jumped out of a rotten potato.

Usually a nursery rhyme; see Opie, Dictionary, p. 376.

Bolton (1888), 113 [Bristol, England].
Gregor (1891), 32 [Scotland]. Two variants, one beginning
   "A-rub, a-dub-dub." Last line omitted.
Turner (1969), 16–17 [Melbourne, ca. 1910]. Begins "The
   butcher, the baker, . . ."

487   **R**umble, rumble in the pot (lot),
King's nail, horse top;
Take off lid!

See also **403**.

Bolton (1888), 3, 109, 112 [New York, New Jersey, Indiana].
   Discusses use of rhyme in a special way of counting out by
   stirring fingers in a cap. Four variants. One ends with a
   "One's all, two's all" rhyme variant (**403**), one with "One,
   2, 3, 4, O-U-T spells out." A variant beginning "Rumzo,
   romzo, hollow pot" ends "One-zo, two-zo, three-zo, four. /
   Kitty is lying on the floor."
Davis (1906), 211.
Wintemberg, *JAF*, 31 (1918), 157 [Roebuck, Ontario]. "Mum-
   bly, mumbly, in the pot, / How many monkeys have I got? /
   One, two, three, and out goes he."

Rumzo, romzo, hollow pot. *See* **403**, **487**.

Rupso, oneso, twoso. *See* **403**.

Rye, chy, chookereye, chookereye. *See* **467**.

488   **R**ytum, tweedle, tweedle, dell,
A yard of pudding is not an ell;
And not forgetting tytherum tie,
A tailor's goose can never fly.

From refrain of the comic song "A Bundle of Truths," 1812.
See Opie, Dictionary, p. 217.

Bolton (1888), 110.

S

489   Saet daet palm flaet,
Hove dove dick,
Dick out, dick in,
Dick upon a riddle pin.

G.W.R., *Old Lore Misc.*, 5 (1912), 7 [Kirkwall].

490   Said the haddock to the skate—Skip the creel, and
shun the bait;
Said the herr' to the eel—Crook you little tail
weel;
Dear Bocht, dear sauld, Seek a sheep frae Jock's
fauld;
Jock's fauld's very close, Tak' the tail frae Jock's
horse.

"Counting-Out Rhymes," *Misc. of Rymour Club*, 2, part 2
(1913), 60 [Scotland].

Sainty, tainty, heathery, bethery. *See* **500**.

491   Salt herrin, penny the pun,
Eat them all, and they'll soon be done.

Gregor (1891), 30 [Scotland].

492   Sam, Sam, the soft soap man,
Washed his face in a frying pan,
Combed his hair with a wagon-wheel,
And died with a toothache in his heel.

*Generally a taunt; also found as a verse of the American
folksong "Old Dan Tucker."*

Bolton, *JAF*, 10 (1897), 321 [western Pennsylvania].
Withers (1946), n.p. [from Brooklyn College students, 1936–
1945].
Daiken (1963), 32 [Dublin]. Begins "Yer auld man's a dirty

auld man"; ends "He combs his hair with the leg of a
chair. / Yer auld man's a dirty auld man."

493 Sando, sando,
Fimma, nocka, dah, dah, doh.
Sucku so fuh me,
Pretty maid and go.

Rutherford (1971), 52 [Browney, England, ca. 1915]. Tune
given.

494 Sandy, he belongs to the mill,
And the mill belongs to Sandy;
He sold his mill for the price o' a gill,
And the mill's no longer Sandy.

Reid, *Misc. of Rymour Club*, 2, part 2 (1913), 70 [Scotland].

495 School's up, school's down,
School's all around the town.
One, 2, 3, out goes she.

Bolton (1888), 111 [Massachusetts].

Scinty tinty heathery beathery. *See* **500**.

Scinty, tinty, my black hen. *See* **213**.

Seentie, teentie,
Tennera, mennera. *See* **500**.

Senny, menny, mitta, ma. *See* **130**.

Senty, tenty, ticity, fae. *See* **129**.

496 Shoe lie, shoe lie, shoe lie, shoe.
Shoe lie, sacaraca, sillababi, cue;
When I see my Billy bab-a-bie,
Come Billy, bab-a-loo.

May be related to the Irish song "Shoolaroon."

Gardner, *JAF*, 31 (1918), 530 [Michigan].

497   Silly Susie tore her pants,
Teaching gentlemen how to dance,
First on the heel, then on the toe,
Cross your legs and out you go.

> *Usually found as a jump-rope rhyme; see JRR, pp. 26–27
> ("Charlie Chaplin went to France").*

Randolph, *SFQ*, 17 (1953), 246 [Arkansas].

Silver Top taxi. *See* **469**.

498   Sing a song, a ming a mong,
A carlin and a kit;
And them 'at disna like butter,
Put in their tongue and lick.

> "Counting-Out Rhymes," *Misc. of Rymour Club*, 2, part 2
> (1913), 59 [Scotland].

Sinkty tinkty, hethery, bethery. *See* **500**.

499   Sinner, sinner,
Come to dinner,
Half past two.
Eat your 'taters,
Alligators,
Out goes you.

> *Cf.* **307**.

Clifton Johnson (1896), 166. "Nigger, nigger, hoc potater, /
    Half past alligater."
Gardner, *JAF*, 31 (1918), 532 [Michigan]. Begins "Little nig-
    ger."
Brewster (1952), 168 [North Carolina, 1925]. Begins "Nigger,
    nigger."
Withers (1946), n.p.
Emrich and Korson (1947), 120. Begins "Little beggar."

Hines, *Daedalian Quarterly*, 17, no. 1 (Fall 1949), 42 [Texas].
   Begins "Little Nigger."
Randolph, SFQ, 17 (1953), 246 [Arkansas].
Evans (1956), 21. Begins "Little sinner."

500   Sinty, tinty, huthery,
   Muthery, banks o' litery,
   Over, dover, dicker, dog,
   San, dan, dush.

A nonsense series which has received much critical atten-
tion is that seemingly derived from "Anglo-cymric" methods
of counting. Because many "Eeny, meeny," "Intery, min-
tery," and "Onery, twoery" rhymes are derived from this
method of counting (usually called "Indian counting" in the
United States) or from some other close linguistic relative, it
is difficult to separate the rhymes grouped below from them.
Basis for the division here has been the inclusion of the
"tether, mether" combination or of a close relative ("ped-
dlera, tothera," etc.). The standard work to which most com-
mentators refer when speaking of the series is A. J. Ellis
reporting in Transactions of the Philological Society,
1887–8–9, pp. 316–372, entitled "The Anglo-Cymric
Score"). See also Newell (1883), pp. 200–201, and Opie
(1969), pp. 47–51. For a discussion of the relationship of this
series to nursery rhymes, see Opie, Dictionary, *pp. 13–15.*
   One widely-reported variant ending is "Up the causey,
down the cross, / There stands a bonny white horse; / It can
gallop, it can trot / It can carry the mustard pot." For
another common ending, see **164**.

Knapp (1976), 24 [colonial U.S., England, Ireland]. Variant
   first lines: "Een teen tuther further fip," "Een tean tether
   mether pimp," "Eina peina puttera pith," and "Eina mina
   pera peppera pinn."
Opie (1969), 43, 46–51 passim [England, Scotland, Wales,
   Rhode Island, since 1820]. Four variants, beginning "Zinti
   tinti / Tethera, methera" (ends "As I sat on my sooty kin / I
   saw the king of Irel pirel / Playing on Jerusalem pipes");
   "Zeenty teenty / Heathery bethery" (ends "Saw the King of
   easel diesel / Jumping over Jerusalem wall / Black fish,
   white trout / Eerie, oarie, you are out"); "Yan, teean, tethera,
   methera, pip"; and "Zeeny, meeny, feeny, fig" (ends "Eeny,
   meeny figgledy, fig" rhyme [**129**]). Mentioned only: "Yan,
   tan, tethera, methera," "Zinti, tinti," "Iny, tiny . . . fethery,
   phips," "Ene, tene . . . fether, fip," "Inty tinty tethery

methery," "Eenty teenty ithery bithery," and "Zeenty teenty tether a mether."

Edward Nicholson (1897), 218–219 [Scotland, 1871]. Three variants, beginning "Scinty, tinty heathery beathery" and "Zinty, tinty, hethery, methery" (Inverness) and "Sinkty tinkty, hethery, bethery" [1871, with an explanation of origins].

Potter, "Eeny, Meeny, Miny, Mo," Standard Dictionary (1949), 340 [Indiana, 1875]. "Eeny, teeny, ether, fether, fip" (first line only).

Sutton-Smith (1959), 66 [New Zealand, 1875]. Begins "Zinte, tinte."

Bolton (1888), 110, 114, 121, appendix [New England, New Hampshire, Connecticut, Indiana, Ireland, Scotland, England]. Nine variants, beginning "Zeinty, teinty, Henry, mothery," "Inty, tinty, tethery, methery," "Eeny, teeny, ether, fether, fip," "Rene, tene, tother, feather, fib," "Aina, peina, para, peddera, pimp," "Ain, tain, fethery, fip," "Ain, tain, tethera, pethera, pimpi," and "Een, teen, tether, fether, fitz."

Gregor (1891), 27, 29 [Scotland]. Four variants, beginning "Zinty, tinty, tethery, bethery," "Zinty, tinty, heathery, meathery," "Iseenty, teenty, hethery, bethery," and "Sainty, tainty, heathery, bethery"; also, "Zeenty, teen-ty, / Tether a-mather" (begins a "Hickory, dickory, dock" rhyme [**216**]).

Stockleridge, JAF, 4 (1891) 171 [Rhode Island]. Begins "Teddery, peddery, slatter, latter."

Blakeborough (1898), 259 [Yorkshire]. Begins "Ena, tena." With a discussion of counting procedure.

Mills and Bishop, The New Yorker (November 13, 1937), 34 [Scotland, nineteenth century and current]. Two variants, beginning "Inty tinty tethery methery" and "Zinty tinty tethera pethera bumf."

Maclagan, Folk-Lore, 16 (1905), 450. Begins "As inty, tinty, lathera, mothera."

Davis (1906), 210, 211, 212 [Scotland; Plymouth, Massachusetts; Indiana]. Four variants: two begin "Een, teen, feather pip"; one begins "Eeny, teeny, other feather hip"; and one begins "Intry, tentry, tethery, methery."

Botkin (1947), 905 [Massachusetts]. "Een, teen, feather pip, / Sargo, larko, bump" (from Davis [1906]).

Waugh, JAF, 31 (1918), 45 [Ontario, 1909].

Reid, Misc. of Rymour Club, 1 (1911), 103 [Edinburgh]. Two variants, beginning "Eenty teenty, heather bell" and "Eenty, teenty, tethery, methery."

Bett (1924), 59–63 [Scotland]. Discusses many local variants, including "Seentie, teentie, / Tennera, mennera" and "Inty, minty."

Boyce and Bartlett (1946), 31. Begins "Inty, tinty."

Withers (1946), n.p. Begins "Een, teen, tether, fether, fip."

Gullen (1950), 16. Begins "Inty, tinty."

Howard, *NYFQ*, 16 (1960), 138 [Australia, from Scotland via New Zealand]. Begins "Hinty, tinty, tethery, minty," with an "Eseentse, teenste, tinnery, nunnery" rhyme ending (**164**).

Bluebells My Cockle Shells (1961), n.p. [Ayrshire]. Begins "A-seenty-teenty, heather beathery"; ends with an "Eseentse, teenste, tinnery, nunnery" rhyme ending (**164**).

G.B. Adams, *Ulster Folklore*, 11 (1965), 94, 95, 97. Three variants, beginning "Sinty, tinty, / Tethery methery," "Zeenty peenty hethery bethery," and "Zeendy, teendy, tethery, methery." One ends "Mounted on Jerusalem stack / Playing on his wee pee poppie puddin pie."

Ritchie (1965), 39, 45 [Edinburgh]. Two variants, beginning "Eentie teentie tithery mithery bamfileerie" and "Eentie teentie heathery beathery."

Sinty tinty
Tethery methery. *See* **500**.

Sinty, vinity, vickety, vy. *See* **129**.

501   Sister, sister, I've been thinking
What on earth have you been drinking?
Looks like water,
Smells like wine—
O my gosh, it's turpentine!

Parody of the song "Reuben and Rachel." Also found as a jump-rope rhyme; see JRR, p. 65 ("Hitler, Hitler, I've been thinking").

Ritchie (1965), 48 [Edinburgh].

Six white horses. *See* **541**.

Skinty, tinty, my black hen. *See* **213**.

Skip, skip, sko. *See* **141**.

502 Sky blue, sky blue,
Who's it? Not you.

See also **412**.

Fowke (1969), 109 [Canada].
Opie (1969), 31 [East Dulwich, England]. Begins "Ip, dip, sky blue"; ends "God's words are true, / It must not be you."

503 The Sky is blue
How old are you?
One, two, three, four, five, etc.

Withers (1946), n.p. [from Brooklyn College students, 1936–1945]. With playing instructions.
Evans (1956), 24.
Bley (1957), 96.
Leventhal and Cray, *WF*, 22 (1963), [California]. With explanation of use.
Knapp (1976), 26. "Blue shoe, blue shoe."
Milberg (1976), 25.

504 Smack, wallop, thump,
You're knocked out.

Opie (1969), 31 [Wilmslow, England].

505 Soldier, soldier, in the battle
Hear his money musket rattle.
One-a-dunna, two-a, three,
Rattle again and out goes she.

Randolph, *SFQ*, 17 (1953), 245 [Arkansas].

506 Some people say that niggers don't steal,
I caught some in my corn meal.
One, two, three, four, five, six, seven,
Eight, nine, ten, eleven, twelve.

Common American folk-lyric stanza.

Maryott, *SFQ*, 1, no. 4 (1937), 54 [Nebraska].

507 Sour-milk Jenny, a pint for a penny,
Stop your horse and give me a drink,
Sour-milk Jenny, you are out.

Reid, *Misc. of Rymour Club*, 2, part 2 (19٤3), 70 [Scotland].

508 Spinnery, spannery, musketue;
Twiddle-um, twaddle-um, out goes he.

Cf. **119**, **410**.

Gardner, *JAF*, 31 (1918), 530 [Michigan].

509 Stick, stock, stone dead,
Blind man can't see;
Every knave will have a slave;
You or I must be he.

Cf. **152**, **222**.

Opie (1969), 22 [since 1810].
Ker (1840) = Bolton (1888), 111 [England].

510 Superman, Superman, fly around,
Around, around *out*.

Knapp (1976), 26.

511 A Swan swam over the sea.
Swim, swan, swim.
Swan swam back again;
Well swam, swan!
O-U-T spells out goes she.

Usually a tongue-twister. See Opie, Dictionary, p. 400.

Bolton (1888), 118 [Hartford, Connecticut].
Emrich and Korson (1947), 119.

512 Sweep the floor, lift the chair,
Sweep below, lay it down;
You are out.

Reid, *Misc. of Rymour Club*, 2, part 2 (1913), 70 [Scotland].

Sybil, Sybil, Fred and Don. *See* **408**.

T

513   Take one-O
Take two-O
Take three-O
Take four-O
Spell potato.

Coats, *HF*, 6 (1947), 73 [Indiana].

514   Tak' up your fit and gie's a pu',
Sax ouks ha'e I been fu';
Sax mair I shall be,
By the land and by the sea;
A' the tailors in the toon,
Up the bank, syne doon.

"Counting-Out Rhymes," *Misc. of Rymour Club*, 2, part 2 (1913), 60 [Scotland].

515   Tarzan, Tarzan in a tree,
Tarzan fell *out*.

Knapp (1976), 27.

516   Tea, and sugar's my delight,
Tea and sugar's out.

Common rhyme ending.

Reid, *Misc. of Rymour Club*, 2, part 2 (1913), 69 [Scotland].

Teddery, peddery, slatter, latter. *See* **500**.

517   Teddy bear, teddy bear, turn around.
Teddy bear, teddy bear, jump up and down.

Teddy bear, teddy bear, go up the stairs.
Teddy bear, teddy bear, say your prayers.
Teddy bear, teddy bear, turn off the light.
Teddy bear, teddy bear, spell good-night.
G-O-O-D, N-I-G-H-T.

Usually a jump-rope rhyme; see JRR, pp. 186–189.

Brill, GMW, 24 (1972), 3.

Teddy on the railway. *See* **447**.

518 Teena, dinah,
Ola, dola,
Dila, dila,
Olla, bolla,
Alabama.
Delia, dillia,
Tela, dila,
Harley, barley,
Delly, jelly,
Tiney, toney,
Teely, toley,
Olam, tolma.

Bolton (1888), 106.

519 Te-witty, te-wally,
Te-melan-co-colly;
Te-niggy, te-naggy,
Te now, now, now.

Reminiscent of nonsense refrain for a number of folksongs.

Bolton (1888), appendix [Indiana].

520 There's a neat little clock, in the centre it stands,
And it points oot the 'oors wi' its twa pretty hands;
The ane shows the meenits, the ither the 'oors,
As aft as ye look to yon high church toors.

"Counting-Out Rhymes," *Misc. of Rymour Club*, 2, part 2
(1913), 62 [Scotland].

521   There's a party on the hill:
Will you come?
Bring your own cup and saucer and a bun:
Who is your loved one?
"John."
John will be there
Kissing Jeanie in the chair—
There's a party on the hill:
Will you come?

> Based on a nineteenth-century song, "Will you come to my wedding, will you come?"

Ritchie (1965), 40 [Edinburgh].
Opie (1969), 60 [Britain].

522   There stands a pretty maid in a black cap.
If you want a pretty maid in a black cap.
Please take she.

> The last two lines are a common rhyme ending.

Courtney (1890), 175 [East Cornwall].
Northall (1892), 350.

523   There was a crookit man
And he walked a crookit mile,
He found a crookit saxpence
Upon a crookit style,
He bocht a crookit cat,
And caught a crookit moose,
And they all lived together
In a little crookit hoose.

> Usually a nursery rhyme; see Opie, Dictionary, p. 289.

Gregor (1891), 32 [Scotland].

524   There was a little man
Who had a little gun;
Over the mountain
He did run.
A belly so fat

And a horse-tail hat
And a pancake tongue.

Howard, *NYFQ*, 16 (1960), 143 [Australia, 1954–1955].

525   There was a little waterman
Who wore a red coat.
Up stairs, down stairs, do you want a boat?
Penny on the water, tuppence on the sea,
Threepence on the railway,
Out goes she!

   Cf. **454**.

Bolton, *JAF*, 10 (1897), 321 [London].

526   There was a miller, stout and bold,
Fed upon beef and brose;
He'd sturdy legs, and shoulder broad,
As ye may weel suppose.

   "Counting-Out Rhymes," *Misc. of Rymour Club*, 2, part 2
   (1913), 61 [Scotland].

527   There was a rat, for want of stairs,
Went down a rope to say his prayers.

   See Opie, Dictionary, p. 361.

Lyle, *Misc. of Rymour Club*, 2, part 3 (1914), 143 [Lothian,
   Scotland].
Gardner, *JAF*, 31 (1918), 535 [Michigan].

528   This little piggy went to market,
This little piggy stayed home,
This little piggy had roast beef,
This little piggy had none,
This little piggy went wee-wee all the way home.

   *Usually a nursery rhyme; see Opie, Dictionary, pp. 349–
350.*

Hines, *Daedalian Quarterly*, 17, no. 1 (Fall 1949), 42 [Texas].

Three horses in a stable. See **541.**

Three little horses. See **541**.

Three men driving cattle. See **325**.

Three mice run up the clock. See **216**.

529   Three potatoes in a pot,
Take one out and leave it hot.

> *Also found as a jump-rope rhyme; see JRR, p. 194 ("Three*
> *wee tatties in a pot").*

Newell (1883), 202 [Pennsylvania].
Bolton (1888), 111 [Pennsylvania].
Opie (1969), 38 [since 1888]. Begins "Three wee tatties"; ends
   "If it's hot cut its throat, / Three wee tatties in a pot."
Withers (1946), n.p.
Justus (1957), 45 [Tennessee].
Ritchie (1965), 48 [Edinburgh]. Begins "Three wee totties";
   ends "If it is, cut its throat. / Three wee totties in a pot."

Three wee tatties (totties) in a pot. See **529**.

Three white horses. See **541**.

Tick (Tic), tack (tac), toe. See **533**.

530   Timothy, Titus took two tees,
To tie two tups to two tall trees,
To terrify the terrible Thomas-a-Tittamus,
O-U-T spells out—goes he.

> *Usually a tongue-twister; see Opie, Dictionary, p. 500.*

Burne (1883), 573 [Shropshire].
Bolton, *JAF*, 10 (1897), 320 [Shropshire].

Tinker, tailor, soldier, sailor. See **473**.

531   Tip, tap, taesie,
Keep your mind aesie,
The tide's comin' in,
If you run a mile awa'
The tide will tak' you in.

Usually a rhyme addressed to a crab to make it run toward the sea.

Maclagan, *Folk-Lore*, 16 (1905), 454.

Tip, tap (top), toe. See **534**.

532   Tish pie addy boom kei smash,
Laddy's going to use the lash.
Mammy's going to kick us both.

Gardner (1937), 229 [New York].

533   Tit, tat, toe,
Here I go.
And if I miss,
I pitch on this.

See Opie, Dictionary, p. 406.

Mill Hill Magazine, 5 (1877), 95 [England and Scotland] = Bolton (1888), 121 = Opie (1969), 30.
Edward Nicholson (1897), 307 [Scotland]. Begins "Tick, tack, toe."
Davis (1906), 211.
Withers (1946), n.p. [Cedar County, Missouri, 1907–1913].
Maryott, *SFQ*, 1, no. 4 (1937), 50 [Nebraska]. Begins "Tick, tack, toe."
"Folk Rhymes" (1944), 4 [Maryland].
Evans (1956), 22.
Howard, *NYFQ*, 16 (1960), 138 [Australia, from Scotland via New Zealand].
Turner (1969), 17 [Melbourne, 1967]. Begins "Tic tac toe" and ends "Where I land / I do not know."
Howard (1977), 212 [Texas, 1910–1912]. Begins "Tic tac toe / Round I go."

534   Tit, tat, to!
Three jolly butcher boys
All in a row.
One says yes,
And the other says no,
Therefore I say, tit, tat, to!

> *See Opie*, Dictionary, p. 106.

Bolton (1888), 117 [Connecticut].
Boyce and Bartlett (1946), 32. "Tip, tap, toe, / My first go. / Ten
   little nigger boys / All in a row, / Stick one up, / Stick one
   down, / Stick one in the old man's crown."
Gullen (1950), 18. Ends "Stick one up, / Stick one down, /
   Stick one in the old man's crown."
Shaw (1969), 47 [Liverpool]. "Tip top toe, out you go, / Four
   jolly sailor boys all in a row."

535   Tobacco, hic, 'twill make you sick,
Tobacco, sick, 'twill make you hic.

Bolton (1888), 111 [New York].
Withers (1946), n.p.

536   Tom Blair is a decent man.
He goes to church on Sunday.
Prays to heaven to give him strength
To whip the boys on Monday.

> *Cf.* **103**.

Maclagan, *Folk-Lore*, 16 (1905), 453.

Tommy on the railway. *See* **447**.

537   Tommy Tinker sat on a klinker;
Then he began to cry,
"Ma, Ma!"
That poor little innocent guy.

Withers (1946), n.p. [from Brooklyn College students, 1936–
   1945].

538   Tom Tit,
       You are it.

Rutherford (1971), 52 [Ushaw Moor, England, 1967]. Begins
    "Ip, dip, tom-tit."
Opie (1969), 30 [Cleethorpes, England].

539   Tom, Tom, titty mouse,
       Laid an egg in my house;
       The egg was rotten
       Good for nothin'.
       Tom, Tom, titty mouse.

Bolton (1888), 119 [Newport, Rhode Island].

Too many horses. See **541**.

540   Trovan, tovan, tin-tin twire-lire,
       Maxfield, northfield, rode on whack.

Musick and Randolph, *JAF*, 63 (1950), 428 [Missouri].

541   Twenty horses in a paddock (stable);
       One jumped out.
       O-U-T spells out
       So out you must go.

   Related to a rhyme used in the game "Hide-and-seek."

Rutherford (1971), 52 [Newcastle upon Tyne, England, ca.
    1919]. "Up the pot! Down the pot! / Twenty horses in a
    stable. / Take one out and skin its navel. / If it says another
    word, / Hit it with a horse's turd."
Guy B. Johnson (1930), 166 [St. Helena Island, North Caro-
    lina]. "Three little horses in de stable, / One fell down
    an' skinned his nable. / All ready? / Not yet. / All ready? /
    Not yet. / Ready, ready? / I'm comin', I'm comin'."
Howard, *NYFQ*, 16 (1960), 141 [Australia, 1954–1955].
Evans (1956), 29. Begins "Too many horses / In the stable."
Ritchie (1965), 40, 48 [Edinburgh]. Three variants; two begin
    "Six (Three) white horses in a stable" and involve "Mable"
    setting the table.
Opie (1969), 38 [best known in north country of England].

Begins "Three white horses"; ends "Pick one out / And call it Mable."
Knapp (1976), 27. "Three horses in a stable, / One runs *out*."

542   Two and two's a tippeny loaf,
An two and two's it.

Gregor (1891), 30 [Scotland].

543   Two, four, six, eight,
Johnny had a rattlesnake.
The snake he died and Johnny cried,
Two, four, six, eight.

Cf. **429**. *Also found as a jump-rope rhyme; see JRR, p. 197.*

Fowke (1969), 109 [Canada].

Two, four, six, eight,
Mary at (Swinging on) the cottage (garden) gate.
    See **421**.

544   Two little sausages
Frying in the pan,
One jumped out and the other went bang!

Howard, *NYFQ*, 16 (1960), 141 [Australia, 1954–1955].

Two tiddlum (tipplin). *See* **574**.

U

545   Uncle Harry, do not tarry,
Lest you be too late;
Nephew John, do go on,
And leave me at the gate.

Reid, *Misc. of Rymour Club*, 1, (1911), 105 [Edinburgh].

546 Up and down the avenue,
One, two, three,
Up and down the avenue,
You're not he.

Turner (1969), 17 [Melbourne, 1967].

547 Up hill, doon brae, doon,
Pell-mell, at the fit I fell.

"Counting-Out Rhymes," *Misc. of Rymour Club*, 2, part 2
(1913), 60 [Scotland].

Upon yonder hill. See **43**.

548 Up the ladder, down the ladder,
See the monkeys chew tobacco.
How many ounces did they chew?
Shut your eyes and think.
"Six."
One, two, three, four, five, six,
And out you must go for saying so.

Opie (1969), 59 [since 1920's].

549 Up the pole
Down the pole
Out goes
Sausage roll.

Ritchie (1965), 48 [Edinburgh]. With playing instructions.

Up the pot! Down the pot! See **541**.

Ury, urry, angry Ann. See **249**, **278**.

V

550 The Vingle, the vangle,
The goose and the gander,
Come roly me bony brandy dip.

Clifton Johnson (1896), 165.

551 Vizzery, vazzery, vozery, vem,
Tizzery, tazzery, tozery, tem,
Hiram, Jiram, cockrem, spirem,
Popular, rollin, gem.

Courtney (1890), 175 [East Cornwall].
Northall (1892), 351.

W

Wannery Too, er, ey, (tooery), Dickery Dairy. *See*
410.

552 Wash my lady's dishes,
Hang them on the bushes,
When the bushes begin to crack,
Hang them on a donkey's (nigger's) back,
When the donkey begins to run,
Shoot him with a leather gun.

Bolton (1888), 113 [New York, Massachusetts, southern
United States]. Two variants.
Maryott, SFQ, 1, no. 4 (1937), 55 [Nebraska].
Withers (1946), n.p.
Leventhal and Cray, WF, 22 (1963), 238 [California].

Watchman, watchman, don't watch me. *See* **460**.

553 W, double-O, D, WOOD;
Sockety peck!
Run round the limb
And stick your bill in—
WOODPECKER!

Withers (1946), n.p.

We are three brethren out of Spain. *See* **208**.

Wee jelly biscuit. *See* **170**.

554 A Wee wee teuchie-bird
Lol lol lol
Laid an egg on the windie-sole:
When the windie-sole began to crack
The wee wee teuchie-bird roared and grat.

Ritchie (1965), 44 [Edinburgh].

555 Wee Willie Root,
You're out.

Maclagan (1901), 250 [Scotland].

556 We had a pie,
Made out of rye,
O' possum was the meat.
The crust was tough,
We had enough,
And more than all could
E-A-T, eat.

Maryott, *SFQ,* 1, no. 4 (1937), 55 [Nebraska].
Withers (1946), n.p.

Wellington City Council, W.C.C. *See* **66**.

557 We'll wash oor face, and kaim oor hair,
And oot to sniff the caller air;

Syne aff for fairin' to the fair
At sax-o-clock i' th' mornin'.

"Rhymes of General and Local Interest," *Misc. of Rymour Club*, 2, part 3 (1914), 113 [Scotland].

558   What colour will you have?
"Red."
R-E-D spells red and O-U-T spells out of the
G-A-M-E, game.

Rodger (1969?), 20 [Scotland].

559   What's for supper?
Pease brose and butter.
Who'll say the grace?
I'll say the grace.
Colour viti, colour voti,
Colour taste, taste, taste.

Gregor (1891), 32 [Scotland].

560   When I cam by the pier o' Leith,
The pier o' Leith cam by me teeth,
White puddin' black troot,
I joise (choose) thee oot.

Johnston, *Old Lore Misc.*, 1 (1908), 296 [Orphir, Orkney].

561   When I was young and had no sense,
I bought a fiddle for eighteen pence,
And all the tunes that it could play
Was "O'er the hills and far away."

Gregor (1891), 31 [Scotland].
Howard, NYFQ, 16 (1960), 140 [Australia, 1954–1955]. Begins "Donald Duck"; ends "Try as he might he could not play; / His beak got in the way. / And O-U-T spells out."

When I went up an apple tree. See **42**.

562   Where are you going, little Sally Brown?
Up to the garden, an apple to bring down;
I'll give it to the best girl here that I see,
But not to this pretty girl, and out goes she.

"Counting-Out Rhymes," *Misc. of Rymour Club*, 2, part 2
(1913), 62 [Scotland].

563   Whimbobo, whambobo, four-bodied draper,
Lilico, balico, sickety sackety;
Dunety, danity, whirligig.

Bolton (1888), 110 [Pennsylvania].

564   Whippence, whoppence,
Half a groat, want a two-pence,
More kicks than half-pence.

Udal (1922), 393 [Dorset].

Who's there? See **355**.

565   Who picked peppers?
Who picked a pocket?
Who stole my lady's locket?
Not you—not me—
This one—that one—
Count and see!

Justus (1957), 46 [Tennessee].

566   Oh, Who will be king in this little game?
Oh, who will be king, I say.
Oh, who will be king in this little game,
A king's part for to play? You!

Notes and Queries, 10th ser., 11 (June 5, 1909), 446 [Orkney].

William . . . See **567**.

567 William a Trimbletoe
He's a good fisherman (water man).
He catches hens
And puts them in pens.
Some lay eggs and some lay none.
Wire, brier, limber-lock,
Three (twenty) geese in a flock.
One flew east and one flew west,
And one flew over the cuckoo's nest.

*This rhyme is often part of a widely-known forfeits game.
See also* **200**, **287**.

Mill Hill Magazine, 5 (1877). Begins "William atrum, atram."
Bolton (1888), 117–118 [Yorkshire, Maryland, North
    Carolina, Virginia, Georgia, New York, Brooklyn]. Six var-
    iants, one from *Mill Hill Magazine*, 5 (1877); "William a
    Trimbletoe," "William atrum, atram," "William T. Trin-
    ity," "William Trimbleton," and "Peter McQuinity." Var-
    iant endings: "Whitefoot, specklefoot, trip and be gone"
    and "Sit and sing till twelve o'clock. / Clock fall down,
    mouse ran 'round. / O-U-T spells out—and be gone!"
Newell (1883), 203 [Georgia].
Perrow, *JAF*, 26 (1913), 141–142 [Virginia and Mississippi,
    1909]. Two variants, one beginning "Rimety, trimety, he's a
    good man" with "Sit an' sing till twelve o'clock" line.
Brewster (1952), 160–161 [North Carolina, 1913]. Four var-
    iants, beginning "William, William Trembletoe" and
    "William Trimbletoe."
Anderson, *Evening Ledger* (May 17, 1916) [South Carolina].
    Two variants, beginning "William o'Trinity" and "William
    the trumpeter." Fourth and final line: "Hecklety, specklety
    (Hecklefoot, specklefoot), trip and begone." Mentions func-
    tion as a finger game.
Parsons, *JAF*, 30 (1917), 207 [Guilford County, North
    Carolina]. Two variants; one begins "William, William
    Trimbletoe"; the other is preceded by the lines "Hentry,
    mentry, coutry corn, / Apple seeds an' briar horn." Both
    have "The clock (flock) fell down, / The mouse ran (cut)
    aroun'" ending.
Cranford, *North Carolina Folklore*, 1, no. 1 (June 1948), 14
    [Montgomery County, North Carolina, ca. 1918]. Begins
    "William Trimatoe."
Smiley, *JAF*, 32 (1919), 377 [Virginia]. Begins "Henry is a
    good fisherman."

Parsons (1923), 203 [Sea Islands, South Carolina]. One line only: "Henry is a good fisherman."

Whitney and Bullock (1925), 137 [Maryland]. Six variants: "William the Conqueror," "William T. Trinity," "William the trumpeter," "William-a-Trumpity." All end with "White foot, black foot, speckle foot" or a variation.

Guy B. Johnson (1930), 165 [St. Helena Island, North Carolina]. Begins "William, William, thrumble toe."

Maryott, *SFQ*, 1, no. 4 (1937), 44 [Nebraska]. Begins "Peter Mutrimity Tram."

Ray Wood (1938), 57.

Brewster, *SFQ*, 3 (1939), 181.

Kenneth Wiggins Porter, *JAF*, 54 (1941), 169 [Ohio]. Begins "Peter Matrimity."

Rowell, *JAF*, 56 (1943), 207 [Virginia, from Pamunkey Indians]. Begins "William Attrivity"; ends "Sit and sing till twelve o'clock. / Clock fell down, mouse ran 'round / O-U-T spells out." With playing instructions.

Horne, *TFSB*, 11, no. 2 (May 1945), 10. "Chick-a-ma-Craney Crow" rhyme mentioned as a version of "Wm. Trimbletoe."

Withers (1946), n.p. Begins "Peter Matrimity."

Williams, *TFSB*, 13, no. 3 (September 1947), 64–65 [Virginia]. Begins "William Trimmeltree." With playing instructions.

Hines, *Daedalian Quarterly*, 17, no. 1 (Fall 1949), 42 [Texas]. Begins "William, William, Trembletoe."

Musick and Randolph, *JAF*, 63 (1950), 427, 428, 429 [Missouri]. Four variants; one begins "William B. Rick-amanee," another "William O-Trinity."

Freedle, *TFSB*, 27 (1961), 28 [Sumner County, Tennessee].

568 Willie Buck, Willie Boo,
Will Buck had a coo;
She lap ower the Brig o'Dee
Like a Cov-en-auter.

Ower Don, ower Dee
Skip the Leys o' Ballochree;
Ballochree and Jenny Fike
Stealt my tike and tak ma ram;
Kent ye blin' Tam?

A variant of the first verse is also found in a version of **43**. *See also* **446**.

Board, *Word-Lore*, 2 (1927), 190 [Scotland].

569   Willy, nilly, nick, nack,
Which one will you tak'?
Which is white and which is black?
Willy, nilly, nick nack.

> *Cf.* **387**.
> Bolton (1888), 115 [Scotland].

Winnery, orrey, hickory Ann. *See* **408**.

Winnery ory, accory ham (han). *See* **408**.

Wire, brier, limber lock. *See* **287, 567.**

570   With a C and a sigh
And a Constant;
With a nople and a pople
And a Constantinople.

> *Usually an entertainment rhyme.*
>
> Bolton (1888), 114 [Pennsylvania, Massachusetts, New York].
> Withers (1946), n.p. [Cedar County, Missouri, 1907–1913].

Wonery (Wonnery), twoery (Tooery) . . . *See* **410.**

571   W.P.A., W.P.A.
You're let out,
Go get your pay.

> Evans (1956), 9.

572   Wring the dish cloth out;
Out, spot, out.

> *Usually a rhyme ending.*
>
> Bolton (1888), 111 [Boston].
> Opie (1969), 31.

Wry, Iry, Ickery Jam. *See* **408**.

Wun a me noory, ikka me Ann. *See* **408**.

Wunnery, unnery (youery), . . . *See* **408**.

Y

Yan, tan (teean), tethera, methera, (pip). *See* **500**.

573 Yellow cornmeal,
Red tomato,
Ribbon cane,
Sweet potato;
Rind melon,
Ripe persimmon,
Little goober peas.

Withers (1946), n.p.

Yen-rie, twa-rie . . . *See* **410**.

574 Yen twa tipples
March mapplin
Mapplin how
How Harry,
Bow Barry,
Biddery gan,
Gan gilly,
Gilly nowd,
Discum towd,
Ten you marry.

G. B. Adams, *Ulster Folklife*, 11 (1965), 93–94. Three variants: two begin "Two tiddlum (tipplin) / March middlum (mapplin)."

Yer auld man's a dirty old man. *See* **492**.

575   Yesterday up on the stair
      I saw a man who wasn't there.
      He wasn't there again today—
      Oh, how I wish he'd stay away.

> *Popular children's poem by Hugh Mearns, often credited to
> "Anonymous."*

Withers (1946), n.p. [from Brooklyn College students, 1936–
   1945].

Ynky, pinky, hallogolum. *See* **126**.

Yokie, pokie, yankie, fun. *See* **227**.

576   You're It,
      You've got a fit,
      And don't know how
      To get out of it.

> *Usually a taunt.*

Withers (1946), n.p. [Cedar County, Missouri, 1907–1913].
Maryott, *SFQ*, 1, no. 4 (1937), 51 [Nebraska].
Evans (1956), 5.
Millard, *NYFQ*, 16 (1960), 149 [New York].

577   You can stand,
      And you can sit,
      But, if you play,
      You must be it.

Maryott, *SFQ*, 1, no. 4 (1937), 60 [Nebraska].

Your mother and my mother were hanging out
   clothes. *See* **375**.

Your shoes are dirty (need cleaning). *See* **291**.

Z

Zaina, daina, dina, disk. See **119**.

578 Zan, pan, musky, dan,
Zan, pan, toosh.

> See also **119**, **410**.

> Gregor (1891), 14, 30 [Scotland]. Two variants, one "Pin, pan, musky by dam, / Eedlem, tweedlem, twenty-one."

Zeanty, teenty, heligo, lum. See **248**.

Zeendy, teendy, tethery, methery. See **500**.

Zeenty, feenty, fanty, feg (fickety, fae). See **129**.

Zeenty, meeny, fickety, fick. See **129**.

579 Zeenty, peenty, feggery, fell,
Ell, ell, dominell,
Zurty, purty, tarry rope,
Zan, tan, tonsy Jock,
Eerie-orie, eerie-orie,
You—are—out.

> Cf. **129**.

> Maclagan (1901), 249 [Argyleshire]. Begins "Inky, pinky, peerie winkie."
> Maclennan (1909), 52 [Scotland]. Begins "Inky, pinky, peerie winkie."
> Simpkins (1914), 186 [Fife]. Begins "Irka, birka stoony rock."
> Gullen (1950), 18 [Ayrshire].
> Sutton-Smith (1959), 71. Begins "Inky pinky fidgety fell."

Zeenty peenty hethery bethery. See **500**.

Zeenty, teenty, fickety, faig (figery, fell). See **129**.

580   Zeenty, teenty, halligo lum,
Pitchin' tawties down the lum.
Wha's there? Johnny Blair.
What d'ye want? A bottle o' beer.
Where's your money? In my purse.
Where's your purse? In my pocket.
Where's your pocket? I forgot it.
Go down the stair, you silly blockhead.
You—are—out.

    See also **111**, **355**.

Maclennan (1909), 53 [Scotland].
Reid, *Misc. of Rymour Club*, 1 (1911), 104 [Edinburgh]. Begins "Eenty, teenty, tuppenny bun."
Gullen (1950), 18.

Zeenty teenty
Heathery bethery (tethera mether, Tether
  a-mather). See **500**.

Zeenty, teenty, tickety, tegg. See **129**.

Zeenty teenty, tippenny bun. See **126**.

Zeenty, tennty, my black hen. See **213**.

Zeeny, meeny, feeny, fig. See **129**, **500**.

Zeeny, meeny, fickety, fick. See **128**, **129**.

Zeeny, meeny, mina, ma (meta, ma). See **130**.

Zeetum, peetum, penny, pie. See **204**.

Zeinty, teinty, Henry, Mothery. See **500**.

581   Zetra detra
Pamphra letra
Hover, dover, dik!

Flett, *Old Lore Misc.*, 3 (1910), 3 [Orkney].

Ziccotty (Zickety) diccotty (dickety), . . . *See* **216.**

582   Zig zag zooligar
Zim zam bum.

Opie (1969), 17 [Manchester].

Zinny, minny, mutta, ma. *See* **130.**

Zinte, tinte. *See* **500.**

Zinti tinti
Tethera methera. *See* **500.**

Zinty, pinkty, halligolum. *See* **126.**

Zinty, tinty, heathery, meathery (hethery,
   methery). *See* **500.**

Zinty tinty tethera pethera bumf (tethery, bethery).
   See **500.**

Zinty, tinty, two-penny bun. *See* **126.**

Works Cited

Asterisks indicate works unavailable to the editors but cited in other sources. Publication information for these works, in some cases incomplete, is derived from the sources quoting them. The later sources present the reprinted rhymes in a counting-out context, but whether the original works specifically assigned this function to the rhymes is uncertain.

Recordings

MacColl, Ewan, and Dominick Behan. *The Singing Streets*. Folkways Record 8501. New York, 1958.

MacColl, Ewan, and Peggy Seeger. *The Elliots of Birtley*. Folkways Record 3565. New York, 1962.

Published Material

Abrahams, Roger D. (ed.). *Jump-Rope Rhymes: A Dictionary*. American Folklore Society, Bibliographical and Special Series, vol. 20. Austin: University of Texas Press, 1969.

Acker, Ethel F. *Four Hundred Games for School, Home, and Playground*. Dansville, N.Y.: F. A. Owen Publishing Company, 1923.

Adams, A. A. "Notes, Queries, and Answers." *Word-Lore*, 3 (1928), 51 n. 106.

Adams, F. G. "A Counting-Out Rhyme." *Journal of American Folklore*, 5 (1892), 148.

Adams, G. B. "Counting-Rhymes and Systems of Numeration." *Ulster Folklife*, 11 (1965), 85–97.

Addy, Sidney Oldall. *Household Tales, with Other Traditional Remains*. London: David Nutt, 1895.

A.H.T. "Girls' Games." *Yorkshire Folklore Journal*, 1 (1888), 214.

Allen, Robert Thomas. "The Tribal Customs of Space-Age Children." *Macleans*, July 6, 1963, pp. 18–19, 42–45.

American Boys' Book of Sports and Games, The. 1864.

Anderson, J. A. Letter in "The Reader's Open Forum." *Evening Ledger* (Philadelphia), May 17, 1916.

Askew, H. "Notes, Queries, and Answers." *Word-Lore*, 2 (1927), 95 n. 56.

Babcock, W. H. "Games of Washington Children." *American Anthropologist*, o.s., 1 (1888), 243–284.

*Baker, A. E. *Gloss: Northamptonshire Words and Phrases*. 2 vols. 1854.

Bassett, Wilbur W. "Illinois Folk-Lore: Some Beliefs of Children and Youths." *The Folk-Lorist*, 1 (1892–1893), 157–158.

* Bates, Clara Doty. *Nursery Jingles.*

Bennett, H. C. "Lyrics of the Pavement." *Children: The Magazine for Parents,* 12 (1927), 20–21.

Bett, Henry. *Nursery Rhymes and Tales.* New York: Henry Holt and Company, 1924.

Birnie, Mrs. "Rhymes from the Huntly District." *Miscellanea of the Rymour Club,* 1 (1911), 89–90, 106–108.

Black, G. F. (collector) and Northcote W. Thomas (ed.). *Examples of Printed Folklore Concerning the Orkney and Shetland Islands. County Folk-Lore,* vol. 3. Publications of the Folk-Lore Society, vol. 49. London: Sidgwick and Jackson, 1901.

Blackwood's Edinburgh Magazine, 10 (August 1821), 36–37. "Voyages and Travels of Columbus Secundus," Chapter 8.

Blakeborough, Richard. *Wit, Character, Folklore, and Customs of the North Riding of Yorkshire.* London: Henry Frowde, 1898.

Bley, Edgar S. *The Best Singing Games for Children of All Ages.* New York: Sterling Publishing Company, 1957.

Bluebells My Cockle Shells. Kilmarnock, Scotland: Cumnock Academy, 1961.

Board, M. E. "Familiar Scottish Rhymes." *Word-Lore,* 2 (1927), 190.

Bolton, Henry Carrington. *The Counting-Out Rhymes of Children.* London: Elliot Stock, 1888.

———. "More Counting-Out Rhymes." *Journal of American Folklore,* 10 (1897), 313–321.

Botkin, B. A. (ed.). *A Treasury of American Folklore,* pp. 769–773, 800. New York: Crown Publishers, Inc., 1944. (From Mills and Bishop [1937] and Newell [1903].

———. *A Treasury of New England Folklore.* New York: Crown Publishers, 1947.

Boyce, E. R., and Kathleen Bartlett. *Number Rhymes and Finger Plays.* London: Sir Isaac Pitman & Sons, 1946.

Brewster, Paul G. (ed.). "Children's Games and Rhymes." In *The Frank C. Brown Collection of North Carolina Folklore,* vol. 1. Durham, N.C.: Duke University Publications, 1952.

———. "Rope-Skipping, Counting-Out and Other Rhymes of Children." *Southern Folklore Quarterly,* 3 (1939), 173–185.

Brill, Melodie. "Folksay—Children's Rhymes." *Green Mountain Whittlin's,* 24 (1972), 3–4.

* Brown, John. *Marjorie Fleming.*

Bryant, Margaret M. "Folklore in the Schools: Folklore in College English Classes." *New York Folklore Quarterly,* 2 (1946), 286–296.

Burne, Charlotte Sophia (ed.). *Shropshire Folk-lore: A Sheaf of Gleanings.* London: Trübner & Co., 1883.

Bury, Eloise. "Notes, Queries, and Answers." *Word-Lore,* 2 (1927), 50 n. 56.

Buspidnick, Melchizedeck. "Cornish Children's Games." In *Cornish*

Notes and Queries, 1st series, ed. Peter Penn. London: Elliot Stock, 1906.

Carey, George G. Maryland Folklore and Folklife. Cambridge, Md.: Tidewater Publishers, 1970.

Cassidy, Frederic G. "Report of a Recent Project of Collecting." Publications of the American Dialect Society, no. 29 (April 1958).

Castagna, Barbara. "Some Rhymes, Games and Songs from Children in the New Rochelle Area." New York Folklore Quarterly, 25 (1969), 221–237.

Chamberlain, A. F. "Folklore of Canadian Children." Journal of American Folklore, 8 (1895), 252–255.

Chambers, Robert. Popular Rhymes of Scotland. 3d ed. Edinburgh and London: W. & R. Chambers, 1841.

Chope, R. Pearce. The Dialect of Hartland, Devonshire. London: Kegan Paul, Trench, Trübner & Co., 1891.

Coats, Nellie M. "Children's Rhymes." Hoosier Folklore, 6 (1947), 73–74.

Cooper, Horton. North Carolina Mountain Folklore and Miscellany. Murfreesboro, N.C.: Johnson Publishing Company, 1972.

"Counting-Out Rhymes." Miscellanea of the Rymour Club, 2, part 2 (1913), 59–62, 93–96.

Courtney, M. A. Cornish Feasts and Folklore. Penzance, Cornwall, 1890.

Covey, E. "Folk Say: Children's Verses," Green Mountain Whittlin's, 12 (1960), 9.

*Cowan, Frank. American Story Book. Greensburg, Pa., 1881.

Cranford, Rachel. "Games and Game Rhymes." North Carolina Folklore, 1, no. 1 (June 1948), 13–14.

Daiken, Leslie. Children's Games throughout the Year. New York and London: B. T. Batsford, 1949.

———. Out Goes She. Dublin: The Dolman Press, 1963.

Davis, William Thomas. Plymouth Memories of an Octogenarian. Plymouth, Mass.: The Memorial Press, 1906.

Devon and Cornwall Notes and Gleanings, 2, no. 18 (June 15, 1889), 87.

Dew, Walter N. A Dyshe of Norfolke Dumplings. London: Jarold & Sons, 1898. Facsimile reprint, Wakefield, Yorkshire, 1973.

*Dickinson, W. Cumberland Glossary (1881).

Dobie, Bertha McKee. "Tales and Rhymes of a Texas Household." In Texas and Southwestern Lore, ed. J. Frank Dobie. Publications of the Texas Folklore Society, no. 6. Austin: Texas Folklore Society, 1927.

Douglas, Norman. London Street Games. 1st ed., London: St. Catherine's Press, 1916. 2d ed., rev., London: Chatto and Windus, 1931.

Elliott, Thorton. "A Bit O' Tayside Taak." Word-Lore, 1 (1926), 95.

Ellis, Alexander J. "The Anglo-Cymric Score." In Transactions of the

Philological Society, 1877–8–9. London: Trübner & Co., 1879.

Emrich, Marion Vallat, and George Korson. *The Child's Book of Folklore.* New York: The Dial Press, 1947.

Evans, Patricia. *Who's It.* San Francisco: The Porpoise Bookshop, 1956. Reprinted in Patricia Evans, *Rimbles.* New York: Doubleday & Co., 1961.

F.B.T. "Counting-Out Rhymes." *Devon and Cornwall Notes and Gleanings*, 2, no. 18 (June 15, 1889), 87.

Findlay, Rev. William. "Scottish Folk Rhymes." *Miscellanea of the Rymour Club*, 1 (1911), 46–57.

Firth, John. In *Old Lore Miscellany of Orkney, Shetland, Caithness, and Sutherland*, 2 (1909), 135.

Flett, Robert. "Counting-Out Rhymes, Orphir." *Old Lore Miscellany of Orkney, Shetland, Caithness, and Sutherland*, 3 (1910), 3.

Flowers, Paul. "Rhymes, Songs, and Ditties." *Tennessee Folklore Society Bulletin*, 10, no. 3 (1944), 7–9.

Folk-Lore, 17 (1905), 77–97, 192–221, 340–349, 439–460.

*Folk-Lore Journal, 1 (1883), 384–385; 5 (1887), 48.

Folk-Lore Record, 4 (1881), 173–177.

"Folk Rhymes and Jingles of Maryland Children." Collected by Children's Literature Class, 1944, State Teachers College, Frostburg, Md.; Dorothy Howard, instructor. Mimeographed.

"Folk Rhymes for Children." *The New York Times Magazine*, November 5, 1944, p. 27. From the unpublished collection of Dorothy G. Howard.

Fowke, Edith. *Sally Go Round the Sun.* Toronto and Montreal: McClelland and Stewart, 1969.

Fraser, Mr. and Mrs. T. A. "Child Rhymes." *Miscellanea of the Rymour Club*, 2, part 2 (1913), 79–80.

Freedle, Martha. "Children's Games and Amusements in Sumner County in 'The Good Ol' Days.'" *Tennessee Folklore Society Bulletin*, 27 (1961), 23–31.

*Games and Sports for Young Boys. 1859.

Gardner, Emelyn E. "Folklore from Schoharie County, New York." *Journal of American Folklore*, 27 (1914), 304–325.

———. *Folklore from the Schoharie Hills.* Ann Arbor: University of Michigan Press, 1937.

———. "Some Counting-Out Rhymes in Michigan," *Journal of American Folklore*, 31 (1918), 521–536.

Gaskell, Alfred. "Children's Games and Jingles in Lancashire about 1900." *Transactions of the Historic Society of Lancashire and Cheshire*, vol. 116 (1964), 207–222. Reprint of "Those Were the Days." Manchester: Swinton and Pendlebury Public Libraries, 1963. Mimeographed.

Goddard, C. V. "Notes, Queries, and Answers." *Word-Lore*, 2 (1927), 163 n. 56.

Goldstein, Kenneth S. "Strategy in Counting Out: An Ethnographic Folklore Field Study." In *The Study of Games*, ed. Elliott M. Avedon and Brian Sutton-Smith, pp. 167–178. New York: John Wiley & Sons, 1971.

Grammer Gurton's Garland, or The Nursery Parnassus. J. Ritson, collector, 1784. Enlarged edition, R. Triphook, 1810. Reprint, 1866.

Grayson, Marion F. *Let's Do Fingerplays*. Washington, D.C.: Robert B. Luce, 1962.

Green Mountain Whittlin's, 12 (1960), 9; 20 (1968), 6; 24 (1972), 3–4.

Gregor, Walter. *Counting-Out Rhymes of Children*. London: David Nutt, 1891.

———. *The Folklore of the North-East of Scotland*. London: Elliot Stock, 1881.

Gullen, F. Doreen. *Traditional Number Rhymes and Games*. London: University of London Press, 1950.

Gutch, Mrs. Eliza, and Mabel Peacock. *Examples of Printed Folk-Lore Concerning Lincolnshire*. County Folk-Lore, vol. 5. Publications of the Folk-Lore Society, vol. 63. London: David Nutt, 1908.

G.W.R. "Counting-Out Rhymes." *Old Lore Miscellany of Orkney, Shetland, Caithness, and Sutherland*, 4 (1911), 165–166; 5 (1912), 6–7, 53.

Halliwell, James Orchard. *The Nursery Rhymes of England*. 1st ed. published by the Percy Society as vol. 4 of *Early English Poetry, Ballads, and Popular Literature of the Middle Ages*. London, 1842. Rev. and enl., 1843, 1844, 1846, 1853, and ca. 1860.

———. *Popular Rhymes and Nursery Tales*. London, 1849 and ca. 1860. (The last edition includes the work above.)

Hansen, Marian. "Children's Rhymes Accompanied by Gestures." *Western Folklore*, 7 (1948), 50–53.

Harris, Harry. "Jumpin' Jive." *The Evening Bulletin* (Philadelphia), May 30, 1949.

Harris, Katherine M. "Counting Rhymes." *Ulster Folklife*, 4 (1958), 73.

———. "Extracts from the Society's Collection (5)." *Ulster Folklife*, 8 (1962), 39.

Heck, Jean Olive. "Folk Poetry and Folk Criticism." *Journal of American Folklore*, 40 (1927), 1–77.

Henry, Mellinger E. "Nursery Rhymes and Game-Songs from Georgia." *Journal of American Folklore*, 47 (1934), 334–340.

———. *Songs Sung in the Southern Appalachians*. London: The Mitre Press, 1934.

Hewett, Sarah. *The Peasant Speech of Devon*. London: Elliot Stock, 1892.

Hines, Joan. "Counting Out Rhymes in Texas." *The Daedalian Quarterly*, 17, no. 1 (Fall 1949), 41–42.

Hoke, N. C. "Folk-Custom and Folk Belief in North Carolina." *Journal of American Folklore*, 5 (1892), 113–120.

Home, Bruce J. "A Selection of Rhymes." *Miscellanea of the Rymour Club*, 1, (1911), 111–113.

Horne, Dorothy. "Chick-a-ma-Craney Crow." *Tennessee Folklore Society Bulletin*, 11, no. 2 (May 1945), 9–11.

Howard, Dorothy. "Counting-Out Customs of Australian Children." *New York Folklore Quarterly*, 16 (1960), 131–144.

———. *Dorothy's World: Childhood in the Sabine Bottom 1902–10*. Englewood Cliffs, N.J.: Prentice-Hall, 1977.

———. *See also* Mills [Howard], Dorothy; "Folk Rhymes and Jingles of Maryland Children"; and "Folk Rhymes for Children."

Hudson, Arthur Palmer. *Specimens of Mississippi Folk-Lore*. Ann Arbor, Mich.: Edwards Brothers, 1928.

Inglis, James. *Oor Ain Folk: Being Memories of Manse Life*. 2d ed. Edinburgh: D. Douglas, 1894.

Ireland, Irma Thompson. "Juggling with Jingles and Jargon." *Recreation*, February 1937, pp. 545, 564.

Jago, Fred W. P. *The Ancient Language and the Dialect of Cornwall*. Truro: Netherton & Worth, 1882.

*Jamieson, [?]. *Scottish Dictionary Supplement*, vol. 2. 1825.

Jennings, Paul. *The Living Village*. London: Hodder and Stoughton, 1968.

Jerrold, Walter. *Highways and Byways of Kent*. London: Macmillan and Co., 1908.

Johnson, Clifton. *What They Say in New England*. Boston: Lee and Shepard, 1896.

Johnson, Guy B. *Folk Culture on St. Helena Island, North Carolina*. Chapel Hill: University of North Carolina Press, 1930.

Johnston, A. W. In *Old Lore Miscellany of Orkney, Shetland, Caithness, and Sutherland*, 1 (1908), 164, 296.

Johnstone, David. "Rhymes and Variants from Annandale." *Miscellanea of the Rymour Club*, 1 (1911), 86–87.

Jones, Bessie, and Bess Lomax Hawes. *Step It Down: Games, Plays, Songs, and Stories from the Afro-American Heritage*. New York: Harper & Row Publishers, 1972.

J.P.F. "Folk Rhymes." *Miscellanea of the Rymour Club*, 2, part 5 (1917), 186.

Justus, May. *Peddler's Pack*. New York: Henry Holt and Company, 1957. Reprinted in May Justus, *The Complete Peddler's Pack*. Knoxville: University of Tennessee Press, n.d. (1967?).

Kelly, J. Liddell. "Children's Rhymes and Rhyme Games." *Miscellanea of the Rymour Club*, 1 (1911), 1–9.

*Ker, John Bellender. *Essays on the Archaeology of Our Popular Phrases, Terms and Nursery Rhymes*. 2 vols. and suppl. Andover, 1840.

*Kirkeys, James. *The Only Child*.

Knapp, Mary, and Herbert Knapp. *One Potato, Two Potato: The*

Secret Education of American Children. New York: W. W. Norton & Co., 1976.

Koch, Mary. "Folk Verse." In *Kansas Folklore,* ed. S. J. Sackett and William Koch. Lincoln: University of Nebraska Press, 1961.

Leland, Charles G. "Children's Rhymes and Incantations." *Journal of American Folklore,* 2 (1889), 113–116.

Leon, Alice. "Variants of Counting-Rhymes." *Journal of American Folklore,* 8 (1895), 255–256.

Leventhal, Nancy C., and Ed Cray. "Depth Collecting from a Sixth-Grade Class." *Western Folklore,* 22 (1963), 159–163, 231–257.

Lomax, Alan. *The Penguin Book of American Folksongs.* Baltimore: Penguin Books, 1964.

Lyle, J [ames]. "An East Lothian Counting-Out Rhyme." *Miscellanea of the Rymour Club,* 1 (1911), 173.

———. "Miscellaneous Rhymes and Variants." *Miscellanea of the Rymour Club,* 1 (1911), 88–89.

———. "A Set of Lothian Rhymes." *Miscellanea of the Rymour Club,* 2, part 3 (1914), 143.

McAtee, W. L. *Grant County, Indiana, Speech and Song.* Privately printed, 1946.

M'Bain, J. M. *Arbroath: Past & Present.* Arbroath, Scotland: Brodie & Salmond, Brothock Bridge, 1887.

McDowell, Mrs. L. L. "Games of Long Ago." *Tennessee Folklore Society Bulletin,* 10, no. 3 (September 1944), 1–4. Three rhymes, reprinted in Flora L. McDowell (ed.), *Folk Dances of Tennessee* (Delaware, Ohio: Cooperative Recreation Service, n.d.).

Maclagan, Robert Craig. *The Games and Diversions of Argyleshire.* London: David Nutt, 1901.

———. "Additions to 'The Games of Argyleshire.'" *Folk-Lore,* 16 (1905), 77–97, 192–221, 340–349, 439–460.

Maclennan, R. J. (comp.). *Scottish Nursery Rhymes.* London, 1909.

McNaughtan, Adam. "Too Old at Eleven." *Chapbook: Scotland's Folk Life Magazine,* 4, no. 1 (n.d. [1967?]), 3–5, 8, 20–22, 32, 34.

Marwick, Ernest W. (ed.). *An Anthology of Orkney Verse.* N.p.: W. R. Mackintosh, The Kirkwall Press, 1949.

Maryott, Florence. "Nebraska Counting-Out Rhymes." *Southern Folklore Quarterly,* 1, no. 4 (1937), 39–62.

Milberg, Alan. *Street Games.* New York: McGraw-Hill, 1976.

Millard, Eugenia L. "You're It in York State." *New York Folklore Quarterly,* 16 (1960), 145–149.

Mill Hill Magazine, vol. 5. June, October, and December 1877. Published by students of Mill Hill School. Mill Hill and London.

Mills [Howard], Dorothy. "Playtime Verses." *Jack and Jill,* 2 (January 1940), 18–19. *See also* Howard, Dorothy.

———, and Morris Bishop. "Songs of Innocence." *The New Yorker,* November 13, 1937, pp. 32–36, 42.

Milne, Colin ("Gamma"). *Times Remembered*. Gourock, Scotland, 1947.

Miscellanea of the Rymour Club, 1 (1911), 1–9, 46–57, 86–90, 102–108, 111–113, 173; 2, part 2 (1913). 59–62, 69–71, 79–80, 93–96; 2, part 3 (1914), 113, 143; 2, part 4 (1915), 169; 2, part 5 (1917), 186.

Monroe, Will Seymour. "Counting-Out Rhymes of Children." *American Anthropologist*, n.s., 6 (1904), 46–50.

Musick, Ruth Ann. *Ballads, Folk Songs and Folk Tales from West Virginia*. Morgantown: West Virginia University Library, 1960.

———. "West Virginia Folklore." *Hoosier Folklore*, 7 (1948), 1–14.

———, and Vance Randolph. "Children's Rhymes from Missouri." *Journal of American Folklore*, 63 (1950), 425–437.

Napier, James. "Singing Games." *Folk-Lore Record*, 4 (1881), 173–177.

Newell, W. W. *Games and Songs of American Children*. New York, 1883. Rev. ed., New York and London: Harper and Brother, 1903.

Nicholson, Edward W. B. *Golspie: Contributions to Its Folklore*. London: David Nutt, 1897.

Nicholson, John. *Folk Lore of East Yorkshire*. London: Hull, Drifield, 1890.

Nicolson, John. *Some Folk-Tales and Legends of Shetland*. Edinburgh: Thomas Allan & Sons, 1920. Facsimile reprint, Norwood, Pa., 1973.

Northall, G. F. *English Folk Rhymes*. London: Kegan Paul, Trench, Trübner, & Co., 1892.

Notes and Queries. 1st series, 10 (1854): (August 12), 124, (September 9), 210, (November 4), 369–370; 11 (1855): (February 10), 113, (March 3), 174, (March 17), 215, (May 5), 352.

———. 3d series, 5 (1864): (May 4), 395.

———. 4th series, 11 (1873): (April 19), 330.

———. 10th series, 11 (1909): (June 5), 446.

———. New series, 16, no. 5 (May 1969), 171–172.

Ogilvie, Mary I. *A Scottish Childhood and What Happened After*. Oxford: George Ronald, 1952.

Old Cornwall, 1, no. 5 (April 1927), 33–34, 41–42; no. 6 (October 1927), 43–44; no. 8 (October 1928), 39–40.

Old Lore Miscellany of Orkney, Shetland, Caithness, and Sutherland, 1 (1908), 164, 296; 2 (1909), 135, 194; 3 (1910), 3, 67; 4 (1911), 5, 165–166; 5 (1912), 6–7, 53.

Opie, Iona, and Peter Opie. *Children's Games in Street and Playground*. Oxford: Oxford University Press, 1969.

———. *I Saw Esau*. London: Williams and Northgate, 1947.

———. *The Lore and Language of Schoolchildren*. Oxford: Oxford University Press, 1959.

———. *The Oxford Dictionary of Nursery Rhymes*. Oxford: Oxford University Press, 1951.

————. *The Oxford Nursery Rhyme Book*. Oxford: Oxford University Press, 1960.

O' Súilleabháin, Seán. *A Handbook of Irish Folklore*. London: Herbert Jenkins, 1942.

Our Meigle Book. Compiled by residents of Meigle, Scotland. Dundee: William Kidd & Sons, 1932.

Parsons, Elsie Clews. *Folk-Lore of the Sea Islands, South Carolina*. Memoir of the American Folklore Society, vol. 16. New York: G. E. Stechert, 1923.

————. "Notes on Folk-Lore of Guildford County, North Carolina." *Journal of American Folklore*, 30 (1917), 201–208.

Perrow, E. C. "Songs and Rhymes from the South." *Journal of American Folklore*, 26 (1913), 123–173.

Porter, Enid. *Cambridgeshire Customs and Folklore*. London: Routledge & Kegan Paul, 1969.

Porter, Kenneth Wiggins. "Children's Songs and Rhymes of the Porter Family." *Journal of American Folklore*, 54 (1941), 167–175.

Potter, Charles Francis. "Counting-Out Rimes." In *Standard Dictionary of Folklore, Mythology and Legend*, ed. Maria Leach, vol. 1. New York: Funk & Wagnalls, 1949.

————. "Eeny, Meeny, Miny, Mo." In *Standard Dictionary of Folklore, Mythology and Legend*, ed. Maria Leach, vol. 1. New York: Funk & Wagnalls, 1949.

Rae, Margery, and Esther Robb. "Salute to Spring." *The Christian Science Monitor Magazine*, March 21, 1942, pp. 8–9.

Randolph, Vance. "Counting-Out Rhymes in Arkansas." *Southern Folklore Quarterly*, 17 (1953), 244–248.

Rawe, Donald R. *Traditional Cornish Stories and Rhymes*. Padston, England: Lodenek Press, 1971.

Reid, Alan. "Edinburgh Children's Rhymes: Counting Out Rhymes," *Miscellanea of the Rymour Club*, 1 (1911), 102–108.

————. "Rhymes and Games from Kingarth School, Bute." *Miscellanea of the Rymour Club*, 2, part 2 (1913), 69–71.

Reisner, Mary Ellen. "An Unrecorded Variant of a Counting-Out Rhyme." *Notes and Queries*, n.s., 16, no. 5 (May 1969), 171–172.

"Rhymes of General and Local Interest." *Miscellanea of the Rymour Club*, 2, part 3 (1914), 113.

Ritchie, James T. R. *Golden City*. Edinburgh and London: Oliver and Boyd, 1965.

Roberts, Warren. "Children's Games and Games Rhymes." *Hoosier Folklore*, 8 (1949), 7–34.

Robertson, Mrs. Donald. "Counting Out Rhymes from Shelburne County, Nova Scotia." *Northeast Folklore*, 3, no. 2 (Summer 1960), 26–33.

Rodger, Jean C. *Lang Strang*. Forfar, Scotland: The Forfar Press, n.d. [1969?].

Rolland, Fred. "Street Songs of Children." *New Masses*, 27 (May 10, 1938), 109.

Rowell, Mary K. "Pamunkey Indian Games and Amusements." *Journal of American Folklore*, 56 (1943), 203–207.

Rutherford, Frank. *All the Way to Pennywell: Children's Rhymes of the North East*. Durham, England: University of Durham Institute of Education, 1971.

Sandburg, Helga. *Sweet Music*. New York: Dial Press, 1963.

Saxby, J. M. E. *Shetland Traditional Lore*. Edinburgh: Grant & Murray, 1932.

Saxon, Lyle, Edward Dreyer, and Robert Tallant. *Gumbo Ya Ya*. Boston: Houghton Mifflin Co., 1945.

Shaw, Frank. *You Know Me, Anty Nelly?* Liverpool: Gear Press, 1969.

Simpkins, J. E. *Examples of Printed Folk-Lore Concerning Fife, with Some Notes on Clackmannan and Kinross-shires. County Folk-Lore*, vol. 7. Publications of the Folk-Lore Society, vol. 71. London: Sidgwick & Jackson, 1914.

Smiley, Portia. "Folklore from Virginia, South Carolina, Georgia, Alabama, and Florida." *Journal of American Folklore*, 32 (1919), 5–383.

Soifer, Margaret K. "The Sidewalks of Brooklyn." *Story Parade*, 6, no. 7 (July 1941), 15–18; no. 8 (August 1941), 26–30.

Somerset and Dorset Notes & Queries, vol. 1, p. 174.

Steele, J. M. N. In *Old Lore Miscellany of Orkney, Shetland, Caithness, and Sutherland*, 2 (1909), 194.

Stockleridge, Frank P. "Notes and Queries." *Journal of American Folklore*, 4 (1891), 171.

Stork, F. C. "Childlore in Sheffield." *Lore and Language*, no. 1 (July 1969), [3].

Stoudt, John Baer. *The Folklore of the Pennsylvania German*. Lancaster, Pa., 1915.

Sutton-Smith, Brian. *The Games of New Zealand Children*. Berkeley and Los Angeles: University of California Press, 1959. Reprinted in Brian Sutton-Smith, *The Folkgames of Children*, American Folklore Society Bibliographical and Special Series, vol. 24. Austin and London: University of Texas Press, 1972.

Taylor, Archer. *English Riddles from Oral Tradition*. Berkeley and Los Angeles: University of California Press, 1951.

*Taylor, Charles. *Magpie, or The Chatterings of the Pica*. Glasgow, 1820.

Taylor, Margaret. *Did You Feed My Cow?* New York: Thomas Y. Crowell Company, 1956.

Thomas, Joseph. *Randigal Rhymes and a Glossary of Cornish Words*. Penzance, Cornwall: F. Rodda, 1895.

Those Dusty Bluebells. Kilmarnock, Scotland: Cumnock Academy, 1965.

T.M. "Shetland Counting-Out Rhymes, Etc." *Old Lore Miscellany of*

Orkney, Shetland, Caithness, and Sutherland, 4 (1911), 5.
Turner, Ian. *Cinderella Dressed in Yella*. Melbourne, Australia: Heinemann Educational Pty., 1969.
Udal, John Symonds. *Dorsetshire Folk-Lore*. Hertford, England: Stephen Austin & Sons, 1922.
"Uncle Sandy" (Young People's Page). *Word-Lore*, 1 (1926), 224–226.
Wallace, R. "Rhymes." *Miscellanea of the Rymour Club*, 2, part 4 (1915), 169.
Watson, W. G. Willis. *The Land of Summer*. Somerset Folk Series, no. 2. London: Somerset Folk Press, 1921.
Waugh, F. W. "Canadian Folk-Lore from Ontario." *Journal of American Folklore*, 31 (1918), 4–82.
Wheeler, Helen M. "Illinois Folk-Lore." *The Folk-Lorist*, 1 (1892–1893), 55–68.
Whitney, Annie Weston, and Caroline Caufield Bullock. *Folklore from Maryland*. New York: G. E. Stechert and Co., 1925.
Williams, Homer N. "William Trimmeltoe." *Tennessee Folklore Society Bulletin*, 13, no. 3 (September 1947), 64–65.
Williamson, L. "Shetland Counting-Out Rhymes." *Old Lore Miscellany of Orkney, Shetland, Caithness, and Sutherland*, 3 (1910), 67.
Wintemberg, W. J. "Folk-Lore Collected at Roebuck, Grenville County, Ontario." *Journal of American Folklore*, 31 (1918), 154–157.
———. "Folk-Lore Collected in the Counties of Oxford and Waterloo, Ontario." *Journal of American Folklore*, 31 (1918), 135–153.
———, and Katherine H. Wintemberg. "Folk-Lore from Grey County, Ontario." *Journal of American Folklore*, 31 (1918), 83–124.
Withers, Carl. *Counting Out*. New York: Oxford University Press, 1946. Annotation of a personal copy sent to R.D.A. indicates those rhymes remembered by the author from his childhood in Cedar County, Missouri, 1907–1913, and those collected from Brooklyn College students, 1936–1945.
———. "Current Events in New York City Children's Folklore." *New York Folklore Quarterly*, 3 (1947), 213–222.
———. *A Rocket in My Pocket: The Rhymes and Chants of Young Americans*. New York: Henry Holt and Company, 1948.
Wood, Clement, and Gloria Goddard. *The Complete Book of Games*. Garden City, N.Y.; Garden City Books, 1940.
Wood, Ray. *The American Mother Goose*. New York and Philadelphia: J. B. Lippincott Company, 1938.
———. *Fun in American Folk Rhymes*. Philadelphia and New York: J. B. Lippincott Company, 1952.
Word-Lore, 1 (1926), 95, 224–226; 2 (1927), 50, 95, 163, 190; 3 (1928), 51.
Yoffie, Leah Rachel Clara. "Three Generations of Children's Singing Games in St. Louis." *Journal of American Folklore*, 60 (1947), 1–51.
Yorkshire Folklore Journal, 1 (1888), 214.